Praise for *Christian Bale*

"When [Cheung] refers to himself as Bale's majordomo, he is not kidding." —N.F. Mendoza, former journalist at *Los Angeles Times, People, TV Guide*

"This intimate and revealing biography of Christian Bale is full of details few people know about Hollywood's most-lauded Batman, and how a child actor—by harnessing his fans on the Internet—became the star he is today."

—BraveNewHollywood.com

"Harrison Cheung's groundbreaking work in Internet marketing during the mid-'90s established Christian Bale as the first major web celebrity, making my work as a journalist that much easier. Thanks to Harrison, many a major publication, including *USA TODAY* and the *Chicago Tribune*, took my profile pitches on this brilliant but largely unknown actor—because of his cyber-popularity."

—Moira McCormick, journalist

"The book is good—a fun, informative read."
—Christopher Heard, author and film historian

Christian Bale

The Inside Story of
the Darkest Batman

HARRISON CHEUNG AND NICOLA PITTAM

BENBELLA BOOKS, INC. | DALLAS, TEXAS

BenBella Books, Inc.
10300 N. Central Expressway
Suite #400
Dallas, TX 75231
www.benbellabooks.com
Send feedback to feedback@benbellabooks.com

Printed in the United States of America
10 9 8 7 6 5 4 3 2 1

Library of Congress Cataloging-in-Publication Data is available
for this title.

978-1-936661-64-0

Editing by Erin Kelley
Copyediting by Eric Wechter
Proofreading by Michael Fedison and Chris Gage
Cover design by Kit Sweeney
Text design and composition by Neuwirth & Associates, Inc.
Printed by Bang Printing

Distributed by Perseus Distribution
perseusdistribution.com
To place orders through Perseus Distribution:
Tel: 800-343-4499
Fax: 800-351-5073
E-mail: orderentry@perseusbooks.com

Significant discounts for bulk sales are available. Please contact
Glenn Yeffeth at glenn@benbellabooks.com or 214-750-3628.

Contents

"I don't want people to know me."

—Christian Bale, *Esquire*, December 2010

"The truth will set you free. But first, it'll piss you off."

—Gloria Steinem

"We know very little about Christian Bale the man because he is intensely private. That is his right, and should be respected, within reason. After all, any serious movie actor who doesn't realize he's choosing the most public of careers when he signs on ought to have his head examined."

—John Farr, *Huffington Post*

Introduction

Here's how it is. I'm always asked two questions about Christian Bale. One: What's he like? Two: How did I end up working for him for almost a decade?

Christian is one of the most secretive and talented stars in Hollywood with a reputation for an incredibly volatile temper and numerous eccentricities. Although pop psychologists can debate nature versus nurture, the fact remains that Christian is a former child actor with an unusual family upbringing and circumstance who grew into a man with a deep need for privacy. In many ways, he is also a man without a country—an actor in Hollywood who's always reminded that he's British—the first foreigner ever to play the iconically American role of Batman. These factors are just part of his development that would cultivate an explosive temper that would rival Mel Gibson's.

My involvement with Christian was initially a fan's dream. I'm delighted to tell the story of how I met Christian and got involved with his career because one of Christian's agents had warned me *never* to tell anyone. The agent thought our story would empower and encourage fans, and that was something he was absolutely against because like any good Hollywood player, he was loath to acknowledge any cultural influences aside from his own.

The influence of The Fan has always been underestimated, indeed scorned in the corner offices of the talent agencies. Why? The agents and the studios want to be the sole influencers of what you watch, rent, wear, and buy. However, when fan power is orchestrated, coordinated, and directed effectively, great things can happen. *Star Trek? Family Guy? Firefly?* Betty White's Facebook campaign to host *Saturday Night Live?* Justin Bieber's discovery on YouTube? There are so many examples of fan-power saving a series, influencing casting, and championing a book. So now you get the limos at Comic-Con—it's Hollywood's begrudging acknowledgment that fans matter.

I started off as a fan of Christian Bale's. I think there are different levels of fandom. You first notice an actor. Then you make a point of watching whatever movie that actor is in. Then there's a big shift to activism—you want all your friends to watch him. You write a fan letter. You meet up with other fans to share experiences. But I managed to reach another level that few fans can achieve: I had the opportunity to directly influence Christian's career.

I ended up taking care of many aspects of Christian's life—as his assistant, publicist, and marketer. I read scripts, followed book projects, got him press coverage, handled his Internet marketing, and replied to his fan mail. I looked after his house and his pets when he was away on location. I took care of his father, his finances, his immigration issues. I had to laugh when people would describe me as the real-life Alfred to his Bruce Wayne.

Through Christian's ups and down, I saw a very talented person struggle to survive in the entertainment industry. Christian was the ultimate Hollywood outsider—a former child actor who was pressured into show business by a determined single parent; a British teen reluctantly relocated to a new country, stuck with the burden of being a foreigner, and both a failed "Disney" and "Spielberg" kid. He dealt with soul-tearing family conflicts and betrayals and faced confidence-shattering discrimination and stereotyping. It's no wonder that he developed his ability into transforming himself physically for different roles. I could see that it was his way of coping, of running away from who he really was.

This book is Christian Bale's biography, but it's also the untold story of a child actor and how he became the Internet's first star. It's the true story of how a British actor got to play a quintessentially American antihero—Batman. There is no other actor in Hollywood in recent times who owes so much to the contribution of his fans.

To the Baleheads, past and present, this book is dedicated to you and what we've collectively accomplished. I remember a certain Christian Bale movie poster and its tagline that empowered us all:

A Thousand Voices. A Single Dream.

Harrison Cheung

1

Empire of the Son

"Difficult boy."
—Empire of the Sun

"The truth is this: if I didn't have to do a single interview, I never would."
—Christian Bale, Tribune Media, July 10, 1992

"*Empire of the Sun* changed my life quite considerably and I didn't like it one bit."
—Christian Bale, *In Focus*, July 10, 1992

The thin boy was sitting quietly, staring intently at an orange he held in his left hand. Across the table sat a seasoned journalist with a tape recorder and a notepad, pen in hand, hoping to continue his interrogation.

Whenever the reporter asked him a question, the boy absently muttered a tired "yes" or "no" until his eyes wandered to the tray on the table covered with remnants of his lunch. He slowly fingered different pieces of cutlery, finally settling on a knife. As the reporter looked on, he began stabbing at the orange, reveling in the spritz of orange rind and the happy scent of citrus, which began to perfume the air. To the boy, this was something tangible and real—something he could do and feel while he ignored any further questions.

Exasperated, the reporter got up and stormed out. This interview was over but the boy, still fixated on destroying his orange, savored the sticky wetness dribbling through his fingers.

A worried publicist ran into the room. "Christian, is everything all right?" she asked.

"Yes. I'd like to go to the bathroom," he announced. Christian then stood up purposefully, wiping orange zest residue off his trousers. He silently walked past the woman and headed out the door and down the hallway.

The woman watched the retreating figure, concerned and troubled at the turn of events. A number of journalists had complained at how poorly their interviews had gone, and Christian's next interviewer was waiting patiently for his allotted appointment.

Instead of returning from the bathroom, Christian decided to make a break for the elevator doors. He was soon walking out through the hotel lobby and heading down the Champs-Elysées. With each step, he felt a weight being lifted off him and happily immersed himself in the anonymity of the noisy streets where everyone was speaking a language he could not understand.

It was 1988 and fourteen-year-old Christian Bale was on his very first press junket for the Warner Brothers film *Empire of the Sun*. As *Empire Magazine* wrote in 1998, Christian "was rude, gave monosyllabic answers and generally proved as uncooperative as possible. His reputation for being difficult was born."

As the next interviewer lost his patience, it soon became apparent that Christian was going to be late for this interview. And the next one. And the two after that. Word would soon spread throughout the hotel that the young star of Steven Spielberg's latest movie was missing.

While a small posse of worried publicists and personal assistants started combing through the streets of Paris, Christian was contentedly sitting in the grass in a park, enjoying the cool weather and the solitude.

Back at the hotel, the publicist had alerted Christian's older sister Sharon, who was just seventeen, and she in turn anxiously called their father, David, who was back home in England. He would know what to do, she thought. He was the only one who could handle Christian.

"You *must* get a hold of Christian at once," David hissed at his daughter. "Tell him he's embarrassing Steven. He *mustn't* do this to Steven!" David was emphatic, his voice edging up in panic. From the very first wonderful review of his only son's major motion picture debut, the future looked absolutely bright. But to have Christian walking out on the all-too-crucial press junket would most certainly get back to Spielberg, and David was worried about Christian's acting future, if word got out that he was throwing tantrums and being difficult.

Christian often tried to describe to me that time period— there was an incredible amount of pressure riding on his small shoulders. He enjoyed making movies, but the publicity junket made him miserable. It was the beginning of his severe dislike of the words "must" and "should." He didn't like being told what he should do or must do—unless it was coming from the director of a movie.

This wasn't something I could understand easily. I always thought that if I had the good fortune of being a celebrity, I'd gladly deal with publicity. But then again, Christian was a child actor and he had a lot of people depending on him at a very early age.

Acting was not his chosen profession but an accident he had cheerfully stumbled into when he was eight years old. Acting was just something he played at, tagging along with his older sisters, Sharon and Louise, when they went to dance and acting workshops. Watching his sisters have fun, Christian jumped right in, glad for the creative outlet to make some noise, conjure up silly faces, and to run around the room. "It was better than just leaving him in the van," explained David.

Christian told the *Daily Mirror* at the time: "I wasn't really interested in acting till I went to see my sister Louise on stage in *Bugsy Malone*. I saw it 27 times and thought it looked fun." Also starring in that 1983 production of *Bugsy*—a stage adaptation of the 1976 Alan Parker movie—was Catherine Zeta-Jones.

But now acting was set to be Christian's profession and his family's livelihood. Christian and his sisters were enrolled in acting workshops while they lived in Reading. Their classmates included Kate and Anna Winslet. Soon, casting agents were picking Christian over his sisters for small parts in television commercials for the now defunct Pac-Man cereal, which capitalized on the video game's popularity in the 1980s, and he was paid £80 for a Lenor clothes conditioner commercial.

"I was one of those annoying kids who peeked around the washing-machine with their dirty football boots," recalled Christian. "I was just eight years old at the time and I had to say: 'Oh mummy, this smells nice.'" Still, movie acting was just a fantasy. Christian's only ambition at the time was to be a Stormtrooper in a *Star Wars* movie.

Commercials gave way to small stage, television, and film roles. Within a space of two years, he had a bit part in the BBC miniseries *Heart of the Country*, based on the Fay Weldon novel. Then, Christian ended up making £12 a night, playing a "noisy, obnoxious American kid" in the West End comedy *The Nerd*, opposite comedian and Mr. Bean star Rowan Atkinson. He had a supporting role in *The Land of Far Away*, a children's film based on a book by Astrid Lindgren, the well-known author of the Pippi Longstocking series. And he was crowned Tsarevich of Russia, as Alexei, in the NBC telefilm *Anastasia: The Mystery of Anna*, opposite Amy Irving, who was then Mrs. Steven Spielberg.

When Spielberg was ready to cast the lead role in *Empire of the Sun*, a film based on the semiautobiographical novel by J.G. Ballard about his childhood in war-torn China, Amy suggested Christian. But Spielberg was not convinced. "Spielberg actually told me he didn't like my performance in *Anastasia*," Christian said. But the boy eventually won the role after many screen tests and readings. It took Spielberg almost seven months to cast the role, and choosing Christian ended up being a perfect casting decision that impressed Ballard when he visited the set.

David and Jenny Bale were thrilled when Christian landed the part. Christian later told *Movieline* that his father was preparing him for a life-changing experience: "Before we started, my dad told me: 'This could be a fantastic experience, but it could also be the worst thing that could happen to you.' There have been moments when I've wished it had never happened . . . You know, when you're a teenager, you just want to be normal."

It seems to me that *Empire of the Sun* was truly the last great American epic, lovingly crafted before today's era of digital effects where crowds of hundreds can be digitally multiplied into hordes of thousands. The sixteen-week shoot involved 500 crew members and more than 15,000 extras. The film used real stunt pilots and real vintage World War II aircraft—not a computerized rendering of aerial battles as in *Pearl Harbor* or *Independence Day*. Shot on location in China and Spain, the film was Spielberg's most ambitious project and an unusual subject matter for him at the time, because it was about the *end* of childhood—innocence brutally lost because of war. *Empire of the Sun* also happened to be the first major Hollywood production shot in China since the 1949 Communist revolution.

The subject matter was unique in many ways because it was set in Shanghai on the eve of World War II during the Sino-Japanese war—not an arena of the war familiar to American moviegoers but painfully known to my family history. I had lost my grandmother during the war, and it was practically a family ritual for my parents to recount the tales of growing up as a child in war-torn China.

Shanghai was the unfortunate first city in history to suffer the devastation of aerial bombardment. Christian played Jamie Graham, a privileged English schoolboy who, like J.G. Ballard, was born and raised in the British section of Shanghai. (Before World War II, Shanghai had a number of European enclaves.) During the Japanese invasion, Jamie is separated from his parents. He is captured and thrown into a Japanese concentration camp where he survives through ferocious skills he learns from two American prisoners.

When production began on *Empire of the Sun*, the cast had grown to include an impressive list of distinguished actors including Nigel Havers, Miranda Richardson, Joe Pantoliano, and John Malkovich. (It also happened to be Ben Stiller's first movie role as "Dainty"—an imprisoned American!) But it was Christian who dominated the screen for the duration of the 154-minute film. It was a striking, career-making debut, and Christian's performance was the heart and soul of the film. Unlike the typical cherubic child actor, Spielberg needed a child who could compellingly portray a concentration camp survivor.

"I really enjoyed working on that film," recalled Christian. "The main thing I remember about it is that it was so well organized. Very well planned indeed. And Spielberg was very friendly to me. But at that age, I didn't know what was going on, which was just as well I suppose. Consequently, I wasn't nervous on the set—it didn't even cross my mind."

Off the set, an English boy stuck in China's largest city was a different story. "There was nothing to do, and everything is very dusty and crowded," Christian recalled. "There's no color anywhere and the Chinese are always coughing."

Though Christian was accompanied by his mother during the

production, he called his father whenever possible and David remembered how lonely Christian was during the shoot.

"He looked forward to playing table tennis with cast and crew, particularly with John Malkovich. But on some days, Malkovich refused to play with Christian and I had to console him and explain that grown-ups don't always like to play games with children."

Once the four-month shoot was finished, Christian was thrilled to be home in England. He told a reporter: "The first thing I did was to head with my sister Louise to the beach and then the local McDonald's. I hated the food in Shanghai."

When it was released in the U.S. at Christmas in 1987, the film itself received mixed reviews as it sugarcoated the nihilism of Ballard's book. With John Williams' "choir of angels" score, no major American stars, and Spielberg's trademark gloss on a part of World War II unknown to most Americans, *Empire of the Sun*, budgeted at $38 million, grossed only $22 million, making it the biggest bomb of Spielberg's career to date.

Worse, *Empire of the Sun* was released just weeks after Bernardo Bertolucci's masterpiece *The Last Emperor*, a film about the last emperor of China, Pu-yi. Spielberg's similarly titled film invited comparison. Both pictures were set in China. Both were centered on a young boy growing up during war and strife. America's pop director set himself up to be compared to Europe's highbrow film maestro, and the critics responded. *The Last Emperor* swept that year's Academy Awards, winning nine Oscars, including Best Picture and Best Director.

But most critics, regardless of how they felt about the film, were impressed by Christian's portrayal, from spoiled, privileged private school brat to feral young prisoner in a Japanese prison camp.

Janet Maslin of the *New York Times* wrote, "Mr. Bale takes the film to a different dramatic plane. This fine young actor is eminently able to handle an ambitious and demanding role."

Roger Ebert, *Chicago Sun-Times*, added, "Kind of a grim poetry that suggests a young Tom Courtenay."

And Michael Atkinson, *Movieline*, praised, "Bale manages so many strange, heartbreaking, transcendent moments that we are continually caught off guard."

At the film's London premiere, Christian was presented to Queen Elizabeth II. It was a glitzy affair that made a deep impression on David, who recalled: "Here I was, a nobody from South Africa, and my son was shaking hands with the Queen!"

Christian's performance earned him an Outstanding Juvenile Performance citation from the National Board of Review and a Young Artist Award. Christian was considered an odds-on favorite to be nominated for an Oscar, but when the nomination failed to materialize, Christian was relieved. "People are ready for recognition at different ages and I wasn't."

Empire of the Sun was my favorite film at the time. I was living in Toronto and belonged to a cappuccino-swilling indie film counterculture; we all dressed like Robert Smith from The Cure and had long outgrown Spielberg movies. But *Empire of the Sun*, with its epic sweep and a subject matter near and dear to my own family history, resonated with me. The bodies of the dead Chinese civilians floating down the river? That brought back to my mind every horrific story my parents had told me about the war. That poor little boy eating potatoes and weevils? I wanted to save him from the Japanese concentration camps!

David was soon making plans for Christian's next film. The *New York Times* reported that Christian had several offers. By March 1988, the *Sunday Express* was reporting that Christian was planning to do a movie with his sister Louise. David had ditched his job to manage his son's career full-time.

But David's post-*Empire* plans were premature. Little did anyone know how Christian would react to the demands of a press junket. By the time Christian found himself in that hotel room in Paris stabbing an orange in frustration, he had been doing ten hours of interviews a day with few breaks. To promote *Empire*, Christian would complete over 160 interviews with newspapers, television, magazines, and radio. In an almost parallel of the movie, Christian now saw himself as a prisoner, only this time his jail was a hotel room as different reporters were marched in and out.

After the Paris press junket, Christian was pretty confident that he no longer wanted to have anything to do with show business. His movie career seemingly over, Christian retreated to his home in Bournemouth in the south of England, happy to be finished with the movie industry.

"I went to my dad and said: 'I don't want to do this, it's not fun anymore.'"

Though Bournemouth was where the Bale family was living at the time and where his mother was from, Christian did not consider it to be his hometown. Years of nomadic living resulted in Christian having no particular allegiances with any of the towns he and his family had moved to and from. Christian was born in Wales but he adamantly did not consider himself Welsh.

Bournemouth was delighted to claim Christian as its biggest celebrity. With a population of 165,000, Bournemouth is a coastal resort town that earned the moniker "The Happiest Place in Britain" after a 2007 survey. It is the seaside town where author J. R. R. Tolkien retired to. And now it had Christian Bale, the local lad who was starring in a Steven Spielberg movie.

Though *Empire of the Sun* had already opened in the U.S. around Christmas to mixed reviews and a poor box office, critics were impressed by Christian's performance. There were high expectations in both the local and national press in the U.K. as they awaited the U.K. premiere. *The Star* declared Christian to be "The Boy Next Door who will be a Millionaire at 15." And on the night of February 17, 1988, all of England waited with baited breath for Christian to land a highly expected Oscar nomination for Best Actor. When the Oscar nomination didn't happen, Christian told the press he wasn't disappointed.

Empire of the Sun had its Royal Premiere in London's Leicester Square for Queen Elizabeth II on March 21, 1988. Christian, father David, mother Jenny, sisters Sharon and Louise were all presented to the Queen. Christian told the local newspaper, the *Bournemouth Daily Echo*: "I've got a white tuxedo which I'll be wearing for the first time." The *Daily Echo* proudly continued to follow the exploits of its favorite son, proclaiming him "Bournemouth's Boy Wonder." The after-party in London went on until 4:00 am and celebrities like Cher and Twiggy were on hand.

So after the Royal Premiere, after his breakdown in Paris during the exhausting international press junket, after the noise and excitement of all the critics' reviews and award nominations from around the world, Christian tried to return to a normal life back in Bournemouth. But when *Empire of the Sun* became Spielberg's biggest box office bomb, Christian became the target of taunts from his school classmates at the Bournemouth School for Boys who jeered that, at the age of fourteen, he was a washed-up has-been. He told a reporter: "Kids would walk up to me saying, 'Where's that kid in *Empire of the Sun*?' and we'd get into a fist-fight. Things like that happened a lot."

In fact, Christian told me that the bullies at school were always trying to cut his face or break his nose, determined to permanently disfigure him to end his career. He told *The People*: "I took a beating from several boys for years. They put me through hell, punching and kicking me all the time."

Christian's mother, Jenny, recalled in a *Sun* interview: "He had a tough time at school. The bullying was quite bad and made him very sad. It really put him off the film and stardom thing. At the time he did not want to do any more acting."

There were perks to being the local celebrity. Christian made money selling his autograph in the school yard and he was surprised to often find himself the target of local gossip.

"On one occasion," Christian recalled, "I was sitting with a friend opposite two girls in a café, and one girl was telling us how she was going out with Christian Bale, and I just sat listening, asking her what he was like. She said stuff, about how he was a good boyfriend, and my friend was crying with laughter. Eventually I told her who I was, she looked mortified and ran off.

"A lot of American journalists commented that I must have been the most popular kid at school after making *Empire*. The complete opposite was true. I walked down corridors with people going: 'Oh look, it's the has-been.' Fourteen-year-old boys would quote me box-office numbers. It was weird how much they wanted the movie to fail. I was mocked for the rest of my school years for having been in the movie."

Suddenly it was *schadenfreude* time, as if Christian were personally responsible for the film's failure.

"I'd go down the public toilets and see things written about me on the wall," he recalled. "Guys would start fights with me. The local paper took pictures of me getting back from school, then wrote features about how I wouldn't open a girls' school fete. I just felt a dick, you know? I was fourteen; I didn't want to stand there next to the mayor with a big pair of scissors, but they started saying I was big-headed, that I'd forgotten where I'd come from." A pause. "I didn't come from there, anyway."

In fact, the school fete was a charity event for the Avonbourne Girls School, which his sister Louise was attending. Even though Louise personally asked him as a favor, Christian declined and said: "I just didn't want to do it." He was furious when the *Bournemouth Daily Echo* ran an article on May 16, 1988, with the headline, "Empire star shuns fair. Won't aid sister's school."

"I told my parents I wasn't interested in doing anything again because the attention ruined it."

But David Bale had other plans in mind. Although he realized that Christian was severely affected by the press junket experience, he also felt that his son had a God-given talent and that he'd inevitably return to the big screen. The problem here was, how long would it take before Christian would snap out of his funk? Their Spielberg connection was fast growing cold. He was also getting discouraging advice from movie industry friends and acquaintances they had made.

"Frank Marshall [longtime Spielberg collaborator and one of *Empire*'s producers] told me that the worst thing to do to a kid would be to pursue a film career," David recalled. But David wanted to move Christian to Los Angeles, the capital of the movie industry with a decidedly different attitude toward actors and acting. "Actors in England," David worried, "are essentially just civil servants. I wanted better than that for Christian."

Nor did David want Christian to follow the British route for actors by attending the Royal Academy of Dramatic Arts (RADA). David boasted, "They had nothing to teach Christian. RADA churns out actors with exactly the same style. You can't tell them apart! Christian's talent is natural and I wanted to keep it that way."

But Christian's mother, Jenny, was very worried about the change in Christian's personality. Before making *Empire*, Jenny recalled: "Christian was a very happy child, who loved to laugh and wore pots on his head singing songs." After the incident in Paris, it was as if her son had become a recluse.

Christian would later tell the *Daily Echo* the same thing about the year following *Empire of the Sun*: "I just don't think it's a good thing for somebody that age to have it happen to them. I had gone from being able to walk about with nobody knowing me, to somebody people pointed at in the streets. It just freaked me out. I didn't leave the house for almost a year after that."

So went the tug-of-war between David and Jenny for the

control of Christian's future. While his father saw Christian's career as his own way into America, Jenny was worried about Christian's already damaged psyche. In Bournemouth, Christian had just started going out with a steady new girlfriend, Natalie, and seemed content with going to university in England.

After the trauma of the *Empire of the Sun* press junket, Jenny was thinking about the fates of other child actors. Hollywood is littered with child actor casualties who couldn't make the transition to a grown-up career. Gary Coleman, Corey Haim, Brad Renfro, Jonathan Brandis, River Phoenix—these were just a few victims of Christian's generation.

But David would twist Christian's mother's concern into something else.

"You see?" David would tell his son, "I have more confidence in you than your mother does." Christian had a lot to think about.

With a Steven Spielberg film on his résumé, David was positive that Christian could launch a major career in Los Angeles. David decided that if Christian were to have a future in film, it had to be in Hollywood, not in England.

David didn't want to overtly pressure his son into the movie industry, but he also didn't want Christian to lose this once-in-a-lifetime opportunity to become a star. Ever since the *Empire* press junket, Christian responded negatively to pressure (no more "must" or "should"), so David treated him with kid gloves, asking him to consider small TV or film roles as paid holidays from school. Christian didn't like his school anyhow and he felt that Bournemouth School for Boys—both the teachers and his classmates—didn't like him, which left him feeling like he was stuck in a downward spiral.

"That school couldn't teach Christian anything," David asserted. "He had been educated by the greatest director in the world and he had traveled to countries his classmates could only dream of going [to]. What did he need that suffering for?"

Like Christian's *Empire of the Sun* character Jim, David believed in the "University of Life" over formal education—a belief that appeared to have rubbed off on his son.

"Basically, I'd turn up late every day," Christian recalled of his school days at Bournemouth School for Boys. "My attendance was probably the lowest of anybody there. I think it was less than 50 percent or something. I remember the teacher saying: 'One day, Christian, you're going to go to an interview and they're going to ask to see your school registration, and when they see all your "lates" on it, they're going to think you're unreliable and you're not going to get the job.' The headmaster was constantly putting me in detention and trying to stop me from working. He succeeded on one movie—purely because of him I wasn't allowed to do it, as he threatened to put me down a year." Being forced to repeat a year of school was a threat that worked.

Christian got his sweet revenge though. Christian heard that he was now one of the "old boys" listed on the school wall. "Which is quite funny because the headmaster couldn't stand me. I can't help but feel smug knowing he has to walk past my name every day."

After *Empire of the Sun*, Christian did not shoot another movie for almost two years. It was a miserable time of retreat and contemplation as Christian agonized about his future. He definitely wanted to get out of Bournemouth but after his first brush with fame, he wanted nothing to do with movies anymore. It just wasn't any fun.

But luckily, David and Christian's U.K. agent came across a perfect project to get Christian back in the saddle. How about an all-expenses paid trip to sunny Jamaica? Fraser Heston (son of Hollywood legend Charlton Heston) was preparing to adapt the classic *Treasure Island*. It would be Fraser Heston's first job as a director, so he was delighted to have an experienced cast and crew on hand. A Heston family project under their Agamemnon

Films production company, Charlton himself prepared to star as pirate Long John Silver. In 1989, Christian, his dad, and sister Louise were enjoying themselves in Jamaica while he shot his first starring role since *Empire of the Sun*.

Playing plucky Jim Hawkins opposite Charlton Heston's Long John Silver, Christian loved sunny Jamaica and he enjoyed working with Fraser Heston.

Charlton Heston described Christian as "fearless" and was impressed that the boy happily did his own stunts. Christian also enjoyed listening to his left-wing father spar with his polar opposite, the conservative icon Heston, over issues like gun control and U.S. politics—something David loved to analyze and criticize.

Fraser recalled: "Christian was a real sport, and a good shipmate. He was seasick the first day out, like a lot of us, but never missed a beat. He'd just lean over the [leeward] side between takes, have a good vomit, put on a brave face, and turn back to the camera for another scene.

"Christian did almost all of his own combats, climbing in the rigging of the Bounty, crossing the waterfall on the rope, diving from the bowsprit, and he (and his father!) were wonderful about it. We were always very concerned about his or any other's safety. But Christian was very game, and was physically adept at doing this stuff, and certainly unafraid of heights. I think the result shows on the screen."

During the shoot of a key scene—the death of Blind Pew—Christian accidentally hit Christopher Lee in the balls. When Lee doubled over in pain, Christian started laughing uncontrollably. Lee demanded that Christian apologize but David interceded and bellowed: "No, my son does not have to apologize! It was an accident." Father and son then had another laugh at Lee's expense.

Fraser recollected: "I think my favorite sequence is the death of Blind Pew, with Christian and his mum [played by Isla Blair, who in real life is married to Julian Glover]. Christian gives Blind

Pew a mighty whack with the empty blunderbuss and he and his mum barely escape out the window. I remember Christian gave Chris Lee a bit too mighty of a whack, and a bit too far below the belt too! It certainly got a very convincing reaction from Chris [Lee]. Now that's what I call realism."

Because *Treasure Island* was a made-for-TV movie on America's Turner Network, Christian didn't need to do publicity. Additionally, David had negotiated top billing for Christian, second only to Charlton Heston—an amazing feat given the caliber of the cast (which included the previously mentioned Christopher Lee, as well as Oliver Reed and Julian Glover). Powered by a spirited Chieftains soundtrack, Fraser Heston's gritty remake of *Treasure Island* earned strong reviews.

Fraser was thrilled with the results: "I think that Christian filled that wonderful role admirably; you really got the feeling by the end of the film that Jim Hawkins had come through a crucible, had been transformed by his ordeal from a boy into a man. The classic Joseph Campbell heroic transformation; the coming-of-age-by-ordeal ritual practiced by many cultures from the Masai to our own. I think our film was also more true to the book, and the spirit of the book, than the other films. I like to think that Robert Louis Stevenson would have liked this version the best."

The reviews ultimately assured Christian (and David) that he still "had it" and that his impressive performance in *Empire of the Sun* wasn't simply a fluke or solely due to Spielberg's expert direction.

David was delighted that *Treasure Island*'s confidence-boosting experience was bringing Christian back to making movies. His mind was made up.

By 1991, Christian had dropped out of sixth-form college and prepared to head off to L.A. to fulfill David's Hollywood dreams, but even though Christian was talented, he obviously wasn't prepared to deal with fans or the press at that early age.

Should David have realized his son was already close to the breaking point after *Empire of the Sun* rather than being more worried about Spielberg being embarrassed? Or did he simply believe that his own charm would somehow rub off on his painfully shy and inwardly angry son?

2

Father Figure

"Christian's profession became David's obsession."
—**Jenny Bale**, *Daily Mail*, **March 8, 2010**

"I was the first one to hold him, all wet and bloody from his mother. I was the one who cut the umbilical cord. When I saw that I finally had a son, I cried out with joy and told Jenny that we had a son. Thank you, God. We have a son!"
—**David Bale**

"No fate but what we make."
—*Terminator Salvation*

Christian Bale's acting career obviously began with his father, David. But don't trust everything you may have read about David Bale. When you look up Christian's name on the Internet, you might have read that his father was an environmentalist, a South African pilot flying food to the starving in Africa, a military pilot for the RAF, or a commercial pilot for British Airways or British Midland. David Bale created an elaborate autobiography after he, Christian, and his daughter Louise had moved to America in 1991. The truth is actually a lot simpler.

Behind every child actor is at least one supportive and ambitious parent. There are scores of books for parents on how to get their child into show business, counseling the ins and outs of auditions, headshots, acting classes, finding an agent, landing a commercial, and so on. And most of those books recommend that in a *two*-parent family, one parent devotes the time and energy to cultivate their child's career while the other parent stays employed, providing the stability and income for the family home. If you look up any former child actor who's been in the news for bad behavior, I'll bet you that they were raised by a *single* parent.

Being the parent of a child in show business is incredibly time-consuming. Parents are chauffeurs, nutritionists, psychologists, dialogue coaches, babysitters, and security. They also must protect the best interests of their child. But there's a thin line between the child's interests and what a stage-parent might see as their *collective* interest. Some stage-parents live through their children, realizing their own childhood dreams of fame and fortune by proxy.

Paul Peterson, president of *A Minor Consideration*—a Los Angeles-based nonprofit organization, dedicated to providing aid to past, present, and future child actors—notes: "Far too many professional stage-parents say: '*We* did a movie last year,' when the truth is that the child learned the lines, hit the marks, and has to deal with the consequences of their success or failure."

People tend to overlook the fact that Christian Bale was a former child actor because *Empire of the Sun* was a box office dud and regarded as one of Spielberg's lesser known films. To understand Christian, you have to understand his father, David, who was the ultimate stage-parent. David loved to tell people about Christian's birth with as much detail and reverence as the birth of Christ. It didn't matter if it was at a dinner party, a Hollywood premiere, or in line for the bank teller—retelling the story gave David so much joy, and he never seemed to tire of telling it.

And in many ways, Christian was indeed David's savior, for it was Christian's film career that would be the answer to David's hopes and dreams of a life less ordinary, away from the drudgery of his years in England. It's one thing to listen to the local school-teacher praise your son; it's an entirely different feeling to have Steven Spielberg do so. In David's eyes, Christian was clearly on track to be the next Richard Burton or Anthony Hopkins, the next great Celtic actor—a confident prediction based on Christian's glowing reviews for his performance in *Empire of the Sun*. Although the film tanked at the box office, it was enough for David to see the reviews and to encourage his son to pursue an acting career with a clear course plotted for Hollywood. He quit his job to manage Christian's career. He wanted Christian to become a movie star in America. Christian explained his father's fear of settling down as: "More because of a restlessness with Britain and an inability to leave it, than anything else."

Standing 6'4", David Charles Howard Bale always made a striking first impression. One evening at dinner at Cozymel's, a Mexcian restaurant in El Segundo, David was talking about his family and that height ran in the Bale family. He said that he loved being tall as he could always look down at women's tits! He was a big man with a big laugh and a hot temper. David's father, Philip, and his uncle Rex were both over 6'3". To explain Christian's acting talents, David often pointed to his family tree. He claimed that his father had doubled for John Wayne in the Duke's 1962 African adventure movie *Hatari*. Uncle Rex, David asserted, was also an actor with more than twenty films to his credit. And Rex's cousin, he said, was none other than Lillie Langtry, a famous Victorian actress from the Channel Islands.

David himself was one of those men blessed with looks that, like a fine wine or Sean Connery, improved with age; he had silver-gray hair, character lines, sad eyes, and a tanned, open, and inviting face. David bore more than a slight resemblance to actor Adam West—television's first Batman.

Yet David's most powerful asset wasn't his physical presence. With a rumbling basso of a voice both theatrical and dramatic in delivery, David had a remarkable gift of gab. He could be undeniably charming, passionate, and insistent. His oratory skills combined with an uncanny ability to mimic different British and South African accents were the centerpiece of his charm. One wanted to applaud at the end of David's magniloquent speeches and pontifications—duly impressed yet certainly relieved as he also had a tendency to be long-winded.

David Bale was born in Cape Town, South Africa, on September 2, 1941. His father, he told me, a retired RAF officer and safari hunter, was a strict disciplinarian. His mother, he fondly described as exactly like the character Patsy Stone portrayed by Joanna Lumley in the British TV comedy *Absolutely Fabulous*. One of David's earliest childhood memories was that of watching Disney's *Song of the South*, which was released in 1946. He loved that movie and often whistled its theme song "Zip-a-Dee-Doo-Dah," under his breath. In Los Angeles, another song he often liked to sing was "They're Coming to Take Me Away, Ha-Ha," a quirky 1966 hit by Napoleon XIV.

When his parents divorced, David followed his mother, attending boarding school to boarding school from Egypt to England and visiting with his maternal grandmother and cousins on tiny Guernsey—one of the Channel Islands between England and France. He spent much of his youth bumming around the beaches of Europe. Said Christian: "He did that for a lot of his life. But what he pointed out to me was that at the time he'd found nothing he was good at. He was quite happy wandering about."

At the age of seventeen, David's mother put him back on a ship to South Africa to be reunited with his father and to pursue an education at the University of Cape Town (UCT).

However, David was no scholar. He loved to drink, and he took the opportunity to party and enjoy student life, though he said that his left-leaning politics and anti-apartheid stance were formed during his years at UCT, which was then a hotbed of anti-apartheid student activism. The lanky David was extremely popular and amusingly garrulous, dominating dinner conversation with tales of his exotic, multinational upbringing. But something else was forming for David. In 1962, his girlfriend, Sandra Thompson, announced that she was pregnant. David was only twenty-one and the surprise pregnancy floored him. Footloose and fancy-free, he wasn't exactly planning to settle down in South Africa with a wife and child, but he nevertheless married Sandra. His first child, Erin, was born that year.

Six months later, David had had enough of playing father. He announced to Sandra that he was returning to England to visit his mother. Sandra Thompson Bale filed for divorce in 1964. Their daughter, Erin, didn't use the name Bale, choosing instead the name of her stepfather, Plessis.

Back in England, David's prospects were decidedly grim. His mother suggested that he learn a trade and enter the workforce—perhaps drive a lorry, he recalled with bitterness. David, who had enjoyed the sunny climes of South Africa, didn't like gray and sullen London, so he headed to Bournemouth to recapture some of the seaside life he preferred.

Destiny found David sleeping at a 24-hour Wimpy restaurant in Bournemouth, one of the few places that would stay open in the conservative and picturesque beach town, about two hours from London by train. Named after the burger-eating character in the Popeye comic strip, Wimpy is a U.K. fast-food chain similar to Big Boy's or Denny's in the U.S. Charming the waitresses, David had settled in a comfortable booth at the back of the restaurant where he could read the newspapers, nurse a mug of tea, and nibble on a plate of chips. "He wouldn't even say he was homeless," Christian said of his father. "To him, it was just another thing he was doing." But there at Wimpy, David met Jenny James, a strikingly beautiful young Joan Collins look-alike. Christian has her piercing eyes.

Jenny James was a very passionate young woman, who was looking for adventure to take her away from quiet Bournemouth. She found it with the silver-tongued David, who was handsome, charming, and told tales of exotic places. She was smitten.

By 1968, David and Jenny had their first daughter, Sharon. They married on February 26, 1972, at St. Laurence's Church in the village of Combe in Oxfordshire. But David was unable to find full-time work. He disliked authority figures, was cheerfully irresponsible, and bristled at the conventional employer-employee relationship. Entrepreneurial in spirit, David attempted to start a number of businesses, all of which ended in disaster. He claimed to have introduced the skateboard to England, but a lack of attention to the distribution contract left David penniless.

When British Midland Airways was actively recruiting for pilots, David borrowed money to attend the airline's Airline Preparation Programme at Oxford Aviation Training, but he never completed it. Jenny gave birth to their second daughter, Louise, in 1972. The growing Bale family needed an immediate source of income.

But instead David decided what the family needed was a return to nature. So the Bales loaded up their VW camper van and headed west to Wales where David planned to find work on a farm. The Bales found themselves in Haverfordwest, the largest town in Pembrokeshire. With its remote calm, beautiful scenery, rugged coasts, clean beaches, and majestic mountains, David felt that Pembrokeshire would be an ideal place to raise a family.

Christian Charles Philip Bale was born on January 30, 1974, in Haverfordwest. To say that David was thrilled would be a gross understatement. After three daughters, he finally had a son. "Those extra couple of ounces make all the difference in the world!" David crowed. David told me that when Christian was born, he held up his new baby to the heavens and whispered a line from Alex Haley's *Roots*:

"Behold, the only thing greater than yourself!"

It was vivid imagery, and I believed every word David told me until I later discovered that *Roots* was published in 1976, two years after Christian's birth. But I didn't doubt the sentiment and could imagine how thrilled David was to finally have a son.

The Bale family continued to move around, avoiding creditors and looking for work wherever available as David tried to find something interesting to do that would pay him a wage. On a couple occasions, Christian told me that the family would find themselves on the streets, evicted from their flat when David missed paying the rent. Christian spent his childhood nomadically, moving to Portugal (as a "gesture of disgust toward England," Christian recalled), then Reading, before the Bales returned to Bournemouth to be closer to Jenny's family.

Christian enjoyed the time the family spent in Portugal, recalling: "We got into a camper van and drove down to Portugal and lived there for a year, and I didn't go to school at all. My parents figured it's an education living in a farming community. All I wanted to do was stay there and work in the horse stables and travel around the mountains of Portugal. I would have been totally happy."

Though David had a disdain for organized religion, he was a spiritual man who was essentially Christian and he named his son accordingly.

Christian recalled: "I always pictured Jesus as Neil Diamond when I was younger. My upbringing was not a religious one, but an inquisitive one. My father was best friends with the bishop and fascinated by religion. I would come back from church, and my dad would put on Neil Diamond. So, I would always picture

Neil Diamond with a big white beard, standing in a tunic and preaching to masses of people."

David was also fascinated with nature and he delighted in waking his children up in the middle of the night to watch falling stars, comets, or eclipses.

While David enjoyed being a father, he was still hard-pressed to make a stable living to support his growing family. David had not finished his university education in South Africa and he blamed conservative, class-conscious British society for his frustrations.

Naturally it fell to Christian's mother, Jenny Bale, to work to support their family. She worked a variety of jobs—as a receptionist, an office clerk at a real estate agency, and for one summer as a dancer in David Smart's Super Circus in Battersea Park in London. During that season, Jenny commuted daily to take care of her children. And thanks to David and Jenny's eventual bitter divorce on June 6, 1991, David would forever tar Jenny as a "circus clown" in Christian's acting bio. It was David's way of demeaning and ridiculing his ex-wife while elevating his own role in Christian's life. She eventually became a therapist and reflexologist.

David and Jenny decided to send Sharon, Louise, and Christian to various dance and acting workshops. Christian was in fact taking ballet lessons and about to enroll in the prestigious Royal Academy of Dance, but David decided against the Academy when he saw how the boys were not allowed to play football or any sport that risked injury.

As Christian began to land TV commercials, David realized that the casting agents were only interested in his son, not his daughters. It looked like his son was going to achieve what he could not—success. David was optimistic and tremendously confident about Christian's potential career. He saw Christian as a golden ticket out of Margaret Thatcher's England, which, he believed, had stymied all of his past ambitions. English class warfare meant more rules about what you should or must do. David, who considered himself a proud Afrikaner, scoffed at English class divisions and the prevalent discrimination by accent and origin—hence David's delight in putting on posh, Cockney, and other accents, a gift of mimicry Christian would inherit.

In 1987, with the money Christian earned from *Empire of the Sun*, David and Jenny bought a large, comfortable two-story brick home on 207 Capstone Road in Bournemouth. Today, the neighborhood is popular for university housing, but back then, it was a regular middle-class home on a broad residential street.

But David was desperate to move to America. David became the ultimate stage-parent, coddling and encouraging Christian to become a Hollywood star. With a Spielberg movie on his résumé, he knew that his son's future would be bright. But those plans hit a wall when Christian had his nervous breakdown in Paris on the press tour for *Empire of the Sun*. David had to treat his son extremely carefully because he could easily retreat into a reclusive shell and quit acting altogether.

British labor laws limited the number of hours a minor could work before the age of sixteen. In fact, Christian would be restricted to making only one movie a year. So while David anxiously waited for Christian's sixteenth birthday, he became obsessed with plans to move to America.

David wanted Christian to pursue the kind of acting career that wasn't possible in England. America was the land of megastardom, big contracts, and big money. To become a true A-list Hollywood star, the only place for Christian to fulfill David's dream was logically in Los Angeles.

However, Christian's mother, Jenny, didn't share David's ambitions to move to L.A. It was one thing to live in Portugal. As British citizens, they could live and work legally anywhere in the European Union. But moving to America was an entirely different matter. To immigrate to the U.S., one generally required a skill or a university degree in an area of demand by the U.S. economy.

Once an immigrant was granted permanent residence, they were awarded "green cards" for identification and employment authorization. Without a green card, David and Jenny would not be allowed to work or stay beyond their visa's expiration date. How, Jenny wondered, could they take that chance?

Unfortunately for David, he personally could never qualify for U.S. immigration. He never finished university and had no work of his own lined up. But he was undeterred because there were other ways into the U.S.—as a proprietor of one's own business or as a sponsored employee of an American company. Surely it was simply a matter of getting Christian to America, becoming a movie star, and then forming a family production company so that Christian could hire his father as the company's president or vice president. Problem solved.

There was just the simple matter of making reluctant young Christian into a star . . .

Jenny was opposed to a move to the U.S. because she realized that unless they had green cards, neither she nor David could legally work and the family would be financially dependent on young Christian who was, at best, ambivalent about acting as his career choice. Jenny was shocked that David would put all this pressure on their young son. Shouldn't Christian stay in England and finish his education instead?

Jenny recalled: "David told me that he and Christian would be moving to the U.S. I had no say in the matter." David was adamant. He wanted to live in America. So he left behind Jenny and Sharon, and uprooted Christian and his sister Louise to move 6,000 miles away on visitors' visas. For Christian, even though he wasn't ready to call Los Angeles home, the California sun and surf were irresistible alternatives to more years at school. And after his miserable years at the Bournemouth School for Boys, he shared his father's disdain for formal education and for England.

Out of the conflict, Jenny Bale filed for divorce on April 22, 1991. It was finalized on June 6, 1991.

David soon discovered what many immigrants to California had learned—he could completely reinvent himself. From 1987 to 1991, while the Bales lived in Bournemouth, in every article about Christian Bale and his fledgling movie career, David described himself as a financial advisor or insurance analyst—a couple of innocuous job titles that wouldn't prompt any investigation into his background. However *Talk Talk* noted that Christian was "often not sure what he did to bring food to the table."

"A lot has gone on that even Christian doesn't know about as he buries his head in the sand about his father and doesn't even seem to realize the role I played in his upbringing," said Jenny.

But after 1991, when David and Christian had moved to Los Angeles, David began to portray himself to Americans as a former RAF pilot, British Airways pilot, or British Midland pilot.

Being the single parent of a celebrity was opening doors for him, and David held a special place in this odd stratum of Hollywood society because Christian held a special place in the pantheon of child actors as a former "Spielberg kid."

Since David could not legally work, he had a lot of free time, which he devoted to networking for Christian's career. He name-dropped frequently, and told producers that he could get them meetings with Spielberg. He socialized with other child actors' parents. He was on the phone for hours, talking to journalists as Christian's publicist.

Much to Christian's chagrin, David played up Christian's Welsh birthplace to Americans, describing his son as the natural successor to other great Welsh/Celtic actors like Richard Burton and Anthony Hopkins. While he made the Hollywood social circuits, lobbying casting agents, producers, and directors to consider his son for roles, David found a ready audience for his interesting combination of social and political views. Thanks to his well-cultivated posh English accent, the proud father could easily spend hours talking about his favorite subjects: his beloved only son, name-dropping Steven Spielberg with empty promises of being able to set up meetings at Spielberg's Amblin Entertainment, or his unusual breed of politics.

Once in California, David set about to reinvent his family background to make it more colorful. David *Charles Howard* Bale became David *Spike* Bale. Christian *Charles Philip* Bale became Christian *Morgan* Bale. David liked the more Celtic-sounding name. As Christian's manager, he named their family production company Morgan Management. Christian would no longer go by Chris as he did back in Bournemouth. David also quickly aligned Christian's bio to core Hollywood interests such as vegetarianism and New Age spirituality. Though David became a vegetarian in California, the burger-loving teenage Christian had a tougher time giving up meat. In an interview, Christian explained his eating philosophy this way: "I don't adhere to vegetarianism because I eat fish and chicken. You could say I'm sort of elitist in what I consider more important life forms. But my theory is that I will eat something that I will kill with my own hands."

Emphatically anti-Republican and anti-Conservative, David was hoping that his politics would be simpatico with Hollywood, California. David was often a walking contradiction with his strange mishmash of twentieth-century liberalism and nineteenth-century British imperialism—in part a result of being raised by a military/safari hunter father in an affluent and privileged white area of South Africa during the apartheid era. He declared that he loved to drive Volkswagens because "Germans make the best cars," but then in the same breath, denounced the Japanese as the race for "whaling and World War II." His privileged upbringing in apartheid South Africa fostered a patronizing attitude toward people of color. He loudly proclaimed that he could tell the difference between Chinese, Japanese, and Koreans and he boasted that he only hired Mexican cleaning women because he was a proponent of minority women's rights.

David didn't realize that he often acted like a stereotypical tourist in America. He hated American food, scoffed at the "culture" (his air quotes), and constantly chuckled at the quality of American acting. He also complained about American politics ad nauseum. "American elections are far too important for just Americans to vote in!" he'd roar. Yet, he never said a word about leaving California with its sun-kissed beaches and balmy oceans.

He was also delighted with Californians' interest in spirituality. The intersection of Eastern and Western religions was like a California Roll—sushi for Western palates. This suited David's own smorgasbord approach to religion and he was happy to attend a variety of churches and temples. He was extremely anti-Catholic and happy to rage about the pope, but oddly enough, David considered St. James Catholic Church in nearby Redondo Beach his primary place of worship. He made a weekly ritual of snipping the "words of wisdom" and "thoughtful quotations" he found on the side of his herbal tea boxes, pasting them into a scrapbook for spiritual guidance.

Though he despised England, he bragged to any American who would listen that the most modern and progressive countries in the world were all former English colonies. But perhaps the most contradictory element of David's behavior was his assertion that he was a feminist even while he blatantly favored and spoiled his only son. Having daughters, he thought, automatically made him a feminist. The reality that I witnessed was that David treated his daughter Louise, who had moved to America with them, like the family maid. She was responsible for cooking and cleaning and laundry so that Christian could concentrate on reading scripts and preparing for roles. David paid scant interest in Sharon's life back in England;

even less so in his first daughter, Erin, back in South Africa. His ex-wives, Jenny and Sandra, he described as "mean-spirited harridans," who had been determined to destroy his dreams.

With such an assortment of views, you would think that having a conversation with David would be an ugly experience. But his undeniable charm, honey-coated with his British accent, only made him colorful and amiable. Back in Britain, Christian recalled that his father was unconventional and "was thought of as a bit odd." But "odd" was the norm in L.A. David became the consummate dinner party guest, delighted to monopolize every conversation with pointed views on virtually every subject.

He eagerly attended Hollywood functions and Democratic Party mixers. He happily portrayed himself as everyone's favorite eccentric uncle who always had something funny or outrageously politically incorrect to say. He came to realize that in L.A. everything sounded better with an English accent. And David was amazed that his gift of gab was more potent in America than it ever was in England.

After spending quite a bit of time with the family, I started to question some of the many inconsistencies of his self-proclaimed biography.

When I asked David what he really did back in England, David laughed and told me: "Oh, Harrison. I was a confidence trickster."

I was puzzled, startled. "Confidence trickster" is not a common term in the U.S. but in England, it's the equivalent of being a con man. From that point on, I realized I'd have to take everything David said with a grain of salt. You didn't need to be a therapist to see that David had had a troubled life filled with disappointments, so to make up for it, he was living vicariously through Christian, holding on tightly to the one thing in his life that could be a success.

But David's social skills would pay off soon enough for both of them.

[3]

Bale-Out

BALE (noun)

> *Etymology:* Middle English, from Old English *bealu*; akin to
> Old High German *balo* evil, Old Church Slavic *boli* sick person
> *Date:* before twelfth century
> 1: great evil
> 2: woe, sorrow
> **—Source: *Merriam Webster***

"I have a very sissy job, where I go to work and get my hair done,
and people do my makeup, and I go and say lines and people
spoil me rotten."
—Christian Bale, *Esquire*

In 1990, after the critical success of *Treasure Island*, which aired
as a TNT TV movie in the U.S., Christian's father, David, was
buoyed by Christian's show business prospects. Christian clearly
still had acting talent!

During this time, however, David was fighting a war with
Christian's mother, Jenny, over their son's future—specifically
whether it was to be in England or in America. In fact, with Christian's girlfriend, Natalie, on Jenny's side, England presented an

attractive option to the young teenager. Christian would return to England, finish school in Bournemouth, and go to university in England with Natalie. Christian enjoyed writing and had an interest in studying English. Jenny and Natalie pointed out other successful child actors like Jodie Foster and Jennifer Connelly, who had taken a break in their movie careers to go to university. Jenny strongly believed that a university education would prepare Christian for a happier future.

But on the strength of *Treasure Island* and a small part in a 1991 British TV movie, *A Murder of Quality*—which starred Denholm Elliot and Glenda Jackson and was based on a book by John le Carré—David managed to get Christian a U.S. talent agent with Triad Talent Agency. This was no small matter because even though Christian had been the star of a Steven Spielberg movie, it was years ago when he was just thirteen. The cruel reality for many child actors was that they were cast for their prepubescent looks, and often grew into unmarketable adults. Think about the post-Spielberg careers of Henry Thomas (*E.T.*), C. Thomas Howell (*E.T.*), Joseph Mazello (*Jurassic Park*), Jonathan Ke Quan (*Indiana Jones and the Temple of Doom*), or Corey Feldman (*The Goonies*). Fortunately for Christian, he didn't have an awkward public puberty—usually the death knell for many a child actor. Instead, young Christian was filling out nicely, growing into a handsome young man, six feet tall, with cheek bones like a male model.

"I've been lucky," Christian told a reporter about transitioning through puberty, "because there wasn't a sudden leap where people were saying: 'Oh what a cute kid,' and then it's: 'Bloody hell, what happened there, he's got zits and hair in his armpits!'"

With the help of Christian's new U.S. agent, David landed a three-picture deal with Disney. Christian would be paid more than $250,000 for his first picture. Not bad for a seventeen-year-old! Of course, you have to subtract the agent's 10 percent fee, and David paid himself another 5 percent as Christian's manager. Minus taxes and the costs of headshots, audition travel, clothes, and grooming, and an actor becomes quite an involved little business. And imagine David doing the math if his son could make at least two or three pictures a year! David triumphantly showed off the contract to Jenny, who could no longer argue about her son's potential in the U.S. She was still worried about Christian's inability to handle pressure, but she had to agree with David that life in America was looking very comfortable and prosperous.

Based in Burbank, California, Disney had a long-established reputation for discovering, developing, and debuting new talent since the days of the Mickey Mouse Club. Many first-time directors (like Kenny Ortega) got their start with Disney projects. And Disney movies and television projects were the ultimate launch pad for many a child actor. Ryan Gosling, Justin Timberlake, Britney Spears, Shia LaBeouf, Christina Aguilera, Lindsay Lohan, Miley Cyrus, and Hilary Duff are just a few stars who got their start in the House that the Mouse built.

But the flipside of being a product of the Disney machinery is that these actors would need to work very hard to progress past their Disney years and prove that they weren't just another fresh-faced, generic, bubble-gum tween that came off the Mickey Mouse assembly line. And at the insistence of the Disney marketing machine, these young actors had to commit to Christian's least favorite chore—publicity!

What finally pushed Christian to the U.S. was his father's unflagging confidence in his abilities and the prospects of lots of movie work. It seemed that Hollywood was truly the Land of Opportunity. While a U.K. project might take years to get production funding, here was David Bale waving around a three-picture Disney deal—an opportunity without parallel in England.

So Christian, who considered himself a serious actor and was hoping to play roles like his heroes, Steve McQueen and James

Dean, flew to Los Angeles in 1991 and prepared to shoot *Newsies*, definitely not the groundbreaking film he had in mind.

"It was either go to college or go to California and do *Newsies*," Christian told *Movieline*. "I decided to do the film."

"Bale's out of Bournemouth!" the *Daily Echo* headlined when the Bournemouth paper discovered that Christian was making the move to Los Angeles. "But I don't feel at home in Hollywood," Christian insisted in the article.

Back in England, David and Jenny had split their assets but decided to rent out the house on Capstone Road in Bournemouth. Sister Sharon had moved to London to pursue a music career, and Jenny was suddenly left alone in a big house she could no longer afford. "It broke my heart," she said. "We'd been a big, fun family and suddenly it was all over."

In early 1991, David first set up house in North Hollywood. He rented a small ranch-style house at 12315 Erwin Street to be close to the major studios in Burbank and Universal City. It was very convenient for Christian who was shooting *Newsies* at Universal Studios. In fact, this NoHo neighborhood was very popular with out-of-town families who had also relocated to Los Angeles for their children's aspiring movie careers. But David was soon annoyed at the nightly noisy flyovers from police and traffic helicopters and the hookers on the street. "This was not a home for a seventeen-year-old boy!" David told me.

Christian agreed at the time, sounding a little homesick. "L.A.'s too big, we can never walk anywhere so we always have to take the car and I talk to most people on the phone. I just wish I could do more work in England."

Christian did make one new friend in North Hollywood. While walking around the streets, Christian noticed a very dirty, scrappy-looking Jack Russell cross wandering the sidewalks. He chased the little dog down an alley where, giving up, the dog flopped to the pavement and fell asleep. Sitting in the middle of a dirty alley, cradling the exhausted dog, Christian looked at the poor dog's worn-down nails and pads. This was a tough little street dog with lots of mojo. Mojo became an official member of the Bale family.

As luck would have it, David was a packrat when it came to making and keeping contacts. David remembered an American fan named Donnie Flaherty, who had actually backpacked his way across England to Bournemouth to look for Christian. Flaherty was a surfer, a photographer, and an aspiring filmmaker. When he had met the Bales in Bournemouth, Donnie had extended an invitation to visit him in Hermosa Beach, one of the three beach cities—Manhattan Beach, Hermosa Beach, and Redondo Beach—made famous by the Beach Boys' song "Surfin' USA."

One sunny morning (are there any other kinds in California?), David made his way to Hermosa Beach, met up with Donnie, and ate at Good Stuff, the local breakfast eatery chain. As the two sat near the boardwalk in the morning sun with the Pacific Ocean roaring and crashing nearby, David was hooked. His family just had to live by the water. There would be so much to see and do and Christian could learn how to surf. And with a friend and fan in Donnie, Christian would enjoy California all the more.

Christian told the *Daily Echo* then: "Even though I would like to live in England, I realize I ought to buy here so it looks like I shall buy a place in an area known as Beach Town, which is about an hour from L.A."

On Friday, May 15, 1992, David bought 3101 Oak Avenue in Manhattan Beach, just north of Hermosa Beach, south of West Los Angeles, which includes Venice, Santa Monica, and Marina del Rey. Christian's monthly mortgage payment was just over $3,300. It was a roomy, two-story, slightly run-down stucco house that was built in 1947 and had an inground pool, a two-car garage, and lots of privacy. Though it was in serious need of updating, compared to their house in Bournemouth, 3101 Oak Avenue was like a tropical resort.

Oak Avenue was a leafy residential street just a block west off busy Sepulveda Boulevard, and right across from the local mall, Manhattan Village. With soaring palm trees and dense greenery, Oak Avenue itself was very quiet and secluded thanks to a privacy wall that ran the length of the entire block. The nearby mall had a Koo Koo Roo restaurant—Christian loved their chicken—a California Pizza Kitchen (the two-in-a-bowl soups were another favorite of Christian's), and an Olive Garden, which featured all-you-can-eat salads and breadsticks. It also had the unfortunately named department store Bullocks, which was the cause of much laughter in the Bale household since "bullocks" had a very different meaning in British slang. And just south of the mall on Sepulveda was the famous (but now defunct) Video Archives store where Quentin Tarantino used to work as a clerk.

The house itself was about 1,800 square feet, had four bedrooms and three bathrooms put together in an unusual layout, thanks to additions from previous owners. You entered the front door and immediately to your right was the staircase to the upper floor. There was a small living room and fireplace, which had a guest room and bathroom to the left by the garage door. Once you walked farther back to the kitchen, there was a dining room that led out to the pool. Off the kitchen was another bedroom where David slept.

Christian had the upstairs master bedroom, with a balcony that overlooked Oak Avenue. His sister Louise had the smaller second bedroom. Brother and sister shared the upstairs bathroom. From the bathroom window, you could climb out over the first floor and jump into the pool—something David sensibly forbade!

Oak Avenue would serve a couple of goals. First of all, David wanted a secure home base for Christian and Louise. He liked its seclusion from the hustle and bustle of Los Angeles. And David felt that the house's distance from Hollywood would also protect Christian from the intrusively competitive costars who would ask to drop over and read scripts with Christian. He was learning very quickly that those friendly visits were actually competitive scouting to see what scripts your agent was sending you.

With the beach just blocks away, the house on Oak Avenue was like a little paradise. But secondly, by buying a house, he had anchored Christian to California and committed the teenager to a mortgage of $3,300 a month—a considerable amount today, a tremendous amount in 1992! Christian would have no help with the house expenses as David had entered the U.S. on a visitor's visa and wasn't legally allowed to work, and Louise had just enrolled on her student visa to study Drama at El Camino College in nearby Torrance.

Adding to Christian's expenses, David leased himself a VW Jetta while Christian drove a Jeep Cherokee—something Louise teased him about because SUVs were not yet in vogue. That didn't change until 1993 when Spielberg's *Jurassic Park* helped spark the Ford Explorer/SUV rage.

Back in England, Jenny was feeling very lonely with the sudden changes in her family. Her eldest, Sharon, had moved to London with her musician boyfriend. And her two youngest had up and left with their father to move 6,000 miles away. With the eight-hour time difference between England and Los Angeles and with David always screening the calls, Jenny found it increasingly difficult to communicate with her children.

I remember David had an interesting way of screening Jenny's calls. He'd often cover the receiver with his hand and say to Christian: "Do you want to talk to mum? I think she wants money." And Christian, by reflex, would wave him off.

But the Oak Avenue house was an important step in establishing a base in the U.S. David outlined their plans:

- Establish a home base for security.
- Draw up plans for short-, medium-, and long-term future.
- Sort out finances.
- Get visas.
- Establish Christian's acting career; get an agent, a manager, and discuss aims and projects.
- Learn how to promote and publicize Christian to the industry and publicize him carefully.

If you've ever moved to another city, state, or province, you know how much work it is to set up a new home. In addition, David had to register Christian with all the appropriate agencies and organizations like the Screen Actor's Guild (SAG) so that they'd have his new agent and contact information in case producers or casting agents were looking for Christian. David was under the gun to set up their new home while Christian was still traveling back and forth between England and L.A. He wanted to make sure that Christian felt happier and more at home in Manhattan Beach than in England.

Newsies was shot in mid-1991, and then later in the year, Christian headed to Prague, Czechoslovakia, to shoot his second Disney picture, *Swing Kids*. The Disney folks recommended to David that Christian sign with a publicist to prepare for *Newsies'* anticipated 1992 theatrical release. Christian was adamant that he did not want one. In Hollywood, personal publicists are either paid by a project (to promote during a specific event, like a film release) or by a retainer. Additionally, every studio has a publicity team that works on a film's release—a studio expense that doesn't cost the actor. Though David set up exploratory meetings with a couple of publicists in L.A.—most notably with Joaquin Phoenix and Josh Hartnett's publicist, Susan Patricola—Christian declined to sign with any of them because of the added expense and the feeling that they could make do with free studio publicity whenever a movie was ready to be released. In between movie releases, Christian saw no need for any coverage.

Christian said to a reporter: "It was definitely a strategy. I like not being in magazines, not being seen on TV, except when I'm actually in a film."

Unlike other young Hollywood hopefuls, Christian was no publicity whore. Publicity was obviously a touchy subject for Christian since his Paris breakdown. David gingerly tried to reach magazine editors on his own. His seventeen-year-old son needed to build an American fan base that had forgotten him by name since 1987's *Empire of the Sun*. With Christian starring in an upcoming Disney movie, David managed to get a couple teen publications to notice. Magazines like *Bop* and *Teen Beat* were interested in covering the handsome English teen—would he pose shirtless with a surfboard? Those kinds of inquiries, David knew, would send his son scurrying into a corner.

Christian was still flying back and forth between London and L.A. as he would finish a project, go "'home" to visit his girlfriend, Natalie, and his mum, then back "home" to L.A. for any auditions David and the agent had arranged. This multinational arrangement added to Christian's internal debate about his future. No surprise, while he was in England, Jenny and Natalie warned Christian to be careful with his money. It was clear to them that David had control of all his funds. And when Christian was back in California, David started his own attack, reminding Christian that his mother was excessively English in her negativity and didn't have confidence in her son's abilities as an actor.

Christian, David, and Louise often complained about English negativity compared to America's can-do spirit. David was particularly anti-England, especially when he lived there under the Conservative Thatcher era. He felt that England was still very class conscious—in particular, how one's accent, whether it be posh or Cockney, could betray your education and social standing. "Who decided," David wondered, "this English system of haves and have-nots?" In fact, Christian agreed with his father after his post-*Empire of the Sun* fallout. It seemed that people were happy to see him fail—back to his station, if you will. But the unpredictability of possible Hollywood movie stardom meant that a poor kid from Wales could suddenly catapult into fame and fortune.

Long an influence in her brother's life, elder sister Louise had this to say about living in America versus England: "I love living in America, and especially in Los Angeles, I love this city. I much prefer the weather, the lifestyle, the ocean, and the variety of people. I don't miss the English weather, or the negativity which is very prevalent in the cities."

The tug-of-war between David and Jenny over Christian swung decidedly in David's favor in 1992. When Christian returned to Bournemouth from a trip to Switzerland in January, he discovered that his two beloved pets, a cat named Kouky and a bird named Percy, were gone.

"Christian was so depressed," David recalled, "but I told him that it wasn't his fault. In fact, I blamed his mum, Jenny, for not caring enough, for not being responsible." To assuage his son's pain, David bought Christian instructional sex books and CDs of rave music for his eighteenth birthday.

Jenny made a fateful decision to take a mother-son vacation to Morocco in the spring of 1992 after *Newsies'* disastrous opening weekend. She wanted to spend some quality time with her son as she felt it was the end of an era. Her little boy was now an eighteen-year-old young man. If David was right, Christian was on the cusp of stardom in Hollywood. But if she was right, Christian could very well buckle under the pressure and competition and return to England in defeat. Jenny was very annoyed that David had saddled Christian with the mortgage on the house in

Manhattan Beach. David could not legally work. Student Louise was not working. It seemed pretty obvious (to her, at least) that David was using Christian to pursue his own dreams of living in America. That entire home base in America was all dependent on her son, and if David wasn't careful, Christian could have another breakdown from the same kinds of pressure he had experienced during the doomed *Empire of the Sun* junket.

On May 17, 1992, just days after Christian and Jenny returned from their Morocco vacation,and two days after David had bought the house on Oak Avenue, Christian was admitted to emergency at Poole Hospital in Bournemouth. He was vomiting violently and had serious diarrhea. Since he had just returned from Morocco, the doctors suspected that he had drunk or eaten something contaminated. In fact, when a panicky David got ahold of Christian by phone, he was told that perhaps he had eaten something with fecal matter in it.

"My son was fed *shite*?" David bellowed at the thought. "This was Jenny's fault. Everyone knows whilst traveling in a third world country that you don't drink the water or eat anything suspect!"

Christian spent a miserable week in the hospital, undergoing test after test. David felt powerless, stuck in Los Angeles while his son was ill in Bournemouth. He did not trust Jenny's ability to take care of his son. And he did not think that Jenny would ask the doctors the right questions.

Additionally, David was very concerned about the severity of Christian's illness. Though actors who are members of the Screen Actors Guild (SAG) have health insurance—and Christian's care in England would be covered under the U.K. National Health—an actor's health is an important part of his/her cast-worthiness. David was worried that if Christian developed a reputation of being sickly, no one would cast him. The issue was a pragmatic one. Producers want to hire actors who are healthy enough to complete a movie shoot.

David blasted Jenny over Christian's illness. Jenny had to concede that David was very effective working the phones, calling the doctors and pharmacists back in Bournemouth to find the best treatment they recommended for his son. But it was cruel for David to use Christian's illness against her and her maternal skills.

A few months later, it would be David's turn to have his parenting skills put to the test.

In December of 1992, David put together a trip to take Christian and Louise back to South Africa to meet their grandfather, Philip, and his second wife, Deborah. Christian recalled, "He had cancer, and he was basically hanging on to meet us." They would spend Christmas and New Year's touring the Transkei Coast and visiting the Hluhluwe-Umfolozi Game Reserve.

A few weeks later, Christian was sick again. In mid-January 1993, he was admitted to Entabeni Hospital in Durban, South Africa, with the same symptoms as his previous illness. Could it be malaria? A burst appendix? David was at wit's end as Christian was transferred from specialist to specialist. Poor Christian spent his nineteenth birthday in a hospital, suffering through another round of tests and painful exploratory surgeries.

By the time Christian, David, and Louise left South Africa in February 1993, they had also left behind Christian's medical bills, which David had hoped SAG would pay. Adding to the family misfortune, David's father died a few months later.

But by November, David had to respond to Dr. Peter Jeffrey, a family friend of his father's who had covered Christian's medical bills.

David remembered telling Jeffrey: "I can only apologize. I am embarrassed and feel that I should never darken your door again. I owe you the unrepayable: my son's life and well-being. Millions would be a mere token, and yet I cannot seem to get even your fee to you. I feel that I must perforce have lost the friendship of people who were very dear to me, and to whom I am eternally indebted, and that is very sad."

As Christian recovered back in his new bedroom on Oak Avenue in the warm California sunshine, David vowed to protect his son even more.

[4]

Newsies

"You say something bad about *Newsies* and you have an awful lot of people to answer to."
—**Christian Bale**

Imagine in some alternate universe, Christian Bale didn't get the part in *Empire of the Sun*. Or imagine if *Empire of the Sun* had been yet another Spielberg blockbuster. How would Christian have handled the superhot stardom that followed the likes of Henry Thomas and Drew Barrymore after *E.T.*? Would he have had more breakdowns? Would he have ended up a hermit on some deserted island? In this could-have, would-have, should-have scenario, imagine if Christian's dad had not tricked his son into starring in *Newsies*. Ah, the mind boggles at the possibilities!

Newsies is the movie that Christian least likes on his filmography. Whenever a movie is released, there's the accompanying press kit that contains the lead actor's biography and filmography highlights in a couple paragraphs. Are you surprised that actors like to leave off any stinkers from their filmography? Actors and publicists call these: OFR (Omitted From Résumé). *Newsies* is Christian's OFR—he is embarrassed by it. And yet the fan-beloved *Newsies* was the pivotal movie that would launch his stardom on the Internet. And in that alternate universe without *Newsies*, Christian would not have become Batman and would not have married his wife. And a guy by the name of Zac Efron would not be the star he is today. I promise, I'll explain!

In early 1991, David had traded Christian's U.K. agent for an American agent with eyes firmly on a goal to move to Hollywood. Just a few years earlier, Christian was telling the press that his heroes were James Dean and Steve McQueen. He had said that he wanted to work with Gary Oldman and Keanu Reeves. So how did he end up starring in a Disney musical?

David, as Christian's manager, screened the scripts submitted to his son. He worked combatively with Christian's agent, like some child-actor parents do. It's the nature of the game. Many show business parents become suspicious of agents and managers, not entirely convinced that they have their child's best interests at heart. David wanted to leverage Christian's experience—having starred in a Steven Spielberg movie and costarred with Charlton Heston—to convince American producers that his son was no untried newcomer. At the age of seventeen, Christian had worked with the biggest American director in the world on a big movie.

When the Disney drama *Hard Promises* came to Christian and David's attention, David was convinced that this was the starring vehicle to relaunch his son's career in America. They had just lost out a chance to audition for *White Fang*, the Disney period action film that helped to build the career of Ethan Hawke. In casting circles, many people thought that Christian looked a lot like a younger Ethan Hawke, so Christian's agent was going after projects that would have been offered to or passed on by Hawke. That's how casting rivalries are born. And Christian would have some famous rivals on his way up: Ewan McGregor, Jake Gyllenhaal, and perhaps most infamously, Leonardo DiCaprio.

But in 1991, the actors Christian and David targeted were Ethan Hawke and River Phoenix. Hawke was another former child actor who was successfully building a career into adulthood. Hawke was only fifteen years old when he starred with River Phoenix in the sci-fi fantasy *Explorers*. And Hawke would win rave reviews in the prestigious Peter Weir film *Dead Poets Society*, with Robin Williams and Robert Sean Leonard, Christian's future *Swing Kids* costar. Based on the Jack London novel, *White Fang* would be a surprise box office hit for Disney and Ethan Hawke.

River Phoenix was the Renaissance man for Young Hollywood of the 1980s and '90s, since he gained attention for his outstanding appearance in *Stand by Me*. He had earned an Oscar nomination for *Running on Empty* (written by Jake Gyllenhaal's mother, Naomi Foner). He was a vegetarian and environmentalist. He, too, was a former child actor, who had gained mainstream attention costarring in Spielberg's blockbuster *Indiana Jones and the Last Crusade*. For the decade after his tragic death in 1993, Phoenix would cast a long shadow over Young Hollywood.

Christian was closer in age to Hawke. Teenage Christian bore a strong resemblance to teenage Hawke. They had similar coloring, the same cheekbones. In fact, they could have been cast as brothers. And quite often at film festivals in the 1990s, Christian would be mistaken for the young Texan.

The wisdom in Hollywood is that a good up-and-coming actor should know how to market himself and follow in the footsteps of successful actors. The career stages in show business:

Who's Tom Cruise?
I want Tom Cruise!
I want a Tom Cruise type!
Who's Tom Cruise?

So for those producers looking for an Ethan Hawke type, David and agent were pleased to offer Christian Bale! Christian met the Disney producers in London to read for *Hard Promises*, a David vs. Goliath drama about a real-life 1899 newsboys strike in New York. The main challenge at the time would be to speak convincingly with a nineteenth-century New York accent. Christian, a gifted mimic, easily won the part.

In 1991, when David moved to Los Angeles, interesting projects were developing at Disney. Under studio chief Michael Eisner, Jeffrey Katzenberg was in charge of Disney's motion pictures division. With Katzenberg at the helm, Disney had entered a critical and commercial renaissance in the late '80s and early '90s, with box office hits like *Who Framed Roger Rabbit*, *The Little Mermaid*, and *Beauty and the Beast*. And the sound of that success was soundtrack composer Alan Menken, who would win best score and best song Oscars for *The Little Mermaid*, *Beauty and the Beast*, *Aladdin*, and *Pocahontas*. Obviously, Disney had the golden touch when it came to family-friendly animation—and they were all musicals.

Disney decided to turn *Hard Promises* into a big-budget musical called *Newsies*. For a nice dusting of Disney box office magic, *Newsies* would be powered by their Oscar-winning composer Alan Menken. The lyrics to the *Ragtime*-like song-and-dance numbers would be written by Jack Feldman, best known for writing Barry Manilow's 1978 hit "Copacabana (At the Copa)." And Disney chose a young Kenny Ortega to direct. This would be Ortega's first time directing, but he was an apt choice to update the live-action musical as a genre for a new generation since he was the influential choreographer of hit movies like *Dirty Dancing* and major music videos for Madonna and Michael Jackson.

Christian's dad was faced with a dilemma. If he told Christian that he was relocating to Hollywood to star in a musical, Christian would probably stay in England. And though Christian had a three-picture deal with Disney, who knew how much longer they'd have to wait for the next "right" project to come along? And the more time Christian spent in England, the more time he was exposed to the influences of his mother and his girlfriend, Natalie, who were both pushing the "stay in England and go to university" option. So David had many obstacles to convince Christian to sign on with *Newsies*. He and Kenny Ortega prepared carefully for their first *Newsies* meeting with Christian.

In an interview with *Seventeen*, Christian recalls that meeting: "I read for the film in England and then Disney flew me to Los Angeles for a screen test. But before I signed a contract, I met the director [Kenny Ortega] and told him I wasn't comfortable with the dancing and singing and I didn't want to be a bloody Artful Dodger in a remake of *Oliver!*, jumping down the street with a big smile on my face. But he told me it wouldn't be like that and he lied to me about all of these different actors who had done musicals, like Al Pacino."

But Christian was still very reluctant: "I didn't want to do a musical specifically. It came my way. I read the script first when it was a drama. By the time I auditioned for it though, it had already become a musical. For the first few auditions, I refused to sing or dance. That didn't last long."

Christian was worried about ending up like Mark Lester, the star of *Oliver!*, the giant 1968 hit musical adaptation of *Oliver Twist*. That movie didn't do much for the career of its young Disney star; Lester gave up acting at the age of nineteen.

But David knew better than to tell Christian that he "should" or "must" take this Disney picture. Skillfully, he persuaded Christian to think of *Newsies* as an actor's challenge on many levels. There was the New York accent and the athleticism of the dance. David also echoed Kenny Ortega's fib that Al Pacino had also started with musicals. In the years before handy Internet resources like the Internet Movie Database (IMDb), there was no easy way for Christian to check if his dad and Ortega were lying to him.

And there was every expectation that this big-budget production, like every other Disney movie in the past ten years, would become a worldwide hit, like Ethan Hawke's *White Fang*. What more could Christian ask for to relaunch his movie career?

Faced with his father's logical arguments and charmed by Kenny Ortega's earnestness, Christian reluctantly agreed. He told *Movieline*: "Eventually I said: 'Fuck it, let's just do it.' But I had a lot of doubts about it—I never liked musicals, and even then I knew I'd never do anything like that again."

Newsies was transformed into a musical, based loosely—*very* loosely—on a real-life 1899 newsboys' strike in New York City. Christian would star as street kid Jack Kelly, who would take a couple brothers, Davy and Les, under his wing to teach them how to hawk papers on the street. Jack eventually falls in love with their older sister, Sarah, and then rallies all the newsboys into a big musical number, a strike against the evil Joseph Pulitzer and his newspaper, *The World*.

Though Christian was not a big enough star to have final casting approval, Ortega generously invited Christian to participate in the auditioning of his character's love interest, Sarah. One actress who did not make the cut was Milla Jovovich, who would go on to star in *Resident Evil*. Though Jovovich could sing, her readings with Christian were abrasive. Christian dismissed any actress he felt was too modern-looking since *Newsies* was set in 1899.

The actress who won the part was nineteen-year-old Ele Keats. Oddly enough, poor Keats could not sing at all, as she later revealed: "I didn't know it was going to be a musical. I am not a singer at all. A vocal teacher spent some time with me to teach me to sing properly. I am totally tone deaf. There was a song in *Newsies* that Sarah was supposed to sing but after trying it a few times with the vocal teacher, Kenny Ortega decided to cut it."

Working with Christian was a little intimidating for Keats. She recalled: "I felt really bad for him when he had to do a scene with me because I freeze up a lot and he always seems cool and natural in front of the camera. I think, at first, we were a little uncomfortable around each other but after a while, we became friends."

In the large cast were two other young actors working on making the transition to grown-up roles. David Moscow had played the younger version of Tom Hanks in *Big*. And Gabriel Damon was the veteran of many TV shows, including *Star Trek: The Next Generation*. Many of the other kids were Disney veterans like Aaron Lohr (*The Mighty Ducks*).

Rounding out the cast in the adult roles were a couple of impressive names: Robert Duvall played Joseph Pulitzer, Ann-Margret would be Medda, a local townhall owner, and Bill Pullman would be the newspaper reporter, Bryan Denton.

Christian tried to get his dog, Mojo, an appearance on *Newsies*, but alas, Mojo—not a little dog that was good with commands or crowds—didn't work out. However, Christian's girlfriend, Natalie, was an extra who appears at the beginning—the schoolgirl wearing a hat who walks by the ogling gang of newsboys. And Christian's sister Louise was also an extra, playing Ann-Margret's maid.

"Working as an extra on *Newsies* was a blast!" Louise remembered. "I had so much fun all summer long. I got to dress in a different period costume every day I worked, and I got to hang out with all the cast, who were so much fun. Being an extra is not easy however. The day usually begins at 6 am, you sit around for 90 percent of the day, and then you're the last to leave the set at around 9 pm."

Though she didn't have any lines as an extra, Louise was thrilled to be very visible in a scene with Ann-Margret.

She recalled: "I was absolutely terrified when I found out that I was in a scene with her, and then even more terrified when I found out how close the camera would be. She made me feel very comfortable, and she was extremely professional. Before we shot the scene where she is trying to get to the Newsie who is getting beaten by the police, she pulled me aside and told me that she was really going to go for it, and that I had better hold her back. Well, I didn't have to act at all! She is a strong lady! I really had to work hard to hold her back, and then dragging her away was a real workout. In the chaos of it all, Ann-Margret accidentally kicked me in the same place in the knee take after take. By the end of the day I had a huge bruise on the side of my knee, and I took a photograph of it. I'm very proud to have a battle wound from Ann-Margret!"

Kenny Ortega had trained under Hollywood legend Gene Kelly (*Singin' in the Rain*), and he believed in being prepared. He set up a two-month *Newsies* camp for the cast to train and rehearse. As many of the cast members were not trained dancers, they had to learn the basics, including jumps and turns. During training camp, Gene Kelly made a set visit and complimented the boys on their work.

Said Christian: "I don't know what kind of dance you would call the *Newsies'* training but we got very fit, jumped around a lot and I got very dizzy."

Ortega was thrilled with the comprehensive regimen: "This was very different for most of them, and obviously very hard work. They had to be in dance class every day, then have voice lessons, dialect and scene studies, gymnastics, and martial arts classes. All this in addition to their regular school studies!"

By all accounts, the *Newsies* set was very boisterous. Managing a large cast of teenage boys would be a challenge. Ever the worrywart, David visited the set daily with a large bag of vitamins and nutritional supplements to keep Christian's energy up. He was always concerned about Christian's health.

It was that insurability issue again. Christian had told me, "Bloody Hollywood. If they think you're sick all the time, you'll never get work! The production companies won't insure you! American actors dripping with syphilis and gonorrhea and they work. But let one English actor cough or wheeze and the producers will send you packing back to England!"

Ele Keats recalled: "I have never worked with a cast that size before, so it was a challenge, but fun. I didn't get too close to a lot of people because most of the boys had worked with each other for weeks already when I came in. But we all became friends. The crowd scenes were fun, but exhausting. Because there were thousands of kids all over the place, it could sometimes take an hour to get everyone in the right spot."

To help the main cast of newsboys bond, the producers arranged frequent social events like softball games or pizza parties. Robert Duvall came out one evening for a bowling party with the young cast. When David asked the Oscar-winning actor for career advice for Christian, Duvall recommended that Christian go to university. Duvall himself had graduated with a degree in drama and had a strong New York theater background when he was roommates in the 1950s with another struggling actor by the name of Dustin Hoffman. "School is a strong foundation for technique and there is nothing like the live theater to train an actor's instincts," David recalled Duvall saying.

"Good advice," David said, "but that wouldn't work for Christian as he's already committed to moving to L.A." And even if David would have allowed Christian to entertain the thought of university, there was the practical matter of where. If Christian remained in England, he would have paid regular tuition fees. In America, he would have had to pay the much higher foreign student rates.

During the making of *Newsies*, cast member Michael Goorjian made a twenty-five-minute home-movie horror spoof called
Blood Drips Heavily on Newsies Square, where "Don Knotts" sys-
tematically kills off the newsboys one by one. The short became
a cult hit on YouTube and offers a peek at the high spirits on set.
Goorjian went on to a successful film and TV career, winning an
Emmy and a number of film festival awards for his short films.
(*Blood Drips Heavily on Newsies Square* would eventually be sur-
passed on YouTube by *F*cking Newsies*, the spoof trailer mashup
of *Newsies* and Christian's foul-mouthed tirade on the set of *Terminator Salvation*.)

Christian told a reporter that the teeming masses on *Newsies*
were also hormonally charged: "It was a massive production, with
hundreds of extras. Apparently there were a few extra kids who
were offering their services to anybody who paid, all during the
time we shot there. There was even a *Newsies* pimp ring. They
used the sets, wherever. They were using my dressing room on
my days off, I heard later."

All Disney movies have a happy ending—an unwritten law
from the early days of founder Walt Disney when he was creating
American interpretations of beloved fairy tales and parables. It
was part of Disney's feeling that American optimism meant that
you could wish upon a star and your dreams would come true.

So for *Newsies*, the happy ending meant the newsboys' strike
against Pulitzer would be successful and that street kid Jack Kelly
would give up his dreams of moving to Santa Fe and stay in New
York with his love interest, Sarah. That did not sit well with
Newsies fans, who openly detested Sarah as the "Destroyer of
Dreams." For a time, Ele Keats was called the most hated woman
in the Balehead World—especially thanks to the "inappropriate
for the time period" tonsil-tickling kiss she has with Christian at
the end of the movie, his first on-screen smooch.

How was Christian as a kisser? Keats said: "I would have to rate

Christian's kiss as a 7 or 8. We were both pretty uncomfortable, and I was going out with someone else at the time, so it was a pretty hard scene to shoot!"

Christian was also amused at how jealous his girlfriend, Natalie, was of Keats. Christian told me that at a house party, Natalie actually starting harassing Ele so badly that Keats locked herself in the bathroom.

Christian also argued with Ortega about the ending of *Newsies*. Would Jack Kelly be willing to give up everything to stay in New York in poverty? Not likely, but Ortega stuck to the script at hand.

And, as the critics were happy to point out, in real life, the newsboys' strike was actually a failure, and Pulitzer's publishing empire was hardly damaged. Pulitzer Prize, anyone?

When *Newsies* wrapped, David arranged for a cast party cruise to Catalina Island. (When the tenth anniversary edition of the *Newsies* DVD was released, David was furious when Ortega, in the DVD extras, mentions the Catalina trip but didn't mention who had paid for it.) It had been a tough shoot but Ortega, Christian, and David were confident that *Newsies* would be the big Disney hit for 1992.

By the fall of 1991, Christian had moved on to begin rehearsals in London for his next Disney picture, *Swing Kids*, which would shoot on location in Prague. It would be another big-budget production with dancing but luckily no singing—a drama about the rise of the Hitler Youth before the outbreak of World War II. With a top-notch cast that included Kenneth Branagh and Barbara Hershey, as well as young stars Robert Sean Leonard and Noah Wyle (*ER*), Christian's future was looking bright. He flew back and forth between L.A. and London to finish the ADR (Automated Dialogue Replacement) sessions on *Newsies*, and he eagerly awaited its opening weekend.

Released in April 1992, *Newsies* was a huge flop. The critics hated the movie and apparently so did the public at large as it grossed a minuscule $2.8 million—an astonishingly small amount of money for a major studio release. It seemed that everyone connected to *Newsies* was covered in the stink of failure. Industry insiders joked that *Newsies* (now sneered as *Flopsies*) was the *Howard the Duck* of the 1990s. Indeed, some Disney insiders claimed that two major bombs helped to end Jeffrey Katzenberg's tenure with the Mouse House in 1994. One bomb was *Newsies*.

The other? *Swing Kids*.

David was filtering to Christian the few positive reviews and blamed Disney for not marketing *Newsies* aggressively, but it was very hard for Christian not to take it personally. His first starring movie role since *Empire of the Sun* was an epic dud. As his son's manager and the guy who pushed the script, David was also very disappointed at the reception to *Newsies*.

David had to search high and low for a good *Newsies* review. Typical reviews looked like this:

New York Times' Janet Maslin, who wrote: "The premise for *Newsies*, an elaborate Disney live-action musical about the New York newsboys' strike of 1899, never sounded all that promising in the first place. But this film's real trouble lies in its joyless, pointless execution. Many of the musical numbers are staged so strangely that the characters, when they begin singing, appear to have taken leave of their senses."

Critic Roger Ebert chimed in with: "What I find hard to believe, however, is that anyone thought the screenplay based on these actual events was of compelling interest. *Newsies* is like warmed-over Horatio Alger, complete with such indispensable clichés as the newsboy on crutches, the little kid, and of course the hero's best pal, who has a pretty sister."

And Desson Howe at the *Washington Post* noted: "In some bright scriptwriter's brain, there's a musical that evokes the heyday of Rooney and Garland and stirs you up with song and dance. Walt Disney's *Newsies* is not that musical."

Disney's great endeavor to revive the live-action musical was over. Later that year Disney returned to more familiar territory—the animated musical—and released *Aladdin* (music by Oscar-winner Alan Menken, the *Newsies* soundtrack composer as well), which would gross $217 million in the U.S., $479 million world-wide. The Mouse had learned its lesson about live-action musicals. It would take another ten years before Australian director Baz Luhrmann would strike live-action musical gold with *Moulin Rouge*.

Why did *Newsies* bomb at the box office? Many other Disney movies have been critic-proof and gone on to box office success. Some industry insiders pointed to the movie's length. It seemed that after Kevin Costner's success with his 1990 *Dances with Wolves*, every director—even a first-time director—wanted director's cut. *Newsies'* runtime: 121 minutes. By comparison, *Little Mermaid*'s runtime: 89 minutes. *Aladdin*: 90 minutes. *Pocahontas*: 81 minutes. *Newsies* was even longer than Ortega's favorite musical, the 1952 classic *Singin' in the Rain*: 101 minutes. *Newsies* fans take great joy in pointing out the continuity errors, clearly the results of Ortega's struggle to edit down his lengthy movie to two hours.

Movie theater owners prefer shorter movies because they can have more show times during the day. A theater owner needs that time in between screenings to clean up the theater and prep it for the next audience.

Another theory why *Newsies* bombed: Because the movie's story line was about the newsboys' strike, this was an unusually pro-union labor movie from Disney. Disney movies were typically nonpolitical in theme, comfortably about fairy tales or the environment or the colors of the wind. As a Disney-fied version of *Norma Rae*, parents were probably looking at the scathing reviews, noticing the lengthy running time, and realizing that this was not a Disney cartoon. Pass. What else is playing at the megaplex?

So 1992 shaped up as a tough year for Christian. After the disastrous opening of *Newsies* in April, David went ahead and saddled Christian with the mortgage on the Manhattan Beach house. Christian went with his mother on that fateful trip to Morocco and fell ill—the case of the fecal matter in the food. The release date for his next film, *Swing Kids*, was being continually pushed back. Originally planned as a Christmas 1992 movie, it was now looking like a 1993 release. The retreating release date was not a good sign.

However, there were a couple people who had seen *Newsies* on the big screen who would have a profound effect on Christian's life. Winona Ryder caught a screening of *Newsies* and fell in love with the movie. Ryder would go on to cast Christian in the movie *Little Women*. And by meeting and befriending Winona, Christian would meet her personal assistant, his future wife, Sibi Blazic. And 2,200 miles away from Los Angeles, I caught the movie at the Kingsway Theater on Bloor Avenue in Toronto, Canada, and began to make a connection with the young actor from *Empire of the Sun*.

As fate would have it, *Newsies* ended up being important to the movie universe. In a couple years following its theatrical release, *Newsies* would thrive as a huge hit on video thanks to an army of Baleheads and Christian's well-orchestrated Internet marketing campaigns. It was the beginning of Christian's rule over the Internet.

Director Kenny Ortega, bitterly disappointed by *Newsies'* original box office failure, would begin to get fan mail from people who loved *Newsies*. One young fan in San Francisco even changed his name to Jack Kelly and started a very popular fan site. In fact, Christian and Ortega received letters from fans around the world who had gotten their high school theater departments or glee clubs to perform numbers from *Newsies*. In 2006, Kenny Ortega would return to the genre and direct all three *High School Musical* TV movies for Disney, launching the careers of a new generation of Disney stars, including Vanessa Hudgens and Zac Efron.

The success of the *High School Musical* movies was one of the influences of the hit 2009 TV series *Glee*. In 2010, Disney quietly registered a bunch of Internet domain names, subtly revealing that they were about to adapt *Newsies* into a Broadway musical. On March 3, 2010, Disney registered newsiesbroadway. com, newsiesmusical.com, newsiesontour.com, newsiesthemusical.com, and newsiestickets.com. Then, on September 15, 2011, *Newsies* opened onstage at the Paper Mill Playhouse in New Jersey—a key theater to beta test Broadway-bound productions—to rave reviews. Newsies opened on Broadway on March 15, 2012, at the Nederlander Theatre. Amazingly, one of Disney's biggest bombs is still popular twenty years later. Not bad for a movie that is OFR!

By the way, Zac Efron's first major pre-*High School Musical* role was in the 2004 TV series *Summerland*, in which his character's name was . . . Cameron Bale.

Christian and I sitting around the pool, making plans for world domination!

[5]

Christian Fail

"Now, before I was a movie star, I had other jobs, you know, low-paying, menial jobs. And I can tell you the best job I ever had was being a professional movie star. Because, as a movie star, I get paid a ridiculous amount of money and I don't have to work that hard. So, to sum it all up, being a movie star? High reward, low effort."

—Mel Gibson, *SNL* monologue

PETER MÜLLER: "You're turning into a fucking Nazi!"
THOMAS BERGER: "Oh, so what if I am?"

—*Swing Kids*

I f you want to be a movie star in Hollywood, you have to be "box office."

It's that simple. That's not cold and that's not cruel, it's just the bottom line. Hollywood is in the business of making money, so stars are the actors who sell movie tickets, drum up movie rentals or downloads, and move DVDs—that's how they are "box office."

If you ask an agent or a producer, who's the best actor in Hollywood, they're going to go by the actor's box office appeal. In an artistic and creative world like moviemaking, you might measure an actor's skill by his awards or reviews, but the bean counters go by grosses.

This is the age-old argument about *quantity* versus *quality*, *movie star* versus *actor*. Ask yourself, what's the best food in the world? Judging by quantity, one could argue that the Big Mac must be the best food in the world. A professional chef in Paris will, of course, gag in his sauce pan, but by sheer quantity, McDonald's has that worldwide "box office" clout that no other restaurant has.

Now ask yourself, who's the best living actor in the world? If you go by grosses, it's arguably Harrison Ford, a movie star who has yet to win an Oscar. His name alone could guarantee that a movie opens at number one at the box office. Will Smith's name could also guarantee a number-one opening, though he, too, has yet to win an Oscar.

So for an up-and-coming actor, the goals are the same. You need to do good work that attracts an audience. And you need to demonstrate to the studios and producers that *your* name in the credits makes them money. If you can attract a large worldwide audience, all the better. No surprise, then, that action movies are the studio's favorites because they translate well worldwide.

When the *Transformer* movies became huge box office hits, you could see the jockeying between the major parties for credit. Was a *Transformer* movie a hit because of director Michael Bay? Because of up-and-coming Shia LaBeouf? Or because of new hottie on the block Megan Fox? As Bay reminded a reporter: "Shia LaBeouf wasn't a big movie star before he did *Transformers*. Nobody in the world knew about Megan Fox until I found her and put her in *Transformers*."

Acting awards are nice trophies for the actor but the studios really don't care about an award unless it helps grosses. Obviously not having an Oscar didn't hurt *Transformers*! But you can bet that career-minded actors will keep alternating their action franchises with films that showcase their acting for an Oscar win. Christian won his Oscar for *The Fighter*, not *Batman*!

Both David and Christian's agent believed in the old Hollywood advice that any actor yearning for a career of longevity and substance had to follow the rule: "Do one for the studio, then one for yourself." Essentially, do a studio film to make the studio money, so you have the freedom to do an indie film of your choice to show off your acting skills.

Initially in 1991, Christian's career was looking pretty good. He had a three-picture deal with Disney, so that took care of his big studio obligations. After shooting *Newsies*, Christian found a small project he wanted to do, *Prince of Jutland*. Most British actors consider Shakespeare's *Hamlet* a true test of acting mettle, and here was an oddball indie film that was going back to the source legends that served as Shakespeare's basis for Hamlet.

Prince of Jutland was an independent film. By comparison, studio films—financed and produced by a major studio—have their own distribution network. A simplified definition of an "independent film" is a film without studio funding and seeking a distributor, presumably after making the tours of film market and festivals.

On paper, this looked like a very prestigious project. Gabriel Axel, an Oscar-winning director, was at the helm, the interpretation of *Hamlet* was inventive and fresh, and the cast was chock-full of impressive British actors. Christian starred as young Prince Amled. His love interest was a very young Kate Beckinsale (*Underworld*) with whom he'd reunite many years later in *Laurel Canyon*. His costars included: Helen Mirren, Brian Cox, Gabriel Byrne (his future *Little Women* costar), Tom Wilkinson, as well as future stars Ewen Bremner (*Trainspotting*) and Andy Serkis (*The Lord of the Rings*).

Unfortunately, Gabriel Axel was seventy-six at the time and in poor health, so, disappointingly, the final cut of *Prince of Jutland* seemed unfinished and uninspired. As a result, the film couldn't find a distributor for a theatrical release in North America. For Christian's fans though, it's an important film, as it featured Christian's first nude scene.

"Yes, it's true," Christian said. "Set foot on Danish soil and clothes seem to become a burden. Almost everyone in the film had a go at a nude scene."

The good-natured production helped Christian relax for his scene where, at night in a barn's rafters, he crawls nude through the hay, bare bubble butt in full view, to hit a prying Steven Waddington on the head with a stick.

Christian recalled: "Axel kept yelling to me: 'No pee-pee! No pee-pee!' So I kept my chest and stomach down and ended up all scratched up by the coarse hay. I had red marks on my body for weeks."

Director Axel also had a laugh at Christian's gestures in a scene with Brian Cox when Cox presents Christian with a foot-long wooden shaft. While the two talk, Christian absentmindedly begins to stroke the upright shaft until Axel had to yell: "Cut! You look like you are playing with your pee-pee!"

Prince of Jutland failed to find a distributor and languished for years until Christian's fans—the mighty Baleheads—campaigned to get Miramax to release it on video, heavily reedited with a new title, *Royal Deceit*.

Prince of Jutland was Christian's first experience with an independent film and all its distribution challenges. And after seeing the uneven work, Christian was happy to add this title to his Omitted From Résumé list.

What a difference twelve months can make. By 1992, Christian Bale's career was looking a little shaky. American producers, if they had heard of him at all, only vaguely knew him as the former child star of Spielberg's biggest bomb, *Empire of the Sun*. By April, Christian was also known as the teen star of Disney's biggest bomb, *Newsies*. His European indie film, *Prince of Jut-land*, couldn't find a distributor. In some Hollywood circles, he had earned the nickname "Christian Fail." Fortunately, Christian thought, he had his next big studio film coming out soon— *Swing Kids*!

Shot in Prague, Czechoslovakia, *Swing Kids* was not released until March 1993. *Swing Kids* was another pricey big production for Disney under their Hollywood Pictures label. Like *Newsies*, *Swing Kids* was also loosely based on a true story. It was about the growing power of the Nazi party and the creation of the Hitler Youth—sort of a Boy Scouts for fascists. In pre–World War II Hamburg, a group of swing kids—German teenagers who loved American big band swing music—defied the Nazis and the peer pressure of the Hitler Youth until they were either beaten and imprisoned or converted into polka-loving Aryans. Nazi Germany eventually banned American jazz music.

It was a terribly flawed movie. Robert Sean Leonard played the defiantly idealistic swing kid, while Christian got to play his first dark character, Thomas, a former swing-kid-turned-Nazi who betrays his family and friends. Kenneth Branagh was rumored to be so unhappy with the final cut of the movie that he requested his name be removed from the credits.

Christian fondly remembered the days before he was a star, when he could wander around Prague during the *Swing Kids* shoot. He told a reporter: "There's a great feeling of being completely anonymous, knowing that I can walk around the city and I'm not going to bump into anybody that I know, at all. It's sort of quite liberating, and you do silly things. I do remember, like, in Prague, for instance, my girlfriend coming up to visit me. We all went to this club. And, you know, we'd all been, the other actors and me, we'd all been going down to these clubs. So we get down there and just act like we always have done each time. Which is like complete and utter knobs. Completely aware that we're in a city that sort of—there aren't really consequences to what we do, that we're gonna be leaving, so it doesn't matter."

Making his big-screen directorial debut, Thomas Carter was best known for his work as a director of the television series *Hill Street Blues*. Though Carter would go on to score a hit with the 2001 dance movie *Save the Last Dance*, he had his hands full dealing with Christian shooting *Swing Kids*.

David recalled dealing with faxes and phone calls from Carter as the director struggled to communicate with Christian: "I had to talk to Thomas Carter about Christian and explain that my son was not rude. He listens but does not necessarily acknowledge. Christian doesn't like unnecessary verbiage."

David tried another tact. He remembered pleading with Carter to help Christian be a better actor: "I asked him to encourage Christian to be emotional and passionate and expressive. He had to understand that my son came from an English background of restraint and repression!"

Christian worked very hard on *Swing Kids*, mastering a light American accent but more importantly, he learned how to swing dance. It looked as if his childhood dance training and *Newsies* experience would come in handy.

"We had a couple weeks of dance rehearsal," Christian recalled. "For *Swing Kids*, we did the Lindy Hop, named after Charles Lindberg's trans-Atlantic flight."

Christian remembered studying the 1941 film *Hellzapoppin'*, which featured the Whitey's Lindy Hoppers, one of the most famous swing dance troupes.

Unfortunately, like *Newsies*, the critics hated *Swing Kids*.

Wrote Roger Ebert: "There are moments here where the movie seems to believe Hitler was bad, not because he mapped genocidal madness but because he wouldn't let the Swing Kids dance all night."

Washington Post's Rita Kempley declared: "*Swing Kids* is a bad idea whose time has not come. It's *Cabaret* as Col. Klink might have envisioned it, a nutty anti-Nazi a-go-go for teenagers, set to American music."

"It's *Footloose* Loose In The Third Reich and, even with your expectations kept knee-high to a kindergarten, you might have at least hoped for some finger-poppin' music and a few great dance scenes. Sorry. Here, too, things come up short," declared the *Globe and Mail*.

And, like *Newsies*, *Swing Kids* was a huge bomb for Disney's Hollywood Pictures subsidiary, grossing just $5.6 million. Christian Fail was getting a reputation as box office poison.

Variety, the pulse of Hollywood, analyzed the movie: "A fascinating footnote of Second World War Nazi Germany is trivialized and sanitized in Hollywood Pictures' odd concoction of music and politics known as *Swing Kids*. It has precious little to entice audiences into movie theaters. It will probably replicate the commercial performance of the company's near-catastrophic *Newsies*."

Critic Leonard Maltin summed it up nicely in his annual movie and video guide: "This year's *Newsies*, and poor Bale is in both."

It was little consolation that *Swing Kids*' retro soundtrack preceded the swing revival of the late 1990s.

Devastated by his second big studio bomb for Disney, Christian decided that one common factor was that he could not work with inexperienced directors again. Both *Newsies* and *Swing Kids* had been helmed by first-time movie directors. Christian vowed not to be anyone's guinea pig again.

The proverb "Success has many fathers, but failure is an orphan" is never more true than in Hollywood. Though David agreed wholeheartedly with his son's assessment that inexperienced directors were to blame for the two Disney bombs, producers would look at the only apparent common element—Christian Bale. Was Christian Fail truly box office poison? Did this mean that Christian's career would begin to backslide from leading man to supporting roles? It was time to rethink Christian's career strategy.

As Christian's manager, David was anxious for Christian to improve his marketability by broadening his skill set. He made plans for Christian to take a number of skill-building lessons like scuba diving, Spanish, martial arts, stunt work, supercross, and tennis. Of course, these plans depended on Christian's actually being in Los Angeles, but Christian was difficult to schedule as he continued to split his time between England and the U.S.

Ask any actor and they'll tell you it's important to have sports skills or a command of dialects and languages when you're looking for work. The more skills you possess, the better your chances of a casting director leaning your way. When Christian was a child, he had landed a small part in *Land of Faraway* because David had assured the casting director that Christian could ride a horse. In the two weeks before starting that shoot, David made sure Christian learned how to ride a horse!

While David was all about positive reinforcement and optimism, he also had to protect Christian's sensitive psyche. Thanks to the trauma by publicity chores for *Empire of the Sun*, Christian abhorred the business and marketing side of movies—something essential for an actor to understand and appreciate if he wanted a Hollywood career. And with two additional box office bombs under his belt, Christian needed a change of luck.

Though David was concerned about Christian accumulating skills that would make him more marketable as an actor, he was beyond overprotective. Most struggling actors who arrive in L.A. get jobs as waiters. It's the perfect job to expose an actor to different people and personalities; an essential skill of acting is to convey a range of human conditions. It's also a job that allows an actor to learn new skills and schedule auditions and workshops throughout the day.

But Christian could not legally work in the U.S. without a work visa, and David didn't think Christian needed to go to acting classes because he had already been educated by his work experience with Spielberg, Heston, and Ortega. "Christian's talent is natural!" David would argue. "He has no need for classes. Acting coaches are just failed actors anyway."

David didn't want Christian to worry about anything except his career. "Stay focused on acting," David would say to Christian, "and Dad will take care of the rest." Christian trusted his father implicitly—had he not been a financial advisor back in England?

So the House of Bale in Manhattan Beach had an odd dynamic. Father David was on a visitor's visa and could not legally work. Sister Louise was on a student's visa and could not legally work. Everyone depended on the fortunes of an eighteen-year-old boy. Unintentionally or not, Christian was surrounded by enablers—a troubling fact of life for a child actor whose career had mutated the traditional roles of parent and sibling.

Balancing being Christian's father, manager, and dependent, David created an unusual atmosphere at 3101 Oak Avenue. David was like Mr. Collins around Lady Catherine de Bourgh from *Pride and Prejudice*. Christian was the absolute young lord and master of the house. Christian often went out in the evenings until the early morning hours and didn't wake up until after noon. When he was sleeping upstairs, everyone had to be quiet. David shushed and silenced himself whenever Christian spoke. Father and son arranged an elaborate way of communication; each step of stairs leading up to Christian's bedroom had neat piles of scripts with David's notes and the railing was feathered with yellow and blue Post-it sticky notes. The notes pointing up on the banister required Christian's attention. When Christian wrote replies, he would point them down.

Every day, David would serve Christian his breakfast in bed—a mug of hot tea, baked beans, scrambled eggs, and toast. "Who's the greatest actor in the world?" David would cheerfully ask at the door. And a sleepy-eyed Christian would meekly reply: "I am! I am!" David happily performed this ritual until Christian married and moved out of that house at age twenty-five.

"You have no idea how difficult it is to be an actor," David would say to me. "My poor son faces rejection every day! His family must be positive and supportive. He must never be criticized!" David loved a pity party, I'd learn.

In his early days in L.A., Christian did face a lot of competition. He was considered for many films, including: *Alive*, directed by *Empire of the Sun* producer Frank Marshall. But the part went to rival Ethan Hawke; two Ridley Scott projects, *1492: Conquest of Paradise* and *White Squall*, which was down to Christian and Balthazar Getty; *Scent of a Woman* (lost to Chris O'Donnell); *A Far Off Place* (lost to Ethan Embry); and most disappointingly, *This Boy's Life*, which Christian lost to rival Leonardo DiCaprio.

Casting agents and producers had no doubt that Christian was a good actor, but in the early 1990s, they questioned whether he could convincingly play an American. There was the matter of physicality. Slender, pale Christian looked very English. The rosiness of his cheeks, Christian complained, was a genetic form of rosacea, common to those of Celtic background. Also, Christian was a British citizen, so producers would have to apply for work visas and have legitimate reasons as to why an American actor wouldn't be an easier choice to hire for the role.

Additionally, casting agents could hear that Christian spoke with a lisp, a product of his embarrassingly large overbite. In fact, Christian could bite his teeth together and stick his finger behind his top front two teeth. Christian would eventually have his teeth fixed for *American Psycho*, but until then, it was another issue that eroded Christian's confidence. He continues to speak with a slight lisp to this day.

Christian's sharp-eyed fans, the Baleheads, noticed that he rarely smiled in photos. This was partly because of his dislike of publicity and partly a reflex that he had developed to avoid showing his teeth. The result was that Christian never looked particularly friendly in photos—a look that could be interpreted as overly serious, or intense.

Said Christian about his serious countenance: "If I have to acknowledge a camera, I tend to look like I'm receiving an injection."

You can imagine that Christian was quite an uphill challenge for his agent to pitch: an actor who lisped, hated publicity, refused to smile, and was a paperwork-ridden foreign hire. To American producers, David pushed Christian's Spielberg experience. To European producers, Christian's British citizenship could satisfy any European investors' quota for European talent.

Christian decided it was racism, plain and simple. "Americans discriminate against the English. They are jealous, because any English actor can out-act an American. That's why they deny me work."

While David was chasing after Christian's opportunities, glued to the phone in his home office/bedroom, he expected daughter Louise to take care of the house. She dutifully tried to cook and clean for her father and brother (both hopeless in the kitchen), juggling her full-time schoolwork at El Camino College, along with her theater work, social life, and assorted waitressing jobs.

David was a terrible cook. He only knew how to make scrambled eggs, beans, and toast. I once showed up for dinner where David's idea of a main course was a nuked cauliflower with dribbles of Cheese Wiz.

Christian was even more helpless in the kitchen. He once stuck a foil-wrapped potato in the microwave and jumped around frantically as sparks and arcing electricity crackled. It was easier for

Christian to run across Sepulveda Boulevard to grab some take-out chicken from Koo Koo Roo's. Or he could wait for Louise to cook something.

Louise Tabitha Bale is only eighteen months older than Christian, but her hopes and dreams of a film career ended back in Bournemouth when a joint brother-sister project fell through. Right after the U.K. premiere of *Empire of the Sun*, *The Sunday Express* had excitedly proclaimed: "The brother and sister double act from Bournemouth are set to take Hollywood by storm." But the movie never happened. Indeed, it was *her* interest in drama, dance, and theater workshops that got Christian involved in show business.

When they were kids, Christian and Louise were practically like twins. David called Louise his "treasure" and called Christian "moosh." He observed that brother and sister were like two peas in a pod, and they were inseparable growing up.

Louise remembered fondly: "Christian and I played together a lot as kids. We often played with other kids on our street, and we played games like 'Family' where we would each take on a role of the member of a family, 'Dad,' 'Mum,' 'Sister,' etc. and re-enact little dramas. We also played in the dirt a lot, dug up worms, made mud pies, rode our bikes down to the local candy shop and we also played in the woods a lot because we grew up in remote areas."

Though Christian's official bio says that he became interested in animal rights after reading *Charlotte's Web*, it was actually Louise who had decided to become vegetarian at the tender age of nine. She recalled: "It was a book called *The Peppermint Pig* by Nina Bawden that I read when I was nine years old that affected me so deeply."

Though close in age, David noticed that brother and sister had different approaches to life. "Louise charges in to scare away the demons," David would say. "While Christian creeps in to avoid them."

Eventually, I could see that Louise began to resent her pseudo-mother role, stuck with the cooking and cleaning and household chores. She and David argued often because David liked to drink and David could be an angry drunk. He was paranoid and critical about Louise's dates and he often jumped to conclusions that any of Louise's boyfriends who had any interest in show business were only interested in getting access to Christian to further their own careers.

In Los Angeles where show business is the primary industry, this wasn't necessarily a wrong conclusion. Siblings of celebrities often need to be wary of their friends and acquaintances' motives. Some families who move to Hollywood are very generous with their connections, hoping that good schmoozing and networking would be good karma and benefit all. Others, like David, are highly suspicious, defensive, and possessive of every hard-earned lead.

David would sigh: "My poor treasure works so hard with school and work, she's a living saint!" But a minute later, David would hiss: "I don't trust any of these boys that hang around Louise. She doesn't realize that they're just using her to get to my son."

Louise had dated a young filmmaker, Darren Doane, who asked Christian to appear in a short film project called *Godmoney*. Though the short was never completed, you can see Christian's performance in the DVD of the full-length version of *Godmoney* as one of the extras. Christian and David were both unhappy that the footage was made public—the grungy performance of a smoking, scrawny, and shirtless Christian went against David's image objectives for his son, and the incorporation of the footage in the DVD only solidified David's suspicions of Louise's friends.

I got to witness firsthand Louise's quiet strength and determination a number of times and I wondered how tough it must be for Louise to be Christian's sister. At the Palm Springs Film Festival in 1996, David, Louise, and I stood in the theater lobby after a screening of Christian's film *Metroland*. As the audience started streaming out, David proudly told people that it was his son who was the star of the movie. A number of people looked at Louise and asked her who she was.

"I'm Christian's sister," she'd reply.

"Why, you're almost as cute as he is!" a couple said.

"Don't you wish you were as talented as your brother?" another couple asked.

"Do you get jealous that your brother is so handsome?" yet another couple asked.

And so on and so on, it seemed that Louise was standing there, unfairly being compared by complete strangers to a kid brother she had introduced to acting. Eventually, Louise began to stay at Oak Avenue less and less as her life steered her away from Christian and David. When she got her own place, visiting relatives would stay at her home, not at Oak Avenue.

David used to say, "There are two important questions that everyone must ask of themselves, and it must be in this order:

Where am I going?

Who is going with me?"

For Christian, after yet another promising start, it seemed as if he was back to square one. However, he would learn soon enough that he'd have new allies.

Christian and his dogs, Mojo and Codger, in Manhattan Beach, California.

6

Baleheads Begin

"They're my loyal, hardcore group of fans who I use to intimidate directors into giving me parts. I think it was a few years ago that someone started saying: 'WE ARE BALEHEADS!' I thought, yeah, I'm all for that—my own little private army."
—Christian Bale, *Hotline Magazine*

Remember the 1990s? (I'm sure some of you younger fans don't!) It's very weird for me to write about the inception of the Internet like a historical event, but in the past twenty years, the way we entertain, inform, and communicate has changed so much thanks to a network that has its origins in military paranoia when they created a way to play a shell game with data in the event of a nuclear attack. Christian's success on the Internet could only have happened in the early 1990s because movie buffs were just finding their voices online. People were craving information and looking for Web sites to visit. If television, radio, and film were the traditional media, dominated and controlled by studios, networks, and advertising agencies, the Internet was like the ultimate public broadcast channel—open and free to all.

And Christian Bale would be its first star.

1992. The Internet was in its infancy as far as commercial use was concerned. There was no Amazon, no eBay, no Craigslist, no Facebook, and no Twitter. If you had a computer at home, it probably had a 486 processor running Windows 3.1, or it was a Macintosh LC. And if you wanted Internet access from your home, it was dial-up and you had a choice of using one of the hundreds of America Online (AOL) start-up disks or CDs they mailed out to you, or you used CompuServe.

That same year, Tim Burton's second *Batman* movie, *Batman Returns*, starring Michael Keaton as Batman, Michelle Pfeiffer as Catwoman, and Danny DeVito as the Penguin was a box office smash, finishing off 1992 as the third-highest grossing film.

But 1992 wasn't looking like a good year for Christian. From an actor's point of view, it's dangerous to have box office bomb after bomb, because producers get scared of anyone who reeks of that fatal cologne, Box Office Poison. Once actors get a box office poison rep, they lose opportunities for leading roles. Worse still, the salary an actor can negotiate—his "quote"—depends on his box office track record. A hot A-list movie star commands top quote, gets gross points (profit-sharing from the movie's gross revenue as opposed to net points), has his choice of roles, his command of cast, and potentially even his choice of directors. An up-and-coming actor? Refer to the proverb "Beggars can't be choosers." Just look up John Travolta pre- and post-*Pulp Fiction* to see how a career can drastically change once you transition from "up-and-coming" to "established."

There was plenty of blame to go around for *Newsies'* and *Swing Kids'* failures. Christian and his dad blamed first-time movie directors Kenny Ortega and Thomas Carter, Disney, for not marketing either picture, and Christian's Triad agent. Taking his father's advice, Christian changed agencies and signed with William Morris, hoping a new agent could help change his luck and improve his opportunities as he searched for his remaining Disney picture in his three-picture deal.

However, *Newsies* did attract a couple of important fans. Winona Ryder loved *Newsies* and promptly ran out to rent everything Christian had appeared in. She was preparing to remake the American classic *Little Women*, based on the book by Louisa May Alcott, and was on the hunt to cast the role of Laurie, the rich young boy next door.

Meanwhile, 2,200 miles from Los Angeles, in Toronto, my own connection to Christian was just beginning, though I hardly knew at the time how deeply involved I'd eventually become with him and his family.

I went to see *Newsies* with my friend Laurie Reid at the Kingsway Theater. We were both movie buffs with broad tastes. I loved everything from big epics to sci-fi (especially *Star Trek*) to David Lynch. Laurie was also a Trekker and a huge fan of old Hollywood musicals, and she was very curious about *Newsies* as Disney was proudly touting it as the first major studio musical to be released in decades. You'd have to look back to *Grease* (1978) or *Hair* (1979) for a major studio live-action musical. By the time disco died, the live-action musical had its last dying breath with the bomb *Xanadu* (1980). As Laurie's future husband, the Canadian crime novelist John McFetridge, would rather have had an appendectomy before watching a musical, Laurie and I wound up seeing *Newsies* on our own.

To say that Laurie was smitten by Christian Bale's performance would be an understatement. She loved his singing voice and she loved his dancing. She told me that Christian looked like a young Jimmy Stewart, who happened to be her favorite actor from Hollywood's Golden Age. He was unlike any other young actor emerging at that time. And when we discovered that this

New York–accented street kid was the same English schoolboy from *Empire of the Sun*, we were both very impressed.

For movie buffs like Laurie and me, Christian Bale appeared to be a classy young actor who was much more talented than his heavily hyped (or self-promoting) American competition at the time—actors like Ethan Hawke, Christian Slater, Stephen Dorff, or Skeet Ulrich. With Christian's singing and dancing talents, and his uncanny ability to reproduce accents, he was like a throwback to Hollywood's golden era when actors had to have a range of skills and do more than just sulk, squint, and look "intense."

Christian was like our own personal discovery. In Canada, if you were an Anglophile, you would've seen all the Merchant Ivory films like *Howard's End*, but here was young Christian, an English talent who wasn't part of that Emma Thompson and Helena Bonham Carter crowd. Christian truly seemed to be an undiscovered young talent.

So we formed the Society to Appreciate Obscure British Actors and made it our mission to watch the films of the actors who were underappreciated and unnoticed by Hollywood. Our favorite actors at the time included Daniel Day-Lewis, Rupert Graves, Kerry Fox, Christopher Eccleston, and Ewan McGregor. While American movie buffs were worshipping at the altar of Tarantino, we were lining up at the Toronto Film Festival to watch the latest from Danny Boyle and Stephen Frears.

It's funny that, for me, if Christian had not done a movie about China and, for Laurie, a couple of musicals, we probably would not have noticed or been so invested in his young and struggling career. *Empire of the Sun, Newsies, Swing Kids, Prince of Jutland*— could a budding actor sustain much more failure without giving up completely?

In retrospect, we were caught up in a moment that moved us from movie buff to fan. A movie buff can talk movies all day long—who's their favorite actor, director, genre. A fan, as we saw it, was a movie buff who actively sought movies by a favorite actor or director. And since we were worried that Christian's career was headed for disaster, we felt he needed fans.

The good news? I was in marketing communications for the largest software company in Canada at the time. I had experience in developing online marketing campaigns, so it felt natural for me to spread the news of Bale in cyberspace. On the Internet, we crossed paths with other movie buffs who had noticed Christian's performance in *Newsies* and *Swing Kids*. But what many people didn't realize, in the days before the IMDb, was that he was the same actor from *Empire of the Sun*. AOL had a large message board area dedicated to Talk About Actors. So did CompuServe. Once we started talking about Christian and his other films, we were quickly converting those movie buffs into Bale fans. We turned musical buffs into *Newsies* fans. We turned Spielberg buffs into *Empire of the Sun* fans. World War II movies your thing? Check out *Swing Kids*. It's like *Cabaret*-lite! Check out *Treasure Island* at your video store! In those days, message boards had a maximum number of posts, so AOL and CompuServe would start new folders for our favorite actor. That's how the seeds of the Christian Bale fan community—Baleheads—were sown. It was audience creation at the grassroots level.

We decided to write Christian letters of appreciation, laud, and encouragement. (Okay, that's just a fancy way of saying "fan letter.") In the years before there were Web sites with agency addresses like fanmail.biz or IMDbPro, we hit the bookstores to find an address for Christian and sent off our letters to his old agent in London.

Fatefully, I received a reply.

It was spring of 1993 when I arrived home to find an envelope with a Los Angeles postmark waiting for me. I opened the envelope to find a handwritten letter from Christian Bale. I was surprised. It was common belief that actors didn't personally respond to fan mail but here was a letter, handwritten no less, from Christian himself. Christian thanked me for my support and wrote that his most recent film, *Prince of Jutland*, had not yet found a distributor.

I decided to send another note to Christian. I told him about our Society for the Appreciation for Obscure British Actors (yes, I did momentarily wonder if he'd be pissed off that we considered him "obscure") and explained that even though his films were not commercial successes, we were promoting lots of chatter on the Internet—particularly on the movie discussion boards of AOL and CompuServe—about overlooked actors. And Christian was a growing topic, especially once *Newsies* was eventually released on video.

A couple of months later, I received another letter from Christian, explaining that he was busy with a new film, *Little Women*, which was going to shoot in Victoria, British Columbia. He was playing the headstrong boy-next-door, Laurie, opposite Winona Ryder's Jo March. "Perhaps," Christian wrote, "you've heard of the book?"

Though my friend was annoyed that Christian had still not replied to her letters, she was thrilled that there was a line of communication developing. She and I continued to work diligently on the Internet, posting news about *The Prince of Jutland* and *Little Women* to anyone asking about Christian Bale. And, of course, we told everyone to rent *Empire of the Sun*, *Treasure Island*, *Newsies*, or *Swing Kids*. The Christian Bale folders on AOL and CompuServe were multiplying and becoming very active.

So Laurie and I decided to prepare a marketing proposal to help Christian take advantage of this growing online activity. It was a comprehensive marketing plan that would use the Internet to alert his fans to his upcoming movies and to check out what was available at the video store. If he authorized it, CCBALE (Cinemaphiles for Christian Bale Appreciation, Laud, and Encouragement) would be the first official online presence for any actor.

A month after we sent out the marketing proposal, there was a voice mail message waiting for me. The voice was a deep, rumbling basso; a rich, theatrical English accent.

"Hello? I . . . am . . . David Bale. I am Christian Bale's father. I understand that you have been writing to *my son*. Would you be kind enough to ring us? Yes, ring us at our Manhattan Beach number."

I replayed the message a number of times before calling Laurie.

"If this is your idea of a joke . . ." I began.

Even Laurie was surprised. No one was expecting a phone call in response to the marketing proposal. A curt rejection letter from the agent? Maybe. A letter asking for more details? Possibly. But definitely not this booming, possibly threatening voice on the phone.

What I remembered the most about the evening when I first called David Bale was that I had to wrap a towel around my head like a turban. I was nervous and sweat was pouring down my forehead. My hair was soaked as I anxiously practiced dialing the number. I had spent several hours analyzing David's voice mail and I was worried that maybe Christian's dad was not at all pleased about my correspondence with his son. On my desk beside the phone, I had a copy of the marketing proposal and a pen ready to take notes.

After I nervously dialed the long-distance number, I still was not quite prepared to hear that same big, booming voice immediately answer.

"Hullo?"

"Yes, hi, hello. Mr. Bale? It's Harrison Cheung from Toronto, Canada, returning your call . . ."

"Why yes, hullo-hullo! Delighted to talk to you, at last, Harrison! Delighted! We've read your wonderful proposal and your bio! Apparently a *fellow* Englishman, I see!" He laughed thunderously.

I moved the phone away from my ear, taken aback by David's volume.

"Yes, Mr. Bale, I was actually born in Scotland. Glasgow."

"Aye, Glaskie!" David roared. "Amazing! Cheung? Now, that's a Chinese name, is it not, Harrison?"

"Yes, my parents are from Hong Kong."

"Noble people, the Chinese! Noble! Hong Kong is an extraordinary place! Honor and integrity abound in your culture and heritage! Be proud! Be *very* proud!"

"Thank you, Mr. Bale."

"Please, call me David! I'm glad you called. You see, Christian and I are fascinated with your proposal, Harrison. Intrigued! We'd like to discuss this at length with you. Using the Internet for publicity is a brilliant idea, brilliant! Do you ever come down to Los Angeles at all?"

"Me? Well, I haven't been to L.A. in a while. I was there—"

"Well, we'll have to have you down! Christian is finishing up in Canada—say, that's where you are, isn't it? Canada! Beautiful country! My father trained in Canada with the RAF. Christian's in Victoria making *Little Women* there with Winona Ryder! Then, he's off to England to visit his mum and he'll be back in L.A. after that. We'll ring you so we can figure out when's the best time to meet.

"I'm so glad we got in touch. I know you and Christian will get along very well, indeed! A godsend! A *Chinese* Scotsman! From Glasgow of all places! Oh dear, look at the time! I'm terribly sorry but I'm running late for an appointment. Good talking to you, Harrison! Good-bye!"

And with that, David hung up. It was like the aftermath of a tornado. My towel was soaked through.

For the next few months, I kept thinking about Christian and his unusual father., According to Christian's official bio at the time, David Bale was a former pilot and now Christian's manager. There wasn't much more. As the weeks passed, I wondered if David had forgotten about our proposal. I debated calling again.

I finally heard again from David in the form of a lengthy fax, apologizing for the long lapse in communication. "I've been terribly ill. But by way of explanation," he wrote, "I'm including a letter from my doctor." The third page of the fax was a letter from a Dr. Charles Crummer, outlining David's heart problems and requesting people's—particularly bill collectors'—forbearance. This was my first indication of just how bizarre David's behavior could be. He signed off, saying that he would be in touch soon.

By the end of November, David finally called.

"Hullo-hullo! Harrison! It's David Bale."

"Hi, David! How are you feeling?"

"Much better, thank you. Say, listen. Christian is coming back to L.A. for the premiere of *Little Women*. We'd like you to come to the premiere. We can talk about your proposal. How does that sound? Have you ever been to a Hollywood movie premiere?"

"No . . ." I tried to sound nonchalant, but in my head I was screaming, *A Hollywood movie premiere? Are you kidding?*

"It's great fun. Now, do you have a nice suit? You need to dress up for these things."

"Oh, yes, of course . . ."

"Wonderful. The premiere will be Sunday, December the 11th. Why don't you come down on Saturday and stay until Monday? How does that sound?"

"December 11th? That's *next* weekend."

"Yes, please say you can make it. I've booked you in a nice English hotel near us. Barnabey's. You'll love it. It's like an old English inn. We can go for a pint and talk about your marvelous proposal. Do you drink?"

"No, actually, I don't."

"Smart lad! Good boy! It's an evil, a sin really. But I'm long past redemption." David chuckled. "And Christian—he drives Americans mad because he simply cannot get drunk. My son can drink pint after pint and he cannot get drunk! It's absolutely amazing, his constitution!"

By the time David had blown through his invitation and hung up, I had made up my mind to go. How could I pass up an invitation to a Hollywood premiere?

I left Toronto on a cold, miserable December morning, and stepped off the plane to the exotic scents of Los Angeles. I could smell jasmine in the air when I stepped outside the Arrivals at four o'clock in the afternoon. I gave the taxi driver the address to Barnabey's Hotel in Manhattan Beach and was surprised at how close it was to the airport. Just half a mile south on Sepulveda Boulevard, Barnabey's sat at the corner of Rosecrans, across from the Manhattan Village Mall. From the outside, the hotel didn't look particularly impressive—rows and rows of faded pink shuttered windows on a two-storey building facing the street.

On the inside, though, the hotel was an amazing replica of a Victorian manor—paneled walls, a plush red parlor. I felt as though I had stepped into Professor Higgins's house from *My Fair Lady*. I checked into my elaborately decorated room, admiring the four-poster bed.

I promptly called David, but no one was home. I left a message that I had arrived, and settled in to wait.

After an hour, I decided to go across Sepulveda for a bite of dinner. Airlines still served meals in those days but the portions were notoriously small and I was famished. I had a quick bite at the California Pizza Kitchen and hurried back to Barnabey's to find a message waiting for me.

"Welcome to L.A.! Giving Christian his dinner. Shall ring again soon."

I had missed the call.

Another half hour passed before I heard a knock at the door. Nervously, I peered through the peephole. I opened the door and found myself staring up at a giant of a man. David Bale was an extremely tall man who bore an uncanny resemblance to Adam West, the actor who played Batman in the 1960s TV series. Tanned, with a deeply lined face and graying hair, David wore a blue denim shirt and black trousers. He smiled broadly, shook hands, and took out a handkerchief to blow his nose.

"Hullo, Harrison! At last we meet! Look at you! Definitely Chinese! Come, my car is outside."

We headed out to David's VW Jetta.

"Christian just arrived last night from London and he is still a bit peevish," David said. "Atrabilious. Pay him no mind. It's just jet lag."

"Oh." I was impressed and a little intimidated by David's vocabulary.

"But he is looking forward to meeting you, Harrison. He's talked about nothing else all day. Absolutely nothing else!"

We drove just a few blocks from Barnabey's, and made our way onto Oak Avenue, a tree-lined street that didn't have sidewalks, making the line of large homes look as if they were on a remote country lane. It was December in L.A. and each house was garnished with enough Christmas lights to guide an airplane for landing and displayed holiday flags with figures of Santa, snowmen, and reindeer.

David made a hard turn into a driveway, and I got my first glimpse of The House of Bale. It looked like an overgrown two-story villa, large, colorful, and sun-bleached. The faded stucco walls, arched and recessed entryway, and slate tile roof seemed homey, and not foreboding. A balcony, painted steel gray and looking like something Evita would stand on, jutted prominently from the second floor. The front yard was wild with tropical plants, flowering bird-of-paradises, orchids, and vines threatening to grow across the stone walkway. Randomly placed throughout the front yard were assorted bowls of what looked like cat food. A giant mature palm tree marked a natural barrier from one neighbor, while a high hedge bordered the other neighbor's yard. Overall the effect was definitely more shabby than chic.

"Welcome to our home!" David had jumped out of the car and was making his way quickly to the front door.

I hurried to keep up; David was already across the yard and fiddling with his key at the door. Stealing a quick glance up at the house's façade, I thought I saw a dark figure at the window at the balcony, but it could have just been my imagination making shapes out of the curtains shifting in the breeze.

By contrast to the house's striking exterior, the inside of the house was a disaster. I first noticed the sharp smell of cat litter. A dirty wall-to-wall gray Berber carpet had clearly seen too much traffic. As if on cue, two cats raced by. A staircase was immediately to the right of the front entrance; each step had a pair of shoes or a pile of scripts. The bannister was covered with sticky notes. In the corner was a small fireplace. A large golden retriever, in obvious need of a bath, was sitting in front of the fireplace, its tail thumping in welcome. I heard a scrabbling noise and saw a Jack Russell terrier racing down the stairs. The little dog ran straight to me, sniffed my leg, and then ran back upstairs.

"That's Mojo checking you out," David explained. "He's Christian's dog. Over by the fire is Codger. They're both rescue dogs. Do you like dogs? We've always had dogs ever since Christian was a baby!"

David beckoned me down the hall to the kitchen. It was a fascinating place. Books, more scripts, and unfinished plates of food were piled on one counter. There were word and phrase magnets on the fridge where someone apparently spelled out their creativity. "He hates to be kept waiting" read one line across the fridge.

Empty cans of dog food were arranged on another countertop. I noticed a line of ants marching steadily from a windowsill to the cans. A large butcher-block kitchen table was covered with boxes and papers and dirty mugs with used teabags still in them. A small moldy block of cheese sat on the table. Although there was an old dishwasher, the sink was piled with dirty plates—it looked like someone loved ketchup.

David directed me to sit at the kitchen table while he put on a kettle.

"Tea?"

"No thanks."

"We love Manhattan Beach. My son, Christian, *loves* the water. We're just a walk away from the beach. You can go to the pier and go surfing or swimming or ride a bicycle on the trails, if you like."

Mojo suddenly ran into the room. He ran to me and put his paws up on my leg.

David laughed. "There's Mojo! There's a boy! Christian named him from The Doors song "Mr. Mojo Rising"? Christian found him. Poor little guy, love him! He had been wandering on the streets of North Hollywood for weeks! His little paws were bleeding from running on the asphalt! Christian stopped his car and chased little Mojo down until the poor little thing could run no more. Then, Christian scooped him up into his arms and brought him home. He wrapped those poor little paws up and nursed Mojo back to health."

I looked at Mojo's eager brown eyes. He seemed like a very happy little dog. Mojo jumped down, rolled over on his back, and looked up with a silly doggy grin, his tongue lolling and tiny white paws waving in the air.

David was thrilled.

"Will you look at *that*, Harrison? He likes you! He trusts you! Animals can sense these things! No animal would expose its stomach to a potential predator!"

I playfully grabbed at Mojo's paws and rubbed his round belly, thankful for the vote of confidence.

"Christian and I are very involved in animal rights. Do you eat meat?"

"Uh, yes."

David's face crumpled.

"What a shame! We can cure you of that illness. Eating meat is a mortal sin, Harrison! How can you eat the flesh of animals to save your own life? That's just wrong! Dead wrong! 'Thou shall not kill,' remember? Did you know that human teeth were never designed to chew meat? Only fruits, nuts, and vegetables! Fruits, nuts, and vegetables! Our teeth are flat! Like our gentle cousins, the gorillas."

I nodded politely. I normally didn't like being lectured about my eating habits but David's charm was irresistible. I got the sense that he might've said the same thing to anyone.

"Ah, here comes Christian now." David turned eagerly to face approaching footsteps. I followed his look, eager for my first glimpse of the young actor.

A lean, lanky figure appeared in the kitchen doorway. Good-looking with short-cropped brown hair, his angular face was immediately recognizable. Though he was tall, standing next to his giant of a father, Christian looked short, almost elfin. Wearing a tight white T-shirt and baggy cargo pants, his skinny body arched slightly with poor posture. His long pale arms were dotted with freckles and moles. *English complexion*, I thought. He seemed tense, almost uncomfortable. His brow was ever so slightly knitted, and his lips were pursed as if he were sucking a sour candy or pretending to be a duck. With his oddly tentative stance at the doorway, he looked like a moody male model, impatiently waiting for his turn down the runway.

Father and son were both staring at me now. David was grinning expectantly. Christian was not.

David made the introductions.

"Christian, this is Harrison, come all the way to visit us from

Canada! And this, of course, is my son [small pause for dramatic effect] Christian Bale!"

"Hi." I stood up to shake his hand. "I'm very pleased to meet you."

Christian mumbled something in reply and we shook hands. I was surprised to hear that his voice was so light and high-pitched. In the movies, his voice sounded a little deeper. And with his refined, almost delicate facial features, I was also surprised that Christian's hands were rough and calloused and his fingernails were chewed to the quick.

Christian turned to his father.

"What does a guy have to do around here to get a clean towel?"

"What? Oh dear! Oh dear!" David scurried to another part of the kitchen toward a small laundry nook. "No worries, Moosh, there are some clean towels in the dryer!" He pulled a couple of gray towels from the dryer and handed them to his son.

Moosh was an odd nickname that I had never heard before. I chalked it up to something English.

Christian grabbed one towel and turned his attention back to me, staring with his penetrating hazel eyes with all the thrill of a botanist examining some new kind of weed.

David jumped in, presumably to cover for Christian's obvious silence: "Harrison, are you hungry? Would you like some chowder? A neighbor down the street made us this huge pot of homemade—"

"I thought she made the chowder for *me*," Christian interrupted.

"Yes, Moosh. But there's plenty left. You already had a couple of bowls, so I didn't think you'd want more."

"I might want more later, Dad." Christian glared at his father and I decided to look out the back door that led to a kidney-shaped swimming pool.

"Of course, Son, of course! There's plenty of chowder for you! Plenty!" By the sound of David's voice, he was clearly used to calming Christian.

"I'm going to take a shower. I'll be right back."

"Don't you want to sit and chat with Harrison?" David pointed to the kitchen table. A copy of my marketing proposal was on the table.

"No, I need to take a shower, Dad. If I had had a clean towel in my bathroom, I wouldn't be keeping our guest waiting, would I?" At that, Christian turned and marched back upstairs. For a moment, there was an awkward silence but David brought over a mug of tea.

"Sit, Harrison! Christian won't be long."

"I think I'll take a stroll outside, David." I headed to the back-yard and started to walk around the pool. A curious Mojo fol-lowed me.

I walked around the pool fifteen times, trying to process every-thing I had seen this strange and wonderful evening, until I heard Christian come down the stairs again. He was wearing tattered blue dress socks and a blue terrycloth bathrobe that was shock-ingly short. If he had sat down or bent over, his modesty would have been lost completely. Christian stomped over to the dryer and pulled out a clean T-shirt and a pair of boxer briefs. He then made his way back upstairs.

I made my way back to the kitchen table while Mojo ran over to the foot of the stairs, waiting for his young master. David smiled.

Christian came back down, now showered and fully dressed in clean clothes. He automatically turned to the kitchen counter where David had a steaming mug of tea waiting for him. Mojo was just at his heels. I was impressed. Clearly David anticipated his son's every need.

The three of us sat around the kitchen table. While David began extolling the benefits of the marketing proposal, Christian was flipping through the pages, looking at each page intently. He read slowly and purposely.

"Christian," David was saying, "you have no idea how revolu-tionary this is! To use the Internet for publicity is brilliant! Your fans could visit a Web site or message board and always know when your movies are coming out or when your videos are to be released. Tell him, Harrison! Tell him how this works."

I cleared my throat. "Well, you see, there are different places on the Internet where movie buffs can post questions. On AOL. On CompuServe. Or in a newsgroup. Thousands of people ask questions like: 'Where are they now?' or, 'Can you help me ID an actor?' That sort of thing."

"Astonishing," David muttered.

"With you, Christian," I suddenly felt awkward as that was the first time I was addressing him by name, "with you and your movies, we often see people posting questions like: 'Whatever happened to the boy from *Empire of the Sun?*' We reply and tell them your name and let them know that your current movies can be rented at the video store. So, you see, we expand your word-of-mouth that way.

"Someone else will post: 'That guy from *Newsies?* Wow, I can't believe it's the same kid from *Empire of the Sun*!' And that gets people curious, so you now have people renting your other titles. They connect the dots and see that you're one and the same person. And that works for *Swing Kids*, too. People who've seen *Swing Kids* may not know about *Newsies* or *Empire*. People who've seen *Newsies* may not know about *Swing Kids*."

"Brilliant!" David muttered again. "Absolutely brilliant!"

"And that's just in the Actors' folders," I continued. "I can hunt down Spielberg fans and remind them of *Empire* and let them know what you're doing now. You know that 'girl in red' scene in *Schindler's List?*"

Christian nodded slowly, looking almost like he was unwilling to concede a point.

"Well, it fascinates a lot of people. So I post in the Spielberg folders that he used that technique first in *Empire*—with your little red school jacket lost in the crowds of Shanghai. I post in the War Movies folders and remind them of *Empire* and *Swing Kids* and I post in the Swing Music folders about *Swing Kids*. That's called cross-pollination."

"Absolutely right!" David muttered yet again, urging me on. "Brilliant!"

I continued: "And it can be used for editorial purposes as well. Fans can write 'letters to the editor.' That impresses a magazine because they always want to know what article generates the most feedback. It helps them gauge what's hot. And reporters can come to the site and read interviews, download your biography, press notes, pictures—lots of stuff."

Christian's nostrils flared, and I wasn't sure if he was impressed or angry. He continued to flip through the pages of the proposal. He was starting to look bored. Suddenly, he jumped up and started pacing around the table, speaking without actually looking at anyone as he thought out each phrase.

"Harrison? Look, I can't stand publicity. I've hated it since I was a child, I'm sure Dad has told you. If we do this Internet thing, I won't have to do anything?"

"No, it's very low effort." I took a deep breath to continue my pitch. "Consider your Web site as your own television network, movie theater, or radio station. Your site tells your audience what you've done, what you're doing, and what you will be working on. Your fans around the world will know what to anticipate— on video, onstage, or in the theaters. Your Web site becomes the Mecca for your fans and helps you tap into an audience that looks forward to your next films. If you do a magazine interview, reprinting or linking it on your Web site multiplies the number of readers. It lets fans know when and where to find articles.

"And most importantly, consider your official Web site to be a 'virtual documentary' of your career. All we'd need is a supply of pictures to post on the site and to be kept up to date with what's happening with your movies. You know, release dates, magazine interviews, things like that. It's a way of getting your fans, your audience, to know what's happening with you, that's all."

"How much will this cost?" Christian asked.

"There are start-up costs," I began. "The Web site will need to be hosted . . ."

David jumped in: "No worries, Christian. I'll iron out those details with Harrison."

"Sure," I continued. "We could run contests for stuff. If your agent or publicist could keep me on a mailing list . . ."

David snorted derisively. "No chance of that. Agents don't know anything about the Internet. Don't worry, Harrison. I'll mail or fax you what you need. And Christian doesn't have a publicist."

"No," Christian cut in. "I don't have one. I don't need one. I can't afford one."

"So what should I do with any press inquiries to the Web site?"

"Send them to my dad for now. You can tell them you are my assistant and acting on my behalf but my dad will answer the questions."

"Okay."

"Good. Well, that's it, really? It looks good. Any details, talk to my dad. He takes care of those things for me. Oh, by the way, your proposal says that this will be my official site? I don't want to sound arrogant or self-serving, so can we make this about the fans?"

"Sure," I agreed. "It's your official site, and it will be the home of the fan club. What do you think of CCBALE? Cinemaphiles for Christian Bale Appreciation, Laud, and Encouragement?"

Christian finally cracked a smile. "No way. Absolutely not. Forget that. Let's just call it the Christian Bale Fan Club." He glanced again at the kitchen clock and marched over to shake my hand. "Nice meeting you, Harrison. We'll see you tomorrow at the premiere, right?" And then he was gone, with Mojo scampering after him.

A delighted David Bale looked at me.

"I think Christian likes you!"

"Really? You can tell from just that?"

"Absolutely. I know my own son. He likes you and respects you because he was impressed with the marketing plan."

"He just flipped through it."

"He loved it! Trust me."

"I don't know." I looked down at the binder, slightly stunned at how the evening had progressed. I wondered if David had already prepped Christian about the proposal. I wondered if they were being nice or if they had recognized an urgent need for my help.

David looked furtively back at the kitchen door. He then leaned toward me and spoke in a conspiratorial whisper.

"I need to take you into my confidence. Can I trust you?"

I nodded.

"I *feel* I can trust you. It is in your honorable Chinese nature." I managed not to flinch at David's overt racism.

"Christian is a young man but in many ways he is still a child." He took a long shuddering breath. "When his mother abandoned us, I had to take over the roles of *both* mother and father. Unfortunately, I can't cook. I can't! I'm just a useless old man, to be honest. A useless old man!" He wiped away a tear. "Because of the abandonment, Christian may not seem very warm or cordial. He was emotionally damaged by his mother's betrayal. He has few friends. How can he possibly trust anyone after his own mother leaves him? How, I ask you, how?"

David's open emotions disarmed me—I had never met such an expressive person before. I was speechless. It was the first, but would not be the last time I heard David bad-mouth Christian's mother.

"So please don't misunderstand his reticence. He *likes* you. I can tell. I *know* you and Christian will get along. Christian likes quiet people."

"And what makes you think I'm a quiet person, David?"

David laughed. "But aren't all Chinese quiet people?" He laughed again at my pained reaction to his stereotyping.

"You shall be a wonderful addition to our family, Harrison. This is a family business and it can't possibly succeed unless we're a united family."

I was shocked by the suddenness of David's offer, but thrilled. Was I really adopting a family? My own family was cautious, full of tales of worry. David Bale was like the dream dad—expressive, encouraging, optimistic. This was heady stuff. I'd gone from just another letter-writing fan to sitting at the kitchen table in Christian Bale's house. But this was it! Officially sanctioned and endorsed, I excitedly thought to the days and weeks ahead to when I'd begin building the first official actor's Web site. A framed movie poster was propped up against the kitchen wall—*Newsies*! The poster featured a painting of Christian dancing on top of a pile of newspapers, looking like Fievel the Mouse. However, the movie's tagline, "A Thousand Voices, A Single Dream," concisely conveyed what I wanted to make Christian's Web site into.

When I returned to Toronto four days later, a package was waiting for me from David. I put aside the box and opened up the letter first.

Dear Harrison,

You are using your skills and training in marketing to do for Christian and his career what normally only a major star would get at great expense from an agency, management team, and studios.

Importantly, you are doing this within the restraints and wishes requested by Christian. Even more importantly, you are honest and honorable about all this—giving a security and trust to Christian that hardly any actor has ever obtained from agency/marketing representation. It is actually not possible to thank you fully, nor appropriate, for by behaving with integrity and upholding Christian's particular and personal wishes, you are being a friend.

It is an obvious fact that an actor has life as such for two reasons: one, that he is good; and two, that people make the decision to go and pay to see him. The first without the second does not work; however the second without the first does! The actor's satisfaction lies in the first, and relies upon the second in order to have life as an actor.

The industry absolutely recognizes that an actor's abilities lie in the number and strength of his fans. Putting Christian on the Internet is a stroke of genius. Your knowledge and expertise in creating a Web page enables Christian to gain and increase recognition on an international basis. The studios all concur that only films with an international appeal can succeed now and in the future.

One does not encounter this kind of unconditional generosity and friendship hardly at all in life. You have me somewhat astonished. Please do understand that for Christian, it is many times more astonishing and personal, compound that with his almost total dislike of publicity due to the extreme pressures put on him at a very young and impressionable age, and it becomes overwhelming.

David Bale

Inside the box was a bottle of Glenfiddich whiskey! What a strange gift, I thought, since I had told him that I wasn't a drinker. On the other hand, David had made a fuss about my Scottish birthplace. It was thoughtful and odd. It was, as I'd soon learn, very David Bale.

I was hooked. I was gobsmacked. This was more than what any fan could hope for.

This was going to be fun.

David and Christian in Palm Springs during the film festival premiere of *Metroland*.

7

Little Women, Big Dreams

"Little Women was definitely a turning point. And not just in career terms. I knew I was doing something new here, something I liked."

—Christian Bale, *Movieline*

Aside from the launch of the Baleheads in cyberspace, Christian's biggest fan on the West Coast was undoubtedly Winona Ryder, who had swooned over his performance in *Newsies*.

In the 1990s, Winona Ryder was a powerful, savvy young actress on her way up. Winona was also a former child actor, making her big-screen debut at the age of fifteen in *Lucas* (1986) with Charlie Sheen and the late teen idol Corey Haim. She connected with her generation as the goth girl in Tim Burton's second feature film, *Beetlejuice* (1988), and then skillfully navigated the "one for the studio, one for yourself" Hollywood maxim as she chose mainstream and indie projects that were both prestigious and challenging. The petite actress preferred to work with talented and experienced directors. Her careful career building in the 1990s yielded fruit. Ryder earned two Oscar nominations— one for *Little Women* (1994), one for *The Age of Innocence* (1993). She won a Golden Globe for *The Age of Innocence*. All this before she was thirty years old!

Aside from her work, Ryder was also known for her active social life. She had been engaged to Johnny Depp (her *Edward Scissorhands* costar) and had dated a number of actors, including Christian Slater, Daniel Day-Lewis, David Duchovny, Chris Noth, and Matt Damon. She also dated musicians, including David Pirner of Soul Asylum as well as Beck. In 1997, *People* named her one of their 50 Most Beautiful People in the World.

Winona Ryder had been friends with producer Denise Di Novi ever since they had met on *Heathers*. When Ryder decided she wanted to remake the classic *Little Women*, she also knew she wanted to work with Di Novi again.

Written in 1868 by American author Louisa May Alcott, *Little Women* is a classic and treasured book for young girls, even today. The book follows the story of Jo March, a headstrong tomboy and her three sisters, Meg, Beth, and Amy, as they grow up and find their ways in the world. Two pivotal male characters are the March sisters' next-door neighbor, the shy rich boy Laurie (short for Theodore) and Professor Bhaer, an older German immigrant.

As a beloved story, *Little Women* was going to be a prestige project and Winona Ryder had lined up a formidable cast of female leads. Susan Sarandon would play Marmie, the March matriarch. Trini Alvarado would play the eldest sister, Meg. Claire Danes would be the sickly Beth. Kirsten Dunst and Samantha Mathis would be the spoiled kid sister, Amy, at two different ages. Ryder herself would star as Jo March. Acclaimed Australian director Gillian Armstrong would direct.

So who would play the male roles?

For a while, Columbia Pictures, the studio behind this latest incarnation of *Little Women*, pushed hard for Hugh Grant to be Professor Bhaer, but Ryder instead chose Irish actor Gabriel Byrne (Christian's costar from *Prince of Jutland*).

And for Laurie, the boy next door? Well, obviously, Columbia and Di Novi thought Laurie should be played by a young Hollywood heartthrob, especially in light of River Phoenix's tragic death.

River Phoenix had defined the young Hollywood archetype of the 1980s and '90s. He was at ease with both big-studio and indie films, ever since he gained notice in *Stand by Me*. He had been nominated for a Best Supporting Actor Oscar for his role in *Running on Empty*. He had starred with Harrison Ford in Steven Spielberg's *Indiana Jones and the Last Crusade*. His 1991 *My Own Private Idaho* with Keanu Reeves would sweep the Independent Spirit Awards. He had a very positive image as an environmentalist and a vegetarian. But his drug-induced death in 1993 became another cautionary tale about Hollywood, and it left a huge void as roles that would have been offered to Phoenix were now chasing after younger and untried new talent.

Columbia and Di Novi thought of tapping an up-and-coming actor like Stephen Dorff for the role of Laurie, but Winona decided to bring in her latest discovery to read for the part.

Recalled Christian: "It was [Ryder's] idea to bring me in to audition for *Little Women*. Winona was very involved in the casting, in every aspect of the film—she'd contacted Gillian about making the film. She wanted me to play Laurie. Talk about someone who's seen a lot of movies—she'd seen everything I'd done."

Ryder's *Little Women* was not immediately ideal. David was grooming Christian to be a leading man, and a supporting role in a large ensemble concerned him. He didn't want Christian to be lost in the crowd in a girl's movie.

The funny thing about Christian was that because of his

nomadic upbringing in England, he had no idea who Winona Ryder was. Nor had he ever heard of the book or previous film incarnations of *Little Women*.

In a *Movieline* interview, Christian was amused when he was scolded by director Gillian Armstrong: "She said: 'Christian, maybe it's a good idea to sort of research who you'll be working with.'"

What did Christian think about taking on the role of Laurie, which had been made famous by Peter Lawford—brother-in-law to John F. Kennedy Jr., uncle of Maria Shriver, and one of the original Rat Pack with Dean Martin, Frank Sinatra, Joey Bishop, and Sammy Davis Jr.?

"I wasn't intimidated due to the fact that I had never heard of it. I went to an all-boys school since I was twelve. *Little Women* was not on the curriculum." Christian added, "I rented the June Allyson version but had to turn it off when I started gagging."

Christian loved the *Little Women* script by Robin Swicord (who would receive a 2009 Oscar nomination for her screenplay *The Curious Case of Benjamin Button*), but David did not want Christian to take a supporting role and make a supporting actor's measly salary. Fortunately, at the time, Christian's new William Morris agent insisted that this Winona Ryder project would be a great career builder.

David was not pleased. Christian had commanded a six-figure quote for his first two Disney movies, and both of those productions had been filmed in 1991. Instead of being offered bigger and better parts, Christian was now being offered a small part in this Columbia Pictures film. As Christian's manager, David grumbled that an agent should be negotiating big bucks and big roles. As Christian's father, David worried that 1993 and 1994 would be very tight financially at Oak Avenue.

Christian would also learn how complicated things could be when you are a British citizen. *Little Women* was to be shot in Canada, so Christian would require a work visa to work in

Canada. He would then need a visitor's visa or work visa every time he wanted to reenter the U.S.

"That's not fair," Christian often complained. "I'm not a visitor! I own a home in the U.S.! I pay taxes here!"

Shot in picturesque Vancouver and Victoria, Canada, Christian enjoyed working with the female cast but confessed to having been irritated when Eric Stolz, who played Laurie's tutor, showed up. Recalled Christian: "I was very possessive on the set of the film. I was experiencing an incredible male possessiveness."

He was also experiencing his first bouts of insomnia. He told a reporter: "On *Little Women*, there was a time when I was having trouble sleeping, and so the producer gave me a bunch of, I think it was NyQuil, tablets. And I found they worked really well.

"And then one morning, I was feeling a little nervous, and I thought: 'Well, I'll just pop a few of these; they'll just make me feel just nice and calm again.' Wrong—on the set, just zzzzzzzzzzzzz, just trying to stay awake for every scene."

Back in Los Angeles, David started to feel the financial pinch. Christian's last big payday had been in 1991 for *Swing Kids* and the creditors were starting to harass the House of Bale. Amazingly, David started faxing out a letter to ask for forbearance and time.

The letter read:

I regret to inform you that Mr. David Bale, who has been diagnosed from serious cardiological problems for at least four years, possibly longer, caused in part by a previous lung disease, diagnosed in 1982, that would normally be terminal, has had severe setbacks in the past six months, and is seriously debilitated.

Regrettably, his situation is compounded by being uninsurable, due to the lung disease and he is thus unable to receive proper treatment. Ideally, he should return to Britain, where he is eligible for treatment under the National Heath; however it is not advisable for him to travel at this time.

Mr. Bale's condition is caused and compounded by a number of extraordinarily stressful family and financial problems and he appears unable to relinquish them mentally. The result is that he exhibits extreme stress and nervousness, which literally places him in a constant danger of a severe physiological failure, probably cardiological. Mr. Bale's records, remitted from Britain by his doctors, and the hospitals that regularly treated him over a period of 15 years, show that he has been advised throughout that time of being in real danger of cardiac failure, in additional to the seriousness of the lung disease, which, incidentally, is a permanent condition that appears at this time to be arrested.

Mr. Bale has requested that we notify a number of people of the situation, as he is overly concerned about legal and financial action being taken against him as a result of his being unable to address certain problems for some period of time now. He has also asked that we give assurances that he will take care of these matters as soon as possible.

Yours sincerely,
Dr. Charles A. Crummer

Interestingly, Dr. Crummer, a former neighbor of the Bale family, is not actually a doctor of medicine. At the time he wrote the letter, he was a lecturer in physics at the University of Phoenix.

It was an odd tactic, something I had never heard of before. Would bill collectors give a damn about your being too sick to pay? I asked David why he would be so forthcoming with his medical details.

"I know, it's not the best way of going about things," he said. "But better than giving people no explanation at all, which would be most rude."

"But, David, shouldn't you tell Christian about your finances?" I asked. "He should take a role that makes better money. One big payday could take care of all your problems."

"NO!" David barked back. "Christian must *never* know about our financial situation. He must remain focused on the work. The worst thing an actor can do is to choose a role just for the money! That's when you become mediocre! That's when your career is over! I will never allow the word 'should' to be dictated to my son!"

David was insistent on sheltering Christian about any "mundane" details like household finances. He didn't want Christian to become a "paycheck" actor so early in his career. As it was early in my relationship with the family, I could only agree with David, though I had misgivings about the deception that was obviously going on between father and son.

Christian finished shooting his scenes for *Little Women* by mid-September and he was impressed at how quickly Columbia was preparing the film for a Christmas 1994 release. In Hollywood, movies released from fall through the end of December are considered top-notch Oscar-bait films (*The Fighter*, anyone?). Films dumped in January and February are titles that the studios don't think have a chance of winning any awards.

The premiere of *Little Women* was on Sunday, December 11, 1994—my first weekend with the Bale family. A limo came up to the Bale house in Manhattan Beach to pick us up. "Is this your first time in a limo?" Christian asked me. I shook my head. But this was my first Hollywood premiere!

"It's nice, eh?" Christian was slouched over—it often seemed he had the worst posture. David and I sat on one side of the car. Christian and Louise were on the other. I tried to act nonchalant, but as we got closer and closer, my mouth dried up and my heart started pounding. I was expecting the limo door to open and a flash of camera lights to start popping, aimed at the car, the eager line of reporters desperate for a view of those of us inside.

When we arrived, Christian insisted I get out first. He hid his face in my jacket. I could hear his funny wheezing laugh in my shoulder blades as he urged me on, "Go! Go! Go!" So Christian, Louise, and I quickly stepped onto the red carpet and raced to the box office, like a crazed conga line. David walked slowly behind, laughing at our antics. No one snapped our picture. They were waiting for Winona Ryder.

The premiere was at the Mann's Theater in Culver City, California, conveniently across the street from the Sony Pictures lot. (Columbia Pictures was a subsidiary of Sony.) I remember very well that during the famous *Little Women* proposal scene, both David and I were in tears. Christian looked over at us and chuckled to Louise, "They're crying!" After the movie, the after-party was held under a giant white circus tent on the studio lot. Inside, the tent was decorated as a winter wonderland to match the Christmas theme of the movie.

To my surprise, I wasn't starstruck at all. I tried to make conversation with *The Nanny* star Fran Drescher, who sat at our table, but she ate her food quietly and seemed depressed. Christian and his costars were walking around the tent, enjoying the post-screening compliments thrown their way. It seemed as though the movie was very well received.

Heathers was actually one of my favorite movies but meeting Winona Ryder in person was a little disappointing. She was petite and porcelain-perfect but chain-smoked and had the mouth of a sailor. To my shock, she sat down beside me and began talking to an oddly familiar looking man at our table. He had a shaved head and was quietly eating French fries.

"Can I have one of your fries?" she sweetly asked the man.

"Sure." He pushed his plate toward her.

Suddenly, Ryder's voice dropped an octave, from sweet cooing to a Linda Blair *Exorcist* voice, as she turned to a woman standing patiently nearby. "Ketchup! Where's some fucking ketchup?" The woman jumped to look for a bottle.

Ryder and the man then turned to look at me.

"Hi," the man said. "What's your name?"

"I'm Harrison," I replied. "I'm a friend of Christian's."

"I'm Michael."

"What do you do, Michael?" I figured I'd make some conversation.

Ryder laughed, and I felt uncomfortably out of place for the first time that evening.

"Well," Michael began, "I'm a musician. I'm in a band called R.E.M."

Shit, Michael *Stipe*. That's why he looked familiar. Later, I'd find that Stipe was very interested in the movie industry. He had been good friends with River Phoenix and he and Christian would become friends, too. Stipe would later produce Christian's glam rock movie, *Velvet Goldmine*.

David ran over to the table and interrupted: "Hello, Winona, I'm David, Christian's father." She smiled sweetly and shook hands.

Then David turned to me, excitedly. "Guess what, Harrison! Do you know who I was talking to?"

I had not noticed. My cheeks were still red with embarrassment for not recognizing Michael Stipe.

"That was Sid Ganis! Sid Ganis! Head of Columbia Marketing! He loved Christian! He thought Christian was tremendous in *Little Women*! Tremendous! He said he wants to build a project around him!"

"That's great, David!"

We both noticed Christian hugging and kissing a woman wearing a black leather dress.

"Oh, that's Christian's agent," David said, his voice darkening.

It was obvious that David didn't like her. I was surprised, since they had only recently changed agents, but David had very high expectations for anyone working on his son's career and David was eagerly waiting for Christian's return to the six-figure pay-days of his Disney projects.

But if David had worried about how small Christian's role would be in *Little Women*, he was thrilled to see the reviews. *Little Women* was both a commercial and critical success, earning two Oscar nominations, including one for Best Actress for Winona Ryder. And Christian was getting lots of attention, especially for the famous proposal scene.

"The effect is magical. The handsome Christian Bale makes a dreamboat out of Laurie, the boy next door to the March family. (If viewers have trouble understanding why Jo wouldn't marry him, Miss Alcott's readers had the same problem.)"

—Janet Maslin, *New York Times*

"As the sensitive but blunt Laurie, Christian Bale turns in a career igniting performance."

—Elizabeth Renzetti, *The Globe & Mail*

"Christian Bale is dashing."   —Joe Baltake, *Sacramento Bee*

"Later, Laurie will tell Jo: 'I have loved you since the moment I clapped eyes on you,' and half the audience will swoon. Bale is excellent."   —James Verniere, *Boston Herald*

Little Women was also the movie that helped to boost Christian's Internet fan base. It was simple demographics. His fans from *Newsies* and *Swing Kids* were 90 percent female. Their ages ranged from high school kid to college student. And a big-screen adaptation of a popular classic young girl's book like *Little Women* meant that the Internet was abuzz with new fans wondering who was that dreamy Laurie and why would Winona turn him down?

Little Women added so many new ways to promote chatter about Christian on the Web. We could track down audiences online and drive them to see the movie.

Louisa May Alcott fan? Check out the movie!

Little Women fan of the 1933 or 1949 movies? Check out the new movie!

Winona Ryder fan? See *Little Women*!

Who played Laurie in *Little Women*? Come to the Christian Bale Web site, Christian Bale AOL folders, or Christian Bale CompuServe discussion boards.

I made a conscious effort to promote Christian to serious movie buffs and to college and university students. When I was in university, I had been the music editor for the school paper. I had the opportunity to talk at length about marketing with a publicist from Capitol/EMI Records. She told me that record companies promoted artists to high school students if they were deemed to be teeny-bopper-teen-idol types. These artists would typically last no more than three records. For serious artists of substance, they would be promoted to college and university students because, she explained, that's when people formulate their tastes for the rest of their lives. This strategy made perfect sense to me to get Christian out of any Disney pigeonholing that people might be doing after *Swing Kids* and *Newsies*.

Following David and Christian's concern about being overlooked in an ensemble cast, I also started to run online contests to get Christian editorial coverage in the major entertainment magazines.

We devised an ingenious method of getting attention. After many publications ran their reviews of *Little Women*, I ran a promotion on Christian's Web site with the Letters to the Editor address, snail mail or e-mail, so that the Baleheads could bombard them with letters asking for an article about Christian Bale. To encourage the letters, my promotion was simple. I announced that everyone who got a letter published would be entered into a drawing for an autographed photo of Christian and a *Little Women* soundtrack on CD. That guaranteed a maximum yield of letters directed at any particular publication.

The letters were orchestrated two ways. Articles that didn't mention Christian—any article that talked about up-and-coming young actors, for example—were bombarded by outraged Bale-heads wondering why Christian had been omitted. And articles that did feature Christian would get an avalanche of letters thanking the journalist for having the smarts and good taste to cover him!

Of course, when I followed up with a call, every journalist brought up how impressed they were that a mere mention of Christian Bale got a tremendous response from their readers! The mainstream print magazines were beginning to notice Christian's Web presence.

Capitalizing on the success of *Little Women*, I redid his press kit and created his demo reel. A demo reel is an actor's video résumé with clips of his best scenes. These tapes are sent out to producers and casting agents in an effort to snag an audition. Christian was the first actor to have an Electronic Press Kit (EPK), trailers, and demo reels available on his Web site. Christian was thrilled to see a slick and professionally produced kit that was considerably nicer than the materials he had had before.

I made sure that each of Christian's press kits was armed with information about Christian's Internet fandom. The Net was still thought of as the domain of geekdom, so I needed to educate the press so that they would take this medium seriously.

In Christian's press kit, I noted:

"Christian Bale's photos have been a very popular download since the release of Little Women. *He's right up there with Brad Pitt and Keanu Reeves . . ."*

—*Margaret Ryan, spokesperson for America Online*

Christian Bale, the talented young actor who first wowed audiences in Spielberg's Empire of the Sun, *and went on to appear in* Henry V, Treasure Island, Newsies, Swing Kids, *and the American classic,* Little Women, *is one of few actors to dominate the Internet thanks to a large and active international fan base that has made Bale the marvel of the cyber age. Word of mouth now has new meaning in this age of the Net! His fans are clearly looking for information in every medium they can!*

How popular is Bale on the Net?

On America Online, Christian Bale's "folders" have been in the Top Ten Most Talked About Actors for the past 2 years!

His WWW Site, which started last summer, has grown rapidly, recently drawing 23,116 visitors in a one week period! The site has been highlighted in various Internet Webzines and was cited in Pointcom's Top Five Percent of all WWW Sites on the Internet. In May, the site was moved to a larger Internet provider because of the volume of traffic.

Bale's WWW Site was chosen by Movie World as one of the Best Movie Sites on the Net and chosen as a Who's Cool in America WWW Site.

Microsoft Cinemania has a Biography page dedicated to Christian Bale.

The Seattle Film Festival Site <www.seattlefilm.com/film/> chose Bale's WWW Site as a Seattle Film Festival Site!

Bale's fan club receives 1,000 e-mails a month!

His fans successfully lobbied the Internet to get Bale his own "newsgroup"—a place for fans to discuss and exchange up-to-the-minute information about Christian and anything even vaguely

Christian at the Sideway Cafe in Venice, California.

related to him! This newsgroup, alt.movies.christian-bale, *is the first of its kind for an actor and draws over 100 posts a day from fans in Australia, Canada, the U.S., the U.K, Japan, and Europe.*

And following Christian and David's wishes, we made sure that the "Christian Bale" brand emphasized that Christian was a vegetarian and an animal rights activist. We debated about how accurate this was. What if a fan caught Christian eating meat? But David was insistent that being a vegetarian and environmentalist had been very good for River Phoenix and aligned with Hollywood sensibilities. It would also endear Christian to his fans as he would be more than an "actor. " He would be a good human being. So on Christian's Web site, years before eBay existed, we began to auction off *Newsies* and *Swing Kids* memorabilia with proceeds going to specific charities. To support one of Christian's charities, the Baleheads raised money to adopt a gorilla named Nahimana through The Digit Fund that was founded by the late Dr. Dian Fossey.

While on location, when Christian heard that one of his *Newsies* bandanas sold for hundreds of dollars, he was impressed. He wrote me:

> *Thanks very much for all of your help. You know it is much needed and I appreciate it very much. Dad has kept me in touch with what you are doing and I think it was a brilliant idea you had to adopt the baby gorilla, Nahimana, through the Digit Fund. As you know, I am uneasy when thinking about fans and all that goes with it, but combining it with something like the adoption seems really sensible.*

Since *Newsies* and *Swing Kids* had been discovered by most fans on video, my first major editorial success for Christian was a large article in *Blockbuster* magazine, a newsletter that the video rental chain used to print and distribute throughout their stores in the U.S. and Canada. *Blockbuster* not only ran an article about Christian's Internet fandom but it smartly listed all of his titles that were available on video.

In spite of Christian's rave reviews from *Little Women* and the growing notoriety of his Internet fame, 1995 was a dry year for Christian. He landed his last and final project for Disney, a supporting character in the animated feature *Pocahontas*, which starred Mel Gibson.

Still, if Christian had not made *Little Women*, he would not have met Winona Ryder and he would not have met her personal assistant, Sibi Blazic, his future wife.

"I owe a lot to her," Christian said in an interview about Ryder.

Christian was depressed and frustrated. What had happened

to the career momentum of *Little Women?* David was furious and blamed Christian's agent for not following up on Sid Ganis's promise to build a project around his son. But according to Christian, his agent threw the blame back at him.

Christian had only acted in period films, so he was definitely in danger of being stereotyped. His slender build and pale complexion made him look stereotypically English. Christian's British citizenship meant that hiring him involved visas and immigration lawyers. And because Christian's publicist was some computer geek in Toronto, none of the press coverage about his Internet fame meant anything to Hollywood producers.

David recalled that Christian's agent was testing Christian's limits: "She wanted Christian to do more publicity. And if he didn't want to do that, then the least he could do would be to show up at more red carpet events so that he could be photographed."

Standing 6'1", Christian was a Young Hollywood rarity because of his height. Christian could be a very popular red carpet date. And attending premieres with starlets would get Christian lots of free press coverage—yet another old Hollywood truism that celeb couples get double the photo ops than a single person. David liked that idea—free publicity, no publicist involved. Would Christian consider that?

"His agent wants Christian to take Natasha Henstridge out!" David squealed with delight one day. Henstridge was a striking 5'10" blonde Canadian model-turned-actress who needed a tall escort for her 1995 *Species* premiere and all subsequent parties and functions to promote the sci-fi gorefest. *Species* would be a surprise hit and Henstridge was stepping out and making her debut in Hollywood.

But no amount of David's careful cajoling worked. Christian refused. It was the first time I heard the two of them argue so loudly. David was desperate for Christian to be seen, while Christian refused to play "The Game."

"Think of your career, Son!" David pleaded.

"I'm an actor, not some bloody male escort!" Christian replied, storming up the stairs to his bedroom. David did not press the matter, lest his easily discouraged son decided to throw in the towel and return to England. No matter how things were going in America, this was a constant worry on David's mind.

Christian was adamant in the face of pressure from his agent and whining from David. He refused to get a Hollywood publicist and play the fame game. He much preferred my approach to publicity, which cost him nothing and was comfortably low-effort.

"Don't worry, Moosh," David assured his son as they made up. "Just focus on your work." As always, David did not want Christian to think about anything except his career.

What Christian did not realize was that his father was at wit's end. If Christian was a single man making indie film wages, he could have done quite nicely. But supporting the House of Bale? That was an entirely different matter. David, the self-proclaimed "financial advisor" had a rude surprise for his son. On July 27, 1995, the state of California slapped a lien against Christian for $29,614 for back taxes.

8

Golden Years

"If the Internet is the ultimate democracy, then Christian Bale has been voted its biggest star."
   —*Entertainment Weekly*

"He is consistently one of the most popular topics on America Online, way ahead of better-knowns like Tom Cruise and Christian Slater."
   —*SPIN*

"For sheer volume of Internet discussion, Christian Bale is in the ranks of megastars Keanu Reeves and Brad Pitt."
   —*USA TODAY*

"Bale is more famous than Leonardo DiCaprio, Ethan Hawke and Christian Slater put together."
   —*The Globe & Mail*

"That man sitting over there in the white suit . . . is the biggest thing to come out of this country since sliced Beatles."
   —*Velvet Goldmine*

The 1990s were, I would argue, the golden era of independent film. Tarantino was the darling of the indie world with his first two films, *Reservoir Dogs* and *Pulp Fiction*. Kevin Smith had just debuted with *Clerks*. And David O. Russell, the guy who would eventually direct *The Fighter*, explored masturbation and incest with his first feature, *Spanking the Monkey*.

"The language of film is universal!" declared the trailer shown before every screening at a Landmark Theatre, a North American chain that focused on independent and foreign films.

It was heady times for actors who wanted a meaty leading role, a labor of love outside the studio system. If the studios wanted movie stars who could guarantee box office success, the indie world was supposed to be all about the craft. This idealism—to cast the right actor for the right role, as opposed to the studio's bean-counter approach to casting a movie star to make the movie profitable—appealed to the up-and-coming actors and the character actors who had a tough time building their careers once they got slotted into a "type" of role.

Infamously, James Woods would find that Tarantino had wanted him to star in *Reservoir Dogs* but Woods's agent turned down Tarantino repeatedly, without even showing the script or mentioning the offer to his client.

For Christian, these indie films were great. His taste in music was eclectic; his taste in books, esoteric. But if he wanted to do an American independent film, he faced the problem of overcoming his reputation. At the time, he was considered a Disney teen star with two bombs under his belt—*Newsies* and *Swing Kids*. Or he was considered something of a Merchant Ivory English actor, a foppish, fey youth who did period films like *Little Women*.

When asked how he chose his roles, Christian replied: "Number one. Did I like the script so much that I didn't want to finish it? Does the character 'fit,' is it a challenge, is this something I would want to see?

"Number two. When's the rent due? Who's doing the catering?"

Christian was only half-joking about his second point. From his heyday of making six-figures with *Newsies*, Christian was now consistently looking at smaller parts. His agent complained that he was too picky and that he wasn't doing enough publicity and therefore couldn't be considered for big studio roles. But his father continued to hide the family finances from Christian so that he wouldn't be pressured into choosing a role based strictly on the size of a paycheck. Chatting about his six-figure paydays, I was astonished to find out that I made more money at my marketing jobs than Christian did making movies!

Concerned about criticism over his lack of publicity, I worked the phones, pitched magazines, and mobilized the Baleheads. Christian was thrilled to be featured in *Entertainment Weekly*, *Movieline*, *USA Today*, *Chicago Tribune*, *Detour*, *Blockbuster Magazine*, *Seventeen*, and more. But David told me that it wouldn't be enough.

"For Christian to be crowned the king of the Internet won't satisfy his agent," David sighed. "Hollywood doesn't recognize the Internet as a legitimate medium because it's outside their control!"

And at the time, that was true. In 1995, I had a conversation with Christian's agent about setting up a business to create Web sites for her actors and for each movie as they were released. She dismissed the Internet as "a fad and the domain of geeks."

Today, of course, every movie has a Web site as part of its marketing; and central to every Web marketing campaign is the ability to build a "fan community." The independent film world loved the Internet from its inception. It was a free medium to promote your film at film festivals or markets or on video. With a Web site, you could compete with anyone else with a Web site on equal footing.

Christian, however, told me that my publicity work on his behalf was hampered by my Toronto phone number, which was considered a joke in L.A. and New York, the two global entertainment headquarters that were notoriously snobby about area codes. In meaner circles, Christian advised me, Canadians were dismissed as "lumberjacks," bumpkins, or worse.

"It would be better if you could move here," Christian said to me one day at lunch at the Sidewalk Café on the Venice Beach boardwalk.

It took me less than ten minutes to agree. I had no dependents, I loved movies, and by then, I had adopted the Bale family as my own. If my own parents could be brave enough to venture to a country where English wasn't even their native language, I could easily move from Toronto to California. I was on one of my regular visits to L.A. Christian and I had become friends, regularly chatting on the phone or communicating by fax. The Bales were hopelessly low-tech and couldn't even get their Mac running to send e-mails. I alternated between calls of supportive optimism with Christian and calls of sympathy with David as he would tell me of their latest financial woes.

"Don't tell Christian, but . . ." was how many of David's phone calls to me would begin.

Their ongoing financial problems also meant that I didn't press my own questions about being paid for the publicity and marketing work I was doing on Christian's behalf. I could see they weren't living in a mansion, they ate crap, and Christian was hardly spending his money on clothes. When I first broached the topic of paying me, David said, "The work you are doing is worth thousands and thousands of dollars. Christian is so lucky that you are both friend and family to him. Of course, we'll pay you once Christian starts to make some decent money. As you can see, we're barely making ends meet as it is."

When I asked David about having Christian sign a contract with me, David warned me that Christian might be offended at such a formality when I was supposed to be a family friend—a relationship, he insisted, founded on loyalty and trust. Nevertheless, Christian replied to my request for a contract with a card that said, "Between true friends, words are not needed."

Because Christian couldn't afford to pay me, our arrangement was on a "deferred" basis, which meant that only when he could afford to would I be paid. At the time, it made sense and I was happy to invest in Christian's career. We made future plans for our production company, imagining the day when we could produce indie films that would suit Christian's eclectic tastes. In the meantime, I found a day job in L.A. in Internet marketing for a software company, and managed to handle Christian's publicity with e-mails and my ever-present Nokia cell phone.

It was easy to move to L.A., in part because I had started to think of the Bale family as my own. I liked David and Christian for their dry British humor. David was a fascinating father character completely different from what I expected in fathers. He was always promoting unconditional dreams and worrying about Christian's low self-esteem, while my parents—conservative Chinese academics—were always worried about the costs or consequences of bad judgments.

Christian, a young man who had been coddled for so long by his father, was amusingly irreverent and rough around the edges. He could be undiplomatically blunt but he loved my cooking and, after he lowered his guard, laughed easily.

The first major sign of our growing friendship happened one evening while I was sitting on the couch in Manhattan Beach, watching TV with David. Christian trotted down the stairs, saw me, then continued down and sat beside me on the couch. He was barefoot, wearing shabby corduroy pants and a white T-shirt. I couldn't help but notice that his toenails were almost dark purple. I wondered briefly (and to myself) what that meant about his blood circulation.

A couple hours later, he retreated upstairs to his bedroom. David summoned me to the kitchen. He was bubbling with excitement.

"Did you see that, Harrison? Christian was barefoot in front of you! He never wanders around barefoot in front of strangers! He likes you! He *likes* you!"

"You can tell from just that?"

"Absolutely! It's just like Mojo rolling over for you. Animals, people, we're all the same! We're all God's creatures! We're not going to expose ourselves to any stranger or predator! What a wonderful development! Christian likes you! He trusts you! This is wonderful!"

David always knew how to make even the smallest of Christian's gestures an sign of hope or good fortune. His optimism was contagious. My eyes lit up. "Great, I'm glad!"

"Oh, Harrison, be more than glad! Be joyous! I want this to work so much! Christian has many people who say they are friends, but he has no one he can really count on."

He leaned toward me conspiratorially. "When we first came to Hollywood, we went to a party where one of Christian's *supposed* friends tried to slip my son a drink laced with drugs. I intercepted the drink and thrashed the young man outside the restaurant for toying with my son's life. Friends indeed! But you, Harrison, you and your Chinese honor and Chinese ways! You come from a culture of loyalty. I can tell you'll take good care of my little son! You shall be Sancho to his Don Quixote! You shall be Samwise to his Frodo! I know it! I *feel* it! I can tell you will become great friends with Christian! Great friends! He and you will do incredible things together! Great and wonderful things! Together, you shall move mountains!"

I could practically hear the trumpets heralding our impending adventure! It was exciting stuff. But there was more.

The next morning, I received my first fatherly note from David slipped under my door. He wrote:

Entreat me not to leave you, or to turn back from following you; For wherever you go, I will go; And wherever you lodge, I will lodge; Your people shall be my people, and your God, my God.

That was a passage from the Bible, Ruth 1:16 to be exact. At the time, I didn't know where the quote was from, but it touched me and I felt as if David and Christian were pulling me ever closer into their orbit. David's occasional but well-timed quotes always added to the moment. We were going to do great and wonderful things indeed.

I looked at Christian as though he was my own needy kid brother. It was good to be needed, mind you. My real kid brother, Les, was living in Toronto; he was quiet and assuredly independent. But here was Christian, odd and awkward, and somehow even more of a stranger in a strange land than I was. I could also keenly identify with Christian's feelings that he was without a country. He definitely did not consider himself Welsh. Being English wasn't helpful to his career in America. And he unquestionably was not American, so he had this curious self-hatred by nationality.

Christian was bizarrely out of synch as a foreigner who had grown up in England without a television; he simply had no point of reference for American pop culture. We would often hang out and just watch TV and I'd have to explain to him who Gilligan was, why Mr. and Mrs. Brady got married, and who that pointy-eared guy was on *Star Trek*.

The other place where Christian was hopeless was the kitchen. Food is a big part of my culture, and after seeing how badly the

Bales fed themselves, I decided I would make the occasional meal for Christian. The very first dinner I cooked for him was a steamed salmon steak. First, I had to clean up the mess of the kitchen and throw out foil-wrapped mystery leftovers in the fridge. Then, it was time to go shopping. I had gone across Sepulveda and picked up salmon steaks from the local Ralph's supermarket, along with rice and asparagus. The salmon marinated in dark mushroom soy sauce for flavor, while I rolled krab sticks in spring roll wrappers for a quick way to make egg rolls. His eyes lit up and he let out a whistle when he walked into the kitchen and saw the dinner preparation. And I had to laugh at dinner when I saw how he argued with Louise over what he thought was the last spring roll. When Louise surrendered the last roll to him, I opened up the oven door to pull out another platter of rolls. Christian promptly threw back the cold one to her and dug into the hot rolls.

I remember one evening when David, Christian, and I went to see a movie at the Santa Monica Promenade. On our drive up from Manhattan Beach, I was sitting in the backseat. Suddenly, I saw one of the newly introduced Volkswagen New Beetles drive by.

"Punch buggy!" I yelled, and I hit Christian on the shoulder. It was the Canadian version of Slug Bug, where you hit someone in the car whenever you spot a VW Beetle.

The effect was instantly catastrophic. Christian yelped, "Dad! He hit me!"

David, who was driving, swerved the car to pull over. He turned to yell at me, his own giant fist raised: "How dare you hit my son!"

But then Christian broke down laughing with his infectious asthmatic Woody Woodpecker laugh as I tried to explain the rules of Punch Buggy to David, while hoping I wasn't about to get punched myself. Christian was very amused.

The heated temper was something that Christian shared with David. They both overreacted out of proportion to any perceived offense. Whether it was bad service at a restaurant, declined credit cards at the rent-A-car, or mix-ups in reservations, both father and son would get huffy and quickly boil into outrage. David was much more vocal about complaining, while Christian would seethe and hiss like some kind of surly snake. Once at an Enterprise Rent-a-Car just a few blocks down from their Manhattan Beach house, Christian was so loudly lecturing the woman at the desk, and he was so angry that she started trembling and pointed to the security camera overhead for protection. Initially, I found it all very entertaining and assumed the Bale huffy-puffery was all about being English. This was so different from my Asian upbringing of stoic tolerance.

What moved me were notes from Christian like this:

Your friendship helps me get closer to fulfilling my goals. I truly appreciate your good nature toward me and value having you on my side.

Love, Christian

As our friendship grew deeper, Christian began to trust my opinions completely, so he fell easy prey to my own highly developed sense of humor. On a trip back to Toronto, I matter-of-factly told Christian that Celine Dion owned the hotel we'd be staying in. That didn't seem too far-fetched as the Air Canada flight we were on featured Celine Dion singing the departure and landing videos with the song "We Were Born to Fly!"

Celine Dion was our running joke of everything he hated about American-style stardom: She was Vegas, showy, a megastar with her own line of Celine Dion Sensational Body Lotion, Celine Dion Belong fragrance, Celine Dion Sensational Eau de Toilette, and Celine Dion Pure Brillance perfume. And, of course, Mister Indie Music could not stand the belting Diva Dion, but as a proud Canadian, I'd always list her as one of the many Canadians

Christian in front of the Ontario Science Centre in Toronto, Canada.

who had made it in Hollywood. So in the hotel lobby at check-in, I was astonished when a normally shy (but very inquisitive) Christian asked the front desk how often did Celine Dion visit.

"Sir?" The surprised concierge said. "Celine Dion?"

"Yes," Christian wanted to know. "Does she personally stay here? Does she inspect your hotel often?"

Only when he noticed that I had run off to laugh did he realize he had been had.

"You lied to me!" he snorted. And it was his turn to playfully hit me on the shoulder. "That's for lying! And that's for making me think of Celine Dion for far too long!"

Christian and little Mojo would often drive up into the Santa Monica mountains for the day. He liked hiking and dirt biking and the solitude of the hills, and he'd take a backpack full of scripts to read outdoors.

While he was out, David swung into action.

David's approach to parenting intrigued me. Coming from a very traditional Chinese family, I thought my parents were over-protective, but compared to David, I was practically a latchkey kid. He poked around Christian's wastepaper basket, looking for any telltale signs that his son was unhappy, using drugs, or mas-turbating excessively. (He didn't wear gloves, by the way.) He knew where Christian kept his journals and poetry and he had keys to Christian's filing cabinet. He made no apologies and got defensive when I questioned him.

"This is Hollywood! How do you suppose a single parent can take care of a young and vulnerable son? I need to know who his friends are, what drugs he's using, and who he's sleeping with. Each one of them could be a dangerous influence on him! I'm his father!"

"What are you doing?" I asked David the first time I followed him on this inspection tour. Christian's room was dark brown with red velvet drapes drawn; call it dorm room macabre. I was shocked that his bed was low to the ground until I realized he didn't have a box spring, just a mattress on the floor. I caught the earthy scent of candles and cigarettes and old books, and then realized that Christian's room had an interesting underlying odor. I was reminded of a song that a Canadian poet, Meryn Cadell, had written about a boy's sweater, noting it had "that slightly goat-like smell that all teenage boys possess." It was no surprise to find hundreds of books piled everywhere. And on top of the books were hundreds of CDs opened and carelessly discarded—Oasis, Bjork, Green Day, The Red Hot Chili Peppers, Belly, Beck, Doves, Badly Drawn Boy, Paul Westerberg. His floor looked like an earthquake had hit a music store. Scripts were all over the floor on a carpet in dire need of a good vacuuming.

A bookshelf held a menagerie of what appeared to be assorted animal fetuses in jars. On the windowsill were a couple of dirty plates, forks, teaspoons, and filthy mugs full of crystallized tea and mold. Closer to his bed was a pile of girly magazines—English titles, I presumed, as I had never heard of any of them.

"I have to see what my son is up to. Is he depressed or not," David explained. He waded through the messy floor and showed me Christian's windowsill, which had an array of little clumps.

"You see," David began, "my poor son has a morbid fascination with death and decay. He enjoys watching things rot and mold on his windowsill."

"Yuck," I said. I took a closer look and tried to identify the blackening clusters on the sill.

"Christian has always had an inquisitive mind," David said proudly. "You see that? He's experimenting with his own bodily fluids on pieces of bread. Some of that is blood. Some is spittle. There's semen there. He wants to see what stimulates the largest amount of mold or takes the least time to decay."

I was horrified as David sniffed through Christian's belongings like a bloodhound. Ever see *Jeepers Creepers*, when the Creeper sniffs through Justin Long's dirty laundry? You get the picture.

If the macabre gallery wasn't enough, David would then grab Christian's latest CD purchases, take them downstairs to the kitchen table, and read the lyrics on the CD insert.

"I need to know what he's listening to," David explained again. "If the music is suicidal or hopeful. If the music is about loneliness or sadness." Sometimes, David would scribble down notes while he read the lyrics so that he could analyze them in depth later. I had never seen anyone behave like this before!

In 1995, during Christian's dry spell, the American Film Institute decided to honor Steven Spielberg with a Life Achievement Award. After years of being criticized as just a pop director with big box office blockbusters, Spielberg impressed the critics with his 1993 *Schindler's List*, demonstrating that the popcorn movie maestro could also create a serious film.

Christian was invited to speak at the tribute. David was ec-static. This would be an important networking opportunity for Christian to reestablish good relations with Spielberg and his prolific producers, Frank Marshall and Kathleen Kennedy. And it would be good for Christian to get out there on a national TV special so that the world could see that the boy from *Empire of the Sun* had grown up into a handsome young man.

Though the producers of the tribute offered Christian help with their writers, he chose to write his own speech. For some reason he didn't have to clear his remarks with any of the producers.

Tom Hanks was the host. Jim Carrey stole the night with a devastating, funny speech that finished with him telling Spiel-berg: "Up yours, man!"

But Christian's homage to Spielberg hit a couple odd notes:

"When I recall working with Steven, I can remember a scene where I had to run down some stairs and say something par-ticular obnoxious. And I was obnoxious throughout the film but this was obviously exceptional because I got slapped for it.

"And we rehearsed this many times so that I wouldn't actually be hit, so that the hand would just miss but it would look for real. We spent a long time perfecting this and then eventually we did a take.

"So Steven shouts: 'Action!' I ran down the stairs and said my line and SMACK! She hit me! And she really wasn't holding back! This was no light tap. And I looked up and Steven said: 'Excellent! Excellent reaction!'

"And I said: 'Well good, I didn't have to do very much because she hit me.'

"And he said: 'Oh, oh dear. Let's make sure Christian doesn't get hit again.'

"So alright. I go back up and we do another take. I run down, I say my line and SMACK! Same thing again. I look up and relo-cate my jaw. And they convince me that it really was just another mistake. It's never going to happen again.

"So I say, all right.

"Anyway, four or five times this happens and finally it dawns on me that she's never going to miss. And what's more, Steven had absolutely no intention of allowing her to miss.

"And whenever I was out of earshot, he was giving her the thumbs up and saying: 'Same again!'"

While the audience tittered and laughed, Spielberg blushed beet red and covered his face. At one point, his wife, Kate Capshaw, turned to ask him if the story was true and you can see Spielberg wringing his hands, nodding.

A couple days later, David called me, upset at a letter Christian had received from Spielberg. Though the letter thanked Christian for speaking at the tribute, David was horrified that Spielberg added: "I think you only got hit once. Any more would have been child abuse."

"Oh dear! What is the meaning of this?" David cried. He was sure that the letter was a thinly veiled warning. And Christian's memories of making *Empire of the Sun*—did that face slapping really happen the way Christian described it? Could his son have been harboring resentment or bad memories all these years?

Christian finished 1995 without doing much work; his only completed project was the voice-over work for Disney's *Pocahontas*. Much to his father's chagrin, his next five films were low-budget but high-prestige indie films shot in Europe.

The first one, *The Secret Agent*, was set in nineteenth-century London and directed by Christopher Hampton. Christian had a small supporting role of Stevie, a mildly mentally challenged boy. Even with the strong cast that included Bob Hoskins, Patricia Arquette, Gerard Depardieu, and an uncredited performance by Robin Williams, the film was poorly received. It was only the second time as director for Hampton, who was better known as a screenwriter. Hampton had won an Oscar for the screenplay for

Dangerous Liaisons and would earn another Oscar writing nomination for 2008's *Atonement*.

The next film Christian did was headed up by director Jane Campion, who was fresh off the success of her 1993 film, *The Piano*, and had decided to adapt the Henry James novel *The Portrait of a Lady* as a starring vehicle for Nicole Kidman. Christian snagged a small part as Ned Rosier, an upper-class twit who falls in love with Pansy, played by Italian actress Valentina Cervi. The film reunited Christian with his *Empire of the Sun* costar John Malkovich, and his *Swing Kids* costar Barbara Hershey.

To get her cast in character, Campion had asked Christian and Valentina to write love letters to each other in character.

Though the film received mixed reviews and minimal box office, Christian enjoyed the shoot that took place in Italy, his favorite place in the world.

Said Christian: "I fell in love 100 times a day in stunning surroundings whilst eating the best pasta in the world. Not a difficult choice. And the wine wasn't bad either!"

In fact, to David's great delight, Christian had split with his longtime English girlfriend, Natalie, and was now dating his costar Valentina Cervi. Campion's love letter assignment certainly must have helped! Christian took Cervi with him to Disney World when he was a presenter at the Discover Awards along with *Star Trek* star, Levar Burton. That was the first major event where Christian got to meet Baleheads in person and they reported back in cyberspace that Christian was charming, taller than expected, but had been spied chomping away on a turkey leg! Since his official bio said that he was a vegetarian (thanks to David), some fans were disappointed and posted their sentiments on Christian's Web site. "I thought he was a vegetarian!" cried a typical post. "I saw him smoking!" revealed someone who was at Disney World.

"I had no idea who the bloke I was presenting with was," Christian later told me.

"That's Geordi La Forge from *Star Trek*! He wears those visors?" I was amused that Christian seemed hopeless when it came to recognizing any actors outside his circle.

Christian was fast getting the reputation for being an actor who got into character for his roles. He had to juggle between characters Ned and Stevie, as production on *The Portrait of a Lady* overlapped with *The Secret Agent*.

He told a reporter: "Because I was filming *Secret Agent* one day and then the next day I'd be rehearsing *Portrait of a Lady* and then straight back on *Secret Agent*, it was quite funny because I would realize just how different I was being. I'd never really realized that I did that before. But I did, on those, because I just would think: 'Christ, if anyone from *Portrait of a Lady* came and saw me on this set, *Secret Agent*, they'd just think I was schizophrenic or something.'"

Metroland, the third in his indie string, was a creative high point in Christian's career. It was also my first opportunity to work on the film's press materials. I designed the original poster and press kit, based on the London Underground logo, which eventually had to be changed from a circle to a square. Based on the book by Julian Barnes, Christian starred as a middle-aged Englishman, Chris Lloyd, who looks back at three stages in his life—as a teenager bored in "Metroland" suburbia, a struggling young photographer in Paris, and as a married-with-child father back in Metroland. A sexy drama costarring Emily Watson, the English actress who had won rave reviews for *Breaking the Waves*, Christian especially liked his raunchy love scenes with French actress Elsa Zylberstein, who played Annick, his girlfriend in Paris.

In real life, Zylberstein and Watson were seven years older than Christian, even though both women played his girlfriends.

Christian became good friends with Watson who enjoyed playing "mother" to his mood swings. In fact, Emily Watson was widely quoted in a number of magazines, including *Angeleno* and *Deluxe*, that she had nicknamed Christian "Tanty" for the tantrums he'd throw on set.

Although Christian had flashed his bare butt for *Prince of Jutland*, to his fans' delight, *Metroland* featured his first hot and heavy love scenes, including a flash of frontal nudity. Christian talked nonchalantly to a reporter: "It comes down to just pulling off your pants and standing there naked. Once they've seen everything, there's nothing else to worry about."

Most actors will tell you that a movie set is the most unromantic place in the world, with bright lights, cameras, and crew milling about. However, in *Metroland*, Christian told me he had a torrid love scene that was shot across an alley in Paris, like a voyeur peeking in. Consequently, Christian and costar Elsa Zylberstein were alone in the apartment, listening to directions radioed across the alley from veteran British TV director Philip Saville, who was watching them from another apartment. In the scene, the young couple comes home and feverishly strip naked. Zylberstein then jumps into Christian's arms so that he can carry her to the bedroom.

"CUT!" Saville radioed across the alley after the end of the first take. "Christian! You've *cocked up* the scene!" The crew across the alley broke up laughing as it was Saville's polite way of telling Christian that his tummy-tapping erection was very much in view.

"There was," Christian jokingly recalled, "a lot of spunk-taneity in that film."

There was another love scene between him and Emily Watson where the two actors were naked in a bed, wrapped in foil to keep warm. Saville, Christian explained, sat at the foot of the bed, giving them directions. But while Saville was talking, Christian felt Saville's hand squeezing his toes. Since both actors' feet were at the foot of the bed, Christian thought that Saville must have thought he was stroking Emily Watson's toes!

When a reporter asked Christian which character he identified with more—Chris, the married-with-child young man, or his best friend, Toni (played by Lee Ross), who remains a bachelor —he replied: "My life has been more like Toni's, in that I don't have and have never had, just in the way that I was brought up, a feeling of having to break free and get out of some place, because we never stayed anywhere long enough for me to get that feeling. I did at some point during, when I was about 12, 13, suddenly just want to be normal. I remember saying that a lot to Mum and Dad, going: 'Why, why am I leaving and going to a different school now?'"

Metroland also offered me a close-up experience with Christian's attitude toward his fans and publicity. When *Metroland* was released on video in the U.S., Universal Studios, the video distributor, invited Christian to a dealer show at the Los Angeles Convention Center to sign autographs for an hour.

"That sounds like fun!" I told him.

"That sounds absolutely miserable," he replied half-asleep on the couch.

But by the day of the show, I had convinced Christian that it would be a good turn to build relations with Universal, and to shore up his growing fan base who had discovered him on video. The Blockbuster chain had been particularly supportive, I reminded him.

To my horror, when it was time to drive over to the Convention Center, I found Christian at home wearing a dirty (formerly) white T-shirt, unwashed khakis, and his favorite desert boots. The T-shirt reeked and had yellow armpit stains. His hair was greasy and he was unshaven, looking as if he had just returned from a weekend-long camping trip, sleeping and wrestling with Mojo.

"You're not going like that!" I exclaimed when I saw him.

"I am and I will. If you dress up for these silly things, you're telling them that they matter. They do not. It's my way of giving them two fingers." He gestured. (The two-finger salute, for non-Anglophiles, is the British version of flipping the bird.)

As much as I tried, Christian would not change his mind. He was determined to show his disdain by looking like crap.

On the drive from Manhattan Beach to the Convention Center, Christian was amused by my eye-rolling every time he stretched out his arm to show off the yellow armpits. And at the Center itself, I stood behind him sniffing out an odor-safe radius from where he was seated signing autographs. Years later, seeing Christian gruff and scruffy during *The Fighter* press junket brought back a flood of memories, complete with offensive scents, and I could imagine it was his way of reluctantly campaigning for the Oscars while passively conveying contempt for the press.

The day after the Convention Center signing, I dragged Christian out to the South Bay Galleria in Redondo Beach to go to the GAP store. I couldn't bear to see him in those nasty old white T-shirts, so I figured he needed to have more options in his closet. He was amused as I picked out several T-shirts in different colors.

"I only wear white," he snapped. But I cut him off and told him that the different colors would accent his eyes and complexion. Before he could complain further, he had a sky-blue shirt on and he was busy admiring himself in the mirror.

I also began to notice the cycles when Christian's hair got pretty greasy. Maybe it was the dark imprints on his pillowcases that gave it away. Maybe it was the bits of lint that stuck to his hair or that I could see (honestly) strands of Mojo's fur stuck to his head. Or maybe it was how his hair was turning black thanks to the accumulation of weeks of oil. I would wait each morning to see if he was going to wash his hair that day. How he could bathe or shower without washing his hair was beyond me. But Christian didn't seem to mind—even when I made an acerbic comment or two about his pillowcases, which started to smell like the inside of a smokehouse.

I decided to ask David to intercede.

David, never the master of subtlety, immediately exploded in full excuse-mode for his son.

"Harrison, in England, because of poor plumbing, because of Margaret Bloody Thatcher, water is a precious resource! She and the House of Bloody Lords have ruined the English economy! It's perfectly normal to take a bath just once a week there."

"But we're not in England, David."

"Bloody Americans!" he roared, changing his attack without skipping a beat. "They waste more water than any other country on Earth! Water, Harrison! Water! The gift of life itself! They waste more petrol than any other country on Earth! Did you know that the world's supply of oil—"

"Yes, David, I know!" I had to cut him off, as I didn't have time for his ecological lectures or political tirades. "I just think that as a celebrity, you know, someone in the public eye, he really needs to wash his hair more often."

David calmed instantly. "Quite right! I understand, Harrison. As always, you are right and you are thinking about Christian's well-being. That's something we appreciate in you. It's your Chinese heritage! Noble and pure of spirit. And your people do love to bathe and wash together, do you not?"

I rolled my eyes, well used to David's comments about the Chinese people. "You're thinking about the Japanese. They take communal baths."

"Bloody Japanese!" he began.

"Yes, David. So do you want to say something to Christian about his hair?"

"You are remarkable! Quite remarkable! Always looking out

for my son! I'll talk to Christian. Rest assured that I will be dis-
creet and subtle and tactful."

The next day, Christian stormed up to me in the kitchen.

"Dad tells me you think my hair is dirty?"

Fantastic. "No, I was just suggesting that perhaps you should
wash your hair more often." Damn, I realized that I used the
word "should."

"Really, Harrison. Hair isn't that important. A true actor has
scant interest in such superficial matters. Look at Ethan Hawke."
At that, he turned around and marched out of the room.

Acting as Christian's publicist was always a challenge. Aside
from pitching story ideas to magazines, arranging the phone interview or in-person interview, I had to deal with the dreaded
photo session. Christian hated being photographed. I think he
just didn't respect the profession and he couldn't stand being told
what to do. Since he had to deal with film directors, I couldn't
understand his dislike of still photography, art directors, and everything that went into it.

For instance, editorial photo sessions typically require a meeting
with the stylist and makeup artist. I had to supply Christian's
measurements in advance since he refused to go in for a fitting.
Of course, as he bulked up and down for different film roles, his
measurements would change wildly, but in between film roles,
Christian measured the following in 2002: Baleheads ready?

Waist	33"
Inseam	31.5"
Neck	16"
Sleeve	36"
Shoe	11
Height	6'1"
Suit	41R
Weight	185lbs

After *Metroland*, Christian landed another small but pivotal role in the 1998 glam rock musical *Velvet Goldmine*. Directed by Todd Haynes (who would be nominated for a Best Original Screenplay Oscar for 2002's *Far From Heaven*), *Velvet Goldmine* was a brash cinematic Valentine to the heady 1970s glam rock scene. Loosely based on the lives of David Bowie and Iggy Pop (the title actually comes from a David Bowie song), Christian played a reporter doing a "whatever happened to" piece on a former rock star. Coproduced by R.E.M.'s Michael Stipe, the cast included Ewan McGregor, Jonathan Rhys Meyers, Toni Collette, and Eddie Izzard.

Producer Christine Vachon described encountering Christian and his dry humor on the set. "I approached Christian Bale to ask if I could get a ride in his car to my apartment. He had only been on set for a couple of days, so I didn't really know him, but he seemed nice enough. He didn't take kindly to my request, though. 'My contract,' he said curtly, 'says I get an exclusive ride to and from the set.' When I started to turn away, he said, 'Christine, I'm kidding.'"

Aside from heavy makeup and some extended frontal nudity from the always brave Ewan McGregor, *Velvet Goldmine* ended with a gay love scene between McGregor and Christian that was literally dusted with sparkles.

To promote *Velvet Goldmine*, Christian participated in an online chat. He talked about the Ewan McGregor scene: "We forewent all the foreplay and to coin a phrase, went straight to taking it up the Gary Glitter. But it was quite tastefully done. We were first on a train and we thought it would be quite graphic and physical, and Todd chose to shoot it from across the way. Which was easier, except Todd chose to not tell us when he cut."

McGregor described the rooftop scene in much more graphic detail when he spoke to *Totalfilm* in 2005. "I was fucking Christian

Bale, Batman, up the arse on a rooftop in King's Cross and the crew was filming from another rooftop on the adjacent building. I hadn't done gay penetrative sex, this was my first shot at it, so I'm standing behind Christian's big naked back, going: 'Wow, this is so . . . Peculiar.' So I start, you know, pumping away slowly and I start to go more like a bunny rabbit, then like a Jack Russell. And I put my head to the side of his head, away from the camera, and I say: 'I'm sure I'd have come by now. I'm going to have a look,' and I glanced back and I saw the crew packing up and walking away! I think Todd [Haynes] had been so respectful of us that he hadn't wanted to interrupt us by saying: 'Cut' . . . Or we didn't hear 'Cut.' It was very funny."

At the time, both Christian and McGregor were pursuing the role of Obi Wan Kenobi in *Star Wars: Phantom Menace*, so there was a friendly rivalry that Christian often experienced with peers in his age bracket.

What Christian didn't realize was that McGregor had already been told that he had won the part midway through the *Velvet Goldmine* shoot, but was sworn to secrecy until the official announcement would take place months later.

McGregor remembered, "I couldn't do anything because I was on set and I wasn't allowed to tell anyone."

However, while on set, McGregor shared with Christian a tale of his own bad experience with the Hollywood studio system when he had lost the starring role in *The Beach* to Leonardo DiCaprio. Directed by longtime McGregor collaborator, Danny Boyle (*Trainspotting, Shallow Grave, A Life Less Ordinary*), McGregor was surprised when he was dumped for DiCaprio.

McGregor told *The Times* in 2009: "Danny [Boyle] and I don't speak, we haven't spoken for years. There was a falling out of sorts over *The Beach* and that was quite a messy and hurtful time."

DiCaprio. The name burned Christian like a branding iron. Leonardo DiCaprio was shaping up to be Christian's primary rival in Hollywood. Over the years, Christian had lost *This Boy's Life* and *What's Eating Gilbert Grape* to DiCaprio. Christian had read for the part of Mercutio in *Romeo & Juliet* but was told that they had decided to cast an African-American in the part instead. Christian, too, had gone up for the part of Jack Dawson in *Titanic* but was told that James Cameron didn't want two British lead actors playing the two leads, who were both supposed to be American. Since British actress Kate Winslet was the starring love interest, the role of Jack had to go to an American actor. Now with McGregor's experience with *The Beach*, it was yet another tale that Christian would keenly remember a few years later when he would go to war with DiCaprio for the lead in *American Psycho*.

Eventually, when I informed Christian that McGregor had won the role of Obi Wan Kenobi, he quietly conceded, "Couldn't have happened to a nicer guy."

Velvet Goldmine won some praise by some critics. Janet Maslin of the *New York Times* described the film as "dazzlingly surreal." But *Empire Magazine*'s Neil Jeffries wrote, "On paper, fine; on celluloid, a Rocky Horror Show of nightmarish proportions." It was nevertheless a small independent film that few people saw in the theaters, grossing little more than $1 million.

The week before shooting wrapped up on *Velvet Goldmine*, Christian was offered a starring role in his final indie film in his five-movie run: *All The Little Animals*, the directorial debut of Jeremy Thomas, who was, ironically, the Oscar-winning producer of *The Last Emperor*, the Bertolucci film that had decimated *Empire of the Sun* critically and commercially back in 1987.

All the Little Animals was a nice change of pace for Christian as it was mostly shot in the remote countryside on the Isle of Man.

"It's a place where they can still birch people legally!" said Christian.

Christian was paid a meager £80,000 for starring in *All the Little Animals* with John Hurt. Yes, a handsome salary for an independent actor, but not even close to enough to keep the House of Bale running back in Los Angeles.

If you watch *All the Little Animals*, you might notice that Bobby, the simple character Christian plays, is remarkably similar to the simpleton character Stevie that Christian played in *The Secret Agent*. I pointed out the similarity to him, noting the only difference was that Stevie couldn't make direct eye contact.

Christian was impressed by my observation. "No one saw *The Secret Agent*, so I could reuse my characterization."

While all five of these independent films opened in limited theatrical release, each of Christian's films did well at film festivals and on video, thanks to Christian's strong worldwide fan following. For the U.S. premiere of *Metroland* at the Palm Springs Film Festival, Paola Freccero, artistic director, wrote, "*Metroland* by far received the most ticket inquiries of any of our films once our line-up was announced. We had a waiting list of ticket-buyers calling in from Washington, Oregon, Northern California, Colorado, Nevada, and Vancouver—obviously Christian has some very loyal fans willing to travel great distances to see his work!"

The entertainment press continued to cover Christian's rise as a cult star on the Internet:

"It was the biggest groundswell of support we've ever gotten for any actor."   —*Entertainment Weekly*

"We were all stunned."   —*Chicago Tribune*

People on the Net just love Christian Bale!"
                    —*Time Out New York*

"He is consistently one of the most popular topics on America Online."   —*SPIN* Magazine

"He has achieved megastardom on the Internet."

—*Interview*

"With secret success stories like Bale's, Hollywood might want to start checking its E-mail."   —*Entertainment Weekly*

I had successfully engineered a writing campaign to lobby Disney for a special fifth anniversary DVD treatment for *Newsies* that was loaded with extras, as well as a direct-to-video release for *Prince of Jutland*, which was renamed and reedited as *Royal Deceit*. The films also provided a lot of footage for Christian's video résumé, which was constantly being updated for his agent to find him his next role. Whether Christian liked it or not, the majority of his fans had discovered him on video and because of *Newsies*. Those fans needed to be marketed to so that they could support his new works.

Oddly enough, I was using a small video editing company in West Los Angeles to update Christian's video résumé. The company was My You Me Productions and it was run by a very pleasant couple, Richard Heene and his wife, Mayumi. Mayumi was a skilled video editor who happily spent time with me and Christian every time we needed to add or remove a clip from his video résumé. (Richard and Mayumi Heene would later become famous for the "balloon boy" incident in 2009, when they claimed that one of their sons had floated away in an experimental balloon over the skies of Colorado.)

While Christian was hopping back and forth across the Atlantic for these indie films, David was scrambling to put together bigger business deals. In 1996, I introduced Christian and David to Santa Monica Studios. Headed by David Rose, Santa Monica Studios and its special effects division, VisionArt, had won multiple Emmys for its work on the *Star Trek* television series and shared an Oscar for Best Visual Effects for its work on *Independence Day*.

As luck would have it, Santa Monica Studios' chief technology officer, Ted Fay, was a fan of Christian's and followed Christian's Internet presence. He had helped me with an early edit of Christian's résumé and was very interested in having him star in a screenplay he was writing. Santa Monica Studios was planning to move into feature films, while David was looking for a company to apply for a green card for Christian.

In Tinseltown, where deals are often done with a handshake, Christian and David tried to negotiate a formal contract that would include a green card and a retainer, while Santa Monica Studios preferred a letter of understanding. By 1997, a contract was signed and Fay recalled that it ended with the phrase, "it is in fact a partnership of faith."

Fay had written a script about pilot Russell O'Quinn, who had famously been asked by the U.S. State Department to head the 1969 food airlift to Biafra during the civil war in Nigeria. Since David often claimed that he had been a commercial pilot for British Airways or British Midland, Fay decided to introduce him to O'Quinn. After meeting with David, O'Quinn remarked: "I doubt he was a pilot of any sort. He definitely was never a commercial pilot!"

On May 13, 1997, the *Hollywood Reporter* announced that Alyssa Milano and Christian Bale would star in *Jungle Croquet*, a romantic adventure film about a small-town librarian who travels to England and finds herself caught up in a romantic scandal with Britain's most eligible blueblood bachelor. It was the first project that marked "a new production partnership between Santa Monica Studios and Bale's production company."

Christian was furious. He exploded at his father. He had not even seen the script for *Jungle Croquet*, much less agreed to be in it. Christian's agent was also shocked to hear about any deal made without her involvement. David, who was hoping to get some momentum from their production deal with Santa Monica

Studios, hastily canceled the project. The partnership of faith was over before it really began.

However, all was not lost. David definitely profited from reading Fay's screenplay about Russell O'Quinn as he began to embellish his own tales of piloting by adding that it was he who had flown food aid airlifts to Nigeria. Fay observed: "David was apparently so impressed with Russell's story, that in a sense he made it his own." Years later, in David's *New York Times* obituary, Paul von Zielbauer would write that David "became a pilot in the hope of establishing air rescue and food supply flights in Africa."

Christian's final small film of the 1990s would be the small part of Demetrius in *A Midsummer Night's Dream*. Shot in 1998 and scheduled to be released on April 26, 1999 (approximately William Shakespeare's birthday), the lavish but very traditional Shakespeare adaptation was a labor of love for director Michael Hoffman (*The Last Station*) and its star, Michelle Pfeiffer, who had always wanted to bring a version to the big screen. Distributed and financed by Fox Searchlight, the film was shot on location in Tuscany, Italy, one of Christian's favorite places, with an all-star cast that included Kevin Kline, Rupert Everett, Stanley Tucci, Calista Flockhart, and Anna Friel.

Reviews were mixed and box office reception was cool, largely thanks to the high expectations set for Shakespeare adaptations by Baz Luhrmann's innovative reimagining of *Romeo & Juliet* in 1996 (which starred Christian's nemesis DiCaprio and his *Little Women* costar Claire Danes) and the witty romantic 1998 comedy and Oscar-hog, *Shakespeare in Love*.

Though Christian loved shooting in breathtaking Montepulciano, a medieval Tuscan town, he didn't find *A Midsummer Night's Dream* particularly fulfilling. His character's love interest was Hermia, played by Calista Flockhart, who was ten years his senior. Chemistry was nonexistent, Christian told me. Christian told a reporter: "To be honest, I didn't really feel attachment to the character at all and I did find, with the language and everything, that really removed me from it."

He began going out with Anna Friel during the shoot. Friel, better known in the U.K. thanks to her pioneering role as a lesbian in the British soap opera *Brookside*, would later costar with Will Ferrell in the box office bomb *Land of the Lost*. It was a relationship that David did not approve of, as he assumed that an English actress like Friel was merely trying to get access to Christian's American agent. More likely, though, David was worried about any relationship that could potentially become serious and cause Christian to think about returning to England.

Christian was getting frustrated with his William Morris agent, wondering why his generally well-reviewed performances in these small European indie films weren't translating into a big U.S. part. She continued to blame his low-profile publicity. Again she said Christian's coverage as the biggest star on the Internet wasn't taken seriously by the studios. However, it was rumored that Christian was also dating Winona Ryder whenever the two were in Los Angeles together and his agent was hoping that Christian would go public with the relationship to get him more publicity.

"We're just friends!" he scolded. He happened to be *very* good friends with Winona. They had clandestine meetings at hotels up the coast or in Las Vegas. She had asked him to come to the final deathbed party for Timothy Leary, her godfather. They were very good friends indeed. Christian, however, bristled at the idea of using his relationship with Ryder for publicity.

That year, Christian's dad had begun dating Charlotte Cornwell, a British acting coach living in L.A. David had need of comforting company. He was depressed and constantly in a state of worry about the family finances and his immigration status. He had long since overstayed his visitor's visa by over eight years.

Christian was not particularly fond of Charlotte, especially since the premiere of *A Midsummer Night's Dream*, when

Charlotte, trying to be helpful, offered Christian acting lessons. "A good English boy should know his Shakespeare," she suggested. I almost burst out laughing at Christian's openmouthed shock at being offered lessons. I quickly steered him to the bar before he could reply.

David was, as always, very upset with Christian's agent. These were desperate times and he blamed her for never following up the promise of Christian's career after 1994's *Little Women*. And now, because of her (or so it seemed to David) the family was drowning in debt.

David, the self-proclaimed "financial advisor" had been fighting and losing a two-front war. To the American Internal Revenue Service (IRS), David told tax collectors that Christian was a British citizen and therefore not required to pay American taxes. To Britain's Inland Revenue, David told those tax collectors that Christian was an American resident and therefore not required to pay U.K. taxes. The result—on February 6, 1998, the IRS filed a lien for the amount of $144,942 against Christian.

It seemed that all of David's plans were backfiring. Just before the lien showed up, David had bought a red 1974 Triumph TR6 for Christian's birthday (1974 was significant as it was Christian's birth year). But a few months later, neither Christian nor David could afford the car, so they suggested that I buy the car with the hope of holding onto it until Christian was financially able to take it back. All the jokes about British cars are true. I had to sell the car a few months later as it couldn't drive for more than ten miles at a time without breaking down.

A Midsummer Night's Dream would be the last time Christian could take on a role without an eye on the paycheck. Christian reluctantly agreed to do a TV movie, *Mary, Mother of Jesus*—the Easter story told from Mary's point of view. It was produced by Eunice Kennedy Shriver, and Maria Shriver, ex-wife of action movie superstar and California governor Arnold Schwarzenegger, was thrilled to see the photos of Christian as Jesus. "Oooh! Sexy Jesus!" she said. Christian's costar would be Swedish actress Pernilla August, who's better known for her role as Schmi Skywalker, Anakin's mom from the *Star Wars* movies.

David was also thrilled. He had been making the rounds in Los Angeles, attending Democratic Party fund-raisers, eager to make

This was Christian's official headshot that I took of him outside an office building in El Segundo in 2002. Christian was insistent that we not use an outside photographer!

connections and network. What better than a connection with the Kennedy family?

However, when Christian declined Eunice Kennedy Shriver's invitation to attend the premiere of *Mary, Mother of Jesus* at the Kennedy Center in Washington, D.C., David was furious. How could Christian turn his nose up at America's legendary First Family, the Kennedys?

No amount of David's begging could change Christian's mind. He would not go to the Kennedy Center. When *Mary, Mother of Jesus* aired on TV, both David and Mojo looked very sad when they saw Christian as Jesus being beaten and crucified. In England, Jenny told me that she, too, had wept during those scenes.

Christian's paycheck from the production had saved the day, and Christian would look on his performance as Jesus with great amusement in contrast to what he would later be known for. That year, Christian's Christmas card featured him as Jesus waving hello.

9

Before Batman,
There Was Bateman

"I had people called up and say: 'This is career suicide,' and I just thought: 'Excellent, that's great!' I was quite turned on by that—by other people thinking it was going to ruin my career."
—Christian Bale, 1999

"I wasn't afraid of being a despicable character from beginning to end. It's my trajectory to become possibly the most hated actor of the year."
—Christian Bale, 2000

In 1999 Christian become the most hated actor on the planet when he took on the role of sadistic serial killer Patrick Bateman. It was a huge career leap for the young actor from Wales that many people thought was career suicide. Remember, his role before this one was Jesus. So it was obviously a calculated risk when he decided to pursue the controversial leading role in *American Psycho*, based on the best-selling novel by Brett Easton Ellis.

The book was an instant hit when it was published in 1991, landing on all the best-seller lists despite its content. The book was originally slated to be published by Simon & Schuster, who had published Ellis's first two novels, *Less Than Zero* and *The*

Rules of Attraction. But the company caved in to protests from the National Organization of Women, led by the feminist Tammy Bruce, and threats of a boycott. So two months before *American Psycho* was due to be published, Simon & Schuster pulled out, something practically unheard of in the publishing world.

Ellis still pocketed the $300,000 advance for the manuscript although he was left shocked by the company's reaction and the consequent arguments over censorship and decency. The book was quickly becoming a cause célèbre. But in early 1991 Vintage Books, a subsidiary of Random House then, quickly stepped in and purchased the rights to the novel, despite all the controversy and protests surrounding it.

After the book was published, Ellis received numerous death threats and hate mail. And it was easy to see why.

The book featured graphic accounts of main character Patrick Bateman's numerous murders, including vivid descriptions of sexual abuse and torture. Many of the murders themselves involved various forms of mutilation including genital mutilation. Ellis wrote graphically of yuppie Bateman examining the internal organs of some of his victims after murdering them. And one particularly horrific scene involved a naked woman, a pipe, some cheese, and a rat.

But none of the material or the public outrage that surrounded the book seemed to bother Hollywood. Plans for a movie went full steam ahead. The hunt was on for a star and a script.

Johnny Depp was the first actor formally attached to the project in the mid '90s, first with Stuart Gordon in talks to direct and then with David Cronenberg officially attached. The project was perfect for Cronenberg who had a reputation for shocking his audiences and was known as the King of Venereal Horror or the Barron of Blood. He had gained popularity with the head-exploding telepathy-based *Scanners* before releasing *Dead Ringers*, in which Jeremy Irons played twin gynaecologists who fall for the same woman, and then he did *The Fly*.

Eventually, Depp passed but Cronenberg remained involved, bringing on Brad Pitt, with Ellis writing the script himself. Pitt was hot off the success of his breakout roles in *Thelma and Louise* and *A River Runs Through It*, but he soon dropped out in favor of playing a cop chasing a serial killer in *Se7en* and the part of Jeffrey Goines in *Twelve Monkeys*, which earned him an Oscar nomination.

Edward Norton also passed on the role of Patrick Bateman. By this time, Cronenberg had lost interest, so producer Ed Pressman offered directing duties to Mary Harron. She signed to do the film on the condition that she could write her own screenplay with Guinevere Turner. Ellis's script was jettisoned because it ended with a big musical number at the Statue of Liberty! While other approaches to the book were more like slasher flicks, Harron and Turner's script was a satiric, feminist take on the book and the narcissistic '80s.

Before *American Psycho*, the Canadian-born, Oxford-educated Harron was probably best known for her 1996 indie film, *I Shot Andy Warhol*, which starred Lili Taylor and was nominated for the Grand Jury Prize at Sundance. *I Shot Andy Warhol* was about the life of radical feminist Valerie Solanas, who wrote the SCUM (Society for Cutting Up Men) Manifesto. That film was produced by long-time Todd Haynes collaborator Christine Vachon, who had just finished producing *Velvet Goldmine*.

Christian had heard about *American Psycho* and was desperate to play Bateman, an American Wall Street broker by day, murderer by night. He met with Harron and convinced her that he was passionate and 100 percent committed to the role. He had been working out on his own to bulk up his body, and he had developed the perfect yuppie American accent.

David did not want his son to even consider the part. "Career suicide" was the key phrase associated with this script, which was based on a book that most people considered unfilmable. David, who was constantly fighting Christian's agent, was now taking her advice that *American Psycho* could ruin Christian's career with a new typecast—that of serial killer/villain. David towed the traditional Hollywood line that a movie star needed to be likeable. Henry Fonda? Tom Hanks? Bruce Willis? Tom Cruise of the 1990s? Likeable. Loveable.

When David learned about Mary Harron's previous work, particularly the SCUM Manifesto, he was very suspicious. He told me: "This Mary Harron will make a fool of my son! He's too innocent to understand that women are the root of all evil. Don't believe me? Look it up in the Bible!"

But Christian was fixated. He loved the dark humor in the script. And while Christian himself was no feminist, he liked Harron's sense of humor and how Harron's script made fun of wealthy, materialistic American stockbrokers of the 1980s. Most importantly, this would be a showy, very American role where Christian could once and for all shed any image of being "just another British actor."

"I don't want to be a movie star," Christian would tell me more than once. "I want to be an *actor*. All this talk of career suicide . . . I rather like that I'm running contrary to what everyone expects."

I was very proud of Christian's position. Sure, he was running against his father's advice, but after reading the *American Psycho* script, with its violence and sex, I could see that Christian would shatter any British actor stereotyping. Worst-case scenario, we decided, the film would be another little-seen indie flick, with minimal negative impact to Christian's career prospects. Best-case scenario, he'd break from the pack of other Young Hollywood men.

Harron told *Salon* why she considered Christian. "When I met with Christian and I watched his face, it wasn't a difficult decision. He reminded me of Lili Taylor in the sense that there was a lot below the surface. He had a sense of mystery and depth in his face. And I hadn't sensed that with anyone else."

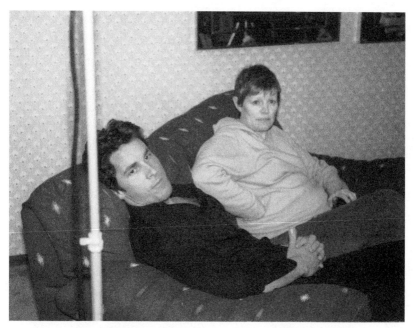

Christian and *American Psycho* director, Mary Harron, chilling in a hotel room at the Sundance Film Festival.

Christian was still not confident the part was his, so he made his move on Harron when he attended the Toronto Film Festival in August 1997.

As luck would have it, while at the festival promoting well-received screenings of *Metroland* with Emily Watson, Christian met Harron's younger sister Kelly, an actress and producer. Knowing who she was, Christian struck up a conversation with her at The Courthouse, a club in downtown Toronto.

He completely charmed Kelly into bed that night *and* also finally won over Mary Harron, and she offered him the part. Kelly Harron had a bit part in *American Psycho* as a bartender and began dating Christian during the shoot, although the relationship soon fizzled shortly after filming ended.

Unfortunately, things started to unravel when Harron took the project to Lionsgate. Christian was very confident that Lionsgate would fund the project. Lionsgate had picked up North American distribution rights for *Metroland* and *All the Little Animals*, and it seemed that they were interested in investing in Christian's career. However, by April 1998, without Harron or Christian's knowledge, Lionsgate offered the part to DiCaprio, who at that point was the most bankable star in the world thanks to the monstrous success of *Titanic*. The movie company had also agreed to pay DiCaprio $20 million for the part—more than triple the small film's original $6 million budget. And to top it off, they wanted Oliver Stone to direct.

So when Lionsgate issued a press release during the 1998 Cannes Film Festival and announced to the world that DiCaprio and not Christian would be starring in *American Psycho*, Harron threatened to resign in protest. She insisted: "Leonardo wasn't remotely right for the part. There's something boyish about him. He's not credible as one of these tough Wall Street guys. Besides, he brought way too much baggage with him. I did not want to deal with someone who had a thirteen-year-old fan base. They shouldn't see the movie. It could've got us into a lot of trouble."

DiCaprio's manager, Rick Yorn, issued a statement during Cannes: "Leo is extremely excited about this script and has decided to make it a priority."

"To have the most romantic man in the movies play someone with no heart or soul will take people's breath away," said Michael Paseornek, president of Lionsgate.

Christian happened to be at the Cannes Film Festival for the premiere of *Velvet Goldmine*. What should have been his time in the sun became a personal nightmare. Christian was beyond livid, ranting: "Losing this role is like having a pencil shoved through my brain."

The day after the Lionsgate announcement, Christian said to a reporter: "I am doing everything I can to keep hold of the part. It was my project and I want to keep it that way. I am shocked that things like this can happen."

To add insult to injury, Lionsgate reportedly offered Christian a consolation prize—a supporting role in DiCaprio's *American Psycho*.

Christian responded with, "I am taking legal advice. I'm not going to do any other role other than the lead."

The Cannes Film Festival finished off on another bad note for Christian. Winona Ryder was also at Cannes, and she was the unfortunate target of Christian's temper after Ryder's friend and *Alien: Resurrection* costar Sigourney Weaver voted against *Velvet Goldmine* for the prestigious Palme d'Or. It would begin the deterioration of their "friendship."

The DiCaprio versus Bale casting struggle suddenly became Hollywood versus Independent Film. It was DiCaprio/Stone versus Bale/Harron. At Cannes, attending actors voiced their outrage because independent film was supposed to be about filmmaking, not deal making.

Perhaps the only person happy about the DiCaprio development was David. He called me, sounding very resigned and tired. "Things happen for a reason. This is a good thing that my son isn't going to end up playing some monster."

The publicity surrounding the casting did not look good for Lionsgate and it intensified when staunch feminist Gloria Steinem began lobbying DiCaprio not to make the film. Steinem wrote to DiCaprio that he would lose his fan base if he made the movie. She was also very concerned that DiCaprio's teen idol popularity might inspire copycat murderers who act out the murders depicted in the book. She drove home the point that his fans consisted of mostly starstruck young teenage girls following his *Titanic* success. Her efforts were successful and he bolted.

Once DiCaprio dropped out, opting to displace Ewan McGregor for the lead in *The Beach*, the project was handed back to Harron on the condition she could make the film for less than $10 million. She said: "I wanted the movie back. I never actually felt like Leo could make that movie because it was such a crazy thing for him to do. The film was so controversial."

She quickly set about assembling an amazing supporting cast on her limited budget, including Chloe Sevigny, Willem Dafoe, Reese Witherspoon, Justin Theroux, Jared Leto, Samantha Mathis, Guinevere Turner, and Josh Lucas. But Lionsgate had final casting approval and they still wanted a lead that had more name recognition and box office appeal.

Christian was in constant contact with Harron, anxiously trying to figure out ways to secure the part. He told a reporter: "I'm sure I harassed her at times because I would lose my temper and give her a call, not mad at her in the slightest but mad at the situation—*how dare they*! And Mary would say: 'Now, Christian, I know, but I'm right in the middle of dinner. I've got friends around. Please, can we do this another day?'"

His tenacity clearly impressed Harron. She told the *Los Angeles Times*: "Christian's family felt that he was deluded."

And that was true. David was very concerned that Christian was burning bridges chasing after this role. He asked him worriedly, "Is it really worth all this, Moosh? Think about it. You've made your point. Producers and casting agents have taken notice! Don't fight against DiCaprio."

One night when the role was still undecided, Christian excitedly told me that he had heard that DiCaprio was at a particular club with his posse.

"Let's go get him!" he exclaimed.

"Get him?"

"Aren't you my bodyguard?" Christian laughed. At the time, he was calling me Oddjob, after the Asian bodyguard and manservant in the James Bond movie *Goldfinger*. "I want to talk to him!"

I talked Christian down, though the idea of the two of us facing off against DiCaprio's well-established posse was amusing . . . from a distance, of course.

But once again Lionsgate insisted on a different leading star and this time offered the part to Christian's *Velvet Goldmine* costar Ewan McGregor. Christian got wind of the offer, and Harron, desperate by this time to get the project off the ground, admitted to Christian that while she wanted him for the role, she would make the movie if McGregor agreed to play Bateman.

So Christian called McGregor and left him a voice mail begging him not to take the part. He pleaded with McGregor to understand the predicament he was in, since McGregor himself had just been screwed out of the lead role in *The Beach*.

Christian believed that McGregor would understand how he felt after they had both been passed over for DiCaprio and bigger box office appeal. McGregor did, and he passed on the part. But Lionsgate was still not convinced Christian should be the lead.

For some reason, Lionsgate decided to run an Internet poll, asking movie buffs who should be cast as the lead. An Internet poll? That was Christian's domain! We organized a Balehead campaign and he handily swept the poll, winning 93 percent of the vote—a victory covered by *Village Voice* and *Spin* before Lionsgate hastily took down the Web page.

Christian was amused at the poll results. He told a reporter: "Lionsgate did mention that, like 'Well, well, my, oh my, that was very positive for you, wasn't it?' They were blindly playing into my hands, there."

He recalled: "It is a controversial role but it's wonderful that Mary had offered it back to me. It got written up in *Variety* and I had people called up and say: 'This is career suicide.' And I just thought: 'Excellent, that's great!' I'm already getting calls from people asking: 'You want to play Satan?' I was committed to go all the way, which is one of the reasons Mary cast me. A lot of actors wanted to do it with a nudge and a wink: 'I'm a really great guy.' But I didn't want to play it that way.

"It's a brilliant book and a brilliant script. I've never met anyone who had as much faith in me as Mary. It's obviously unlike any character I've done before and it's really nice to meet a director who doesn't just look at your past work and do versions of what you've already done. It was wonderful having her recognize that, yes, I can do the part and really fighting for me."

Filming began in Toronto, Canada, in March 1999. To prepare for the role, Christian spoke to Harron on the phone before filming began, giving her his thoughts on how his version of Patrick Bateman should be portrayed.

They would have long conversations about, according to Christian: "How Martian-like Patrick Bateman was, how he was looking at the world like somebody from another planet, watching what people did and trying to work out the right way to behave."

When people have asked Christian how he created the character of Bateman, he usually mentions that he had seen superstar Tom Cruise on late-night U.S. chat show *David Letterman* and his alien-like behavior had been his inspiration for Bateman.

There was another source for his inspiration. On his downtime, Christian channel-surfed television but was fascinated by an odd character he saw who was not quite human but obviously tried to imitate all the appearances of life.

"Who is this Mr. Data?" Christian asked me after being entranced by Brent Spiner's performance on an episode of *Star Trek: The Next Generation*. He knew I was a Trekker, so I happily explained the android character and how Mr. Data differed from the half-Vulcan, half-human Mr. Spock.

"Mr. Data," I said, "is someone who desperately wants to be human, while Vulcans are a race who have suppressed all emotions and are not interested in being human."

Spiner's portrayal of Mr. Data interested Christian and as he began to test voices and accents for Patrick Bateman, there was a time when he sounded very much like Mr. Data attending an Ivy

League school. And to a Trekker, perhaps Patrick Bateman bears more than a passing similarity to Mr. Data's evil brother, Lore.

Around this time while Christian was preparing for the role of Bateman, I gave Christian a number of books about serial killers and man's inhumanity to man. He was eager to understand Bateman's mind-set and detachment. One book I gave him was *Invisible Darkness: The Strange Case of Paul Bernardo and Karla Homoka* by Stephen Williams. Bernardo and his wife, Homoka, were infamous Canadian serial killers. The other book was *The Rape of Nanking* by Iris Chang, which is a collection of eyewitness reports about the mass murders in Nanking by occupying Japanese troops during WWII. Christian's interest in this book would eventually lead him to the 2012 project *The Flowers of War.*

He might have found his inspiration for the interior of fiction's most twisted killer, but Christian still needed to get the exterior right. He would have several nude scenes, so he began the first of his many transformations for a movie role.

Before *American Psycho*, Christian had rarely worked out or visited a gym, telling a reporter: "Being English I tend to enjoy going down to the pub far more than going to the gym, so it was very unnatural for me. I just had to convince myself that I love it, which was the most difficult thing about playing this part."

But hit the gym he did, spending six months while the casting battle raged on working out on his own, confident that DiCaprio would drop out and the part would be his. Then once he knew he had the part, Christian started working out with a trainer and taking his creatine supplements, ready to strip down and flex his muscles in the scene where he shares a threesome with a street hooker and a high-class call girl, while all the time checking himself out in the mirror.

The infamous "looking in the mirror" sex scene has been copied and aped by other actors since. In 2009, British actor Christian

Cooke pulled the same posture in a naked romp for the raunchy ITV series *Trinity*. And American actor Miles Fisher remarkably re-created the *American Psycho* sex scene for his music video cover of The Talking Heads' "This Must be the Place." Fisher portrayed Tom Cruise in the 2008 comedy *Superhero Movie.*

Christian said: "The character is so vain and obsessed with his looks. While the psychology of the character was something that I could perform, you can't fake the physicality. Working out is incredibly boring. I swear it's true that the bigger your muscles get, the fewer brain cells you have. I found I had to stop thinking when I was in the gym because if I thought about it, I'd realise how ridiculous it was that I was pumping iron when I could've been out having a drink and a cigarette and enjoying some lunch.

"I did three hours a day for six weeks with a personal trainer and some time before that. I ate an awful lot during training and then almost nothing during filming."

While he was sculpting his body for *American Psycho*, Christian would lift weights in the middle of the night at a 24-hour gym in Manhattan Beach. One day, he told me that he was stuck under the free weights for almost an hour before someone else showed up to rescue him.

And aside from muscle tone, he began to bake himself on the tanning beds to get rid of his English complexion, that Celtic rosacea he complained about constantly. Contrary to speculation, Christian did not take any steroids, because he was worried about the consequences. One day after a workout, Christian told me that he was in the sauna when he saw a well-known movie star walk in. This actor had recently gotten buff for a jungle movie role, and Christian reported that the fellow had "next to no nutsack!" That was enough to scare Christian off any steroid experimentation.

All of this worried David and me to no end. Lifting weights without a spotter, overdosing on the tanning bed? I teased Christian

that hitting the tanning bed without sunscreen would age him pre-
maturely but he was determined to burn away his old appearance.

Christian would be required to get naked for the threesome
scene and several other scenes in the film and had to wear what's
called in the industry a "cock sock." For *American Psycho*, a different
kind of cock sock was created by costume designer Patrick Antosh.
Antosh recalled: "There was a scene with Christian running around
naked. Because he didn't want to do full frontal nudity, I developed
a fleshtone spandex pouch that fits around the entire genitalia, so
he could run around without anything popping out."

Antosh later took his cock sock design to his work on the TV
series *Queer as Folk*. Antosh was proud to say that actor Hal
Sparks called his cock sock, "Mr. Bale."

According to one of Christian's costars, he was so comfortable, he'd parade around the set wearing nothing but his cock
sock and his shoes. Guinevere Turner, who played Elizabeth, also
went as far as to mock Christian and the size of his sock as she
told *Fashion Wire Daily* during shooting: "Christian was walking
around the set with a sock on his penis and shoes and socks. It
was a brown sock, more like a tiny stocking. Oh, correction, a
smallish stocking!"

When he heard about Turner's comments, Christian defen-
sively insisted that he needed something definitely larger than
a "smallish stocking." He claimed: "Goddamn her! Not so tiny a
sock, thank you."

But the size of his cock sock was really the least of his worries
on set. Christian had to constantly keep up his American accent,
and to do that he stayed in character both on and off the set.

He would even call up family and friends and leave them
chilling messages in the voice of Patrick Bateman.

One friend revealed: "It was really creepy. He would call up
and go: 'It'sssssssssss Patrick!' as soon as you answered the phone
in that perfect American accent. And even if he wasn't on set,

Christian would still leave these bizarre messages on the voice mail completely in character. It would freak me out."

Christian even stayed in character for interviews, using his accent, with the result that many U.S. and foreign reporters had no idea that he was, in fact, British. But when asked by one reporter about his dead-on American accent he revealed that for him, finding the accent was like finding the character.

He said: "I change my accent because it gives me more choice, more choice of roles. If you are born in America and have a non-regional American accent, then you are probably going to get the widest choice of roles around but still you're going to be restricting yourself from playing roles all around the world. And very much a part of finding a different character is the voice. It's so essential to who we are, you start taking in a different accent and you're not going to feel like yourself whatsoever and it's a matter of you just keep doing it until you feel like somebody again. It's nice to make those transformations."

But his accent and even his acting didn't go down well with the real American actors on set. Costar Josh Lucas claims he thought Christian was going to ruin the entire movie with his "boring" performance.

Lucas, who plays Craig McDermott in the movie, told City-Beat.com: "We all thought the same thing: 'What's he doing? He's really boring. Really vacant.' All of us New York actors were looking at him like: 'What the f***'s he doing?'"

During the shoot in Toronto, there were protesters who were angry that a movie was being made of such a notorious book. A group called Canadians Concerned about Violence in Entertainment protested when the city of Toronto was issuing film permits for the production. Leading the protests was Debbie Mahaffy, whose daughter, Leslie, had been a victim of Canada's own infamous serial killer, Paul Bernardo. Bernardo loved books about serial killers and reportedly had a well-worn copy of *American Psycho* on his nightstand.

But it seemed Christian knew exactly what he was doing. When *American Psycho* debuted at the Sundance Film Festival on January 21, 2000, the buzz for the movie was so intense that passes to the screening were being scalped for up to $200 a ticket. However, the movie itself polarized audiences and critics, with some showering the movie with praise and others pouring scorn.

During the screening Q&A, Harron tried to explain the ending of *American Psycho*, which left the audience wondering if all the murders were just a dream of Bateman's. She compared the ending to *The Talented Mr. Ripley*. "I never meant for the ending to be ambiguous," she said. "The murders happened. Patrick Bateman discovers that he's too rich, white, and upper class to be considered a murder suspect—even when he's trying to confess."

In the book, one of Bateman's murder victims was Paul Owen. But in the movie, Harron had changed the name to Paul Allen. She insisted that her film was not making any "die yuppie scum" comment about the most famous Paul Allen in the world, the cofounder of Microsoft.

After Sundance, Lionsgate was loving the publicity that *American Psycho* continued to generate. Before it could be released theatrically, the Motion Picture Association of America (MPAA) demanded that some cuts be made or else it would be rated NC-17. In the U.S., an NC-17 is the kiss of death as many theater chains refuse to screen a movie with the same rating as a porn flick. Surprisingly, it wasn't the violence that offended the MPAA review, but the threesome sex scene. There were one too many thrusts and an implication of anal sex that supposedly put the MPAA over the edge. Once the cuts were made (later restored on DVD), *American Psycho* was released with the R rating.

When the movie was released worldwide in April 2000, it generally received positive reviews from critics. The *New York Times* called it: "A mean and lean horror comedy classic," while respected critic Roger Ebert gave it three out of four stars. He went on to praise Christian's performance as "being heroic in the way he allowed the character to leap joyfully into despicability; there is no instinct for self-preservation here and that is one mark of a good actor."

Bloody Disgusting also praised Christian's performance, writing: "Christian Bale's disturbing/darkly hilarious turn as serial killer/Manhattan businessman Patrick Bateman, a role that in hindsight couldn't have been played by any other actor . . . At its best, the film reflects our own narcissism and the shallow American culture it was spawned from, with piercing effectiveness."

American Psycho did a respectable turn at the box office. Harron had eventually finished the movie under budget at around $8 million, an easier task to do when Christian's salary was just scale plus ten—approximately $2,000/week in those days—far less than the $20 million DiCaprio was offered for the role, and even less than the makeup artist was paid for the shoot. Lionsgate, however, did pay for Christian's new teeth; his embarrassing overbite was finally gone.

The film made just over $15 million at the U.S. box office and close to $20 million overseas, which in financial terms made it a very profitable movie. If Lionsgate had hoped for a bigger hit with all the press and controversy, they'd be disappointed. Sex may be salacious, but it does not sell movie tickets. In Edward Jay Epstein's 2010 book, *The Hollywood Economist*, he notes: "The top 25 grossing films since 2000 contained no sexually oriented nudity. In fact, the absence of sex—at least graphic sex—is often key to the success of Hollywood moneymaking movies since it increases the potential of children in both the domestic and foreign markets."

Given Christian's dislike of musicals, *American Psycho* has an interesting postscript as it was being workshopped in September 2011 to become a Broadway musical. Imagine a Tony Award Show with *Newsies* competing with *American Psycho*!

Christian was also finally a hit with directors and producers who scrambled to cast him in their next projects. The film also changed Christian's attitude about stardom. He told the *Village Voice*: "The *American Psycho* thing changed my view on that— simply, it was offered to someone much better known. So, I'll get better known. Really, I didn't want to keep fucking around and getting fucked."

Because Mary Harron had also been with William Morris during the *American Psycho* casting debacle, Christian decided to change agencies, going to the Creative Artist Agency (CAA).

David was delighted at the move as he had long blamed Christian's William Morris agent for the low pay and small films that Christian did during the later part of the 1990s. However, when David, who loved Hollywood rumor and gossip, heard that Christian's William Morris agent was blaming *his* poor management skills, David lashed out. He drafted a withering memo to the William Morris Board of Directors:

October 14, 1998
Board of Directors
William Morris Agency

To The Board:

There is apparently some confusion as to why Christian Bale recently left William Morris Agency. To put the matter quite simply, his agent was not providing the service and support required of an agent. While Christian had been most patient with his agent, her indifferent approach toward his career eventually led him to realize that he would have to regain his career momentum elsewhere.

More specifically:

WMA did not capitalize on the critical and commercial success of Little Women *(1994).*

Sid Ganis of Columbia said that he wanted to build a project around Christian after seeing Little Women *but she did not follow up.*

After the success of Little Women, *Christian surprisingly en-tered into a long period of unemployment with only voice-over work [for]* Pocahontas *(1995).*

In 1996, when his agent blamed Christian's lack of publicity for his lack of roles, Christian's staff landed him major features and articles in Entertainment Weekly, Movieline, USA Today, Chicago Tribune, Detour, Blockbuster Magazine, Seventeen *etc. . . . Even when faced with this flurry of press coverage, she neither acknowledged nor acted upon it.*

More interestingly, when Entertainment Weekly, USA Today, Movieline *and other major nationwide publications were all taking note of Christian's preeminence on the Internet—she did nothing to take advantage of this new medium.*

Cathleen Schine, author of The Love Letter, *sent in a letter to WMA and to Dreamworks (Kate Capshaw producing) to recom-mend Christian for the lead—no response from her.*

The publisher of Snow Falling on Cedars *sent a letter to WMA to suggest Christian for the lead. No response from her—and the part eventually went to Ethan Hawke.*

She did nothing with Christian's list of directors and actual nominated film projects.

Christian entered into another long period of unemployment end of 1996/1997.

In the case of The Talented Mr. Ripley, *she did nothing for two years despite many requests and reminders.*

The most recent American Psycho *casting fiasco was another example of her inaction. She didn't get a pay or play agreement with producer, Ed Pressman. And she was noticeably absent in the eyes of the industry press ever since the news hit Cannes.*

She ignored Christian and Loeb & Loeb's instructions with regard to the A Midsummer Night's Dream *contract which in effect left him with the worst contract he has ever had.*

All film projects came to Christian directly from directors and producers, sometimes years in advance. All WMA had to do was to receive the details. In all his years with WMA, Christian never received any effort, promotion or lobbying on his behalf.

In fact, the only one film that ever came about through WMA was the film Metroland—*and that was through WMA's London office. Of course, WMA UK providing misleading and erroneous information with regard to financing on that project!*

Aside from specific project foul-ups, she also did not provide Christian with any personal support one would expect from an agent. For example:

She never visited Christian on the sets of Velvet Goldmine *or* Metroland—*even when she was in London on business.*

She would not return Christian's calls for months.

She never attended any film festival screenings of his films.

She continually blamed Christian for being selective in his script choices.

She did not acknowledge the phenomena of his proactive fan base.

She allegedly told Francis Ford Coppola that Christian didn't like to read scripts.

She booked appointments that could not be met—most recently, Tim Burton.

She made emotional pleas to Christian not to take a meeting with Nick Stevens or to socialize with other agents.

She made her attacks personal by badmouthing his family.

With this lackadaisical approach to Christian's career, there should be no doubt as to why he had to leave if he wanted to continue to work and thrive as an actor. For her to blame anyone else is simply scapegoating.

David Bale

While Christian's career was heating up, so was his personal life. Just days after *American Psycho* premiered at Sundance, Christian eloped with Sandra "Sibi" Blazic in Las Vegas.

The couple began quietly dating in the summer of 1999, after reportedly meeting at a backyard barbeque thrown by Winona Ryder and managed to keep their relationship under the radar of any press. Standing 5 feet 11 inches tall, stunning Sibi had attended USC, did some fashion modeling, and even appeared in celebrity makeup artist Kevyn Aucoin's book *Face Forward* before she began working as a personal assistant for Ryder.

The couple tied the knot on January 29, 2000, just a day before Christian's twenty-sixth birthday.

While David was all smiles to the newlyweds, in reality, he did not take the news well. It was dawning on him that he was losing control of his son. Christian had defied his career advice about *American Psycho*, and it had paid off. And Christian was beginning to question some of the financial decisions his father had made on his behalf.

A few nights after Christian and Sibi got married, David and I sat together at the pub in Barnabey's Hotel in Manhattan Beach. He was wallowing in his fourth pint, bemoaning the fact that his son had married suddenly and secretively. I was doing my best to console him.

"David, I'm sure Christian had his reasons."

"You don't understand!" David was practically weeping. "I've lost my son! I've lost my son!"

"I'm sorry, David . . ."

But then David angrily shook his head, raised a pint to the heavens, and bellowed,

"HOW MUCH SHARPER THAN A SERPENT'S TOOTH IT IS TO HAVE A THANKLESS CHILD!"

The pub went silent. I wanted to crawl under the table.

The year 2000 would be a major turning point for Christian and David. Adding to David's misery over his son's marriage, David had more problems. The INS (Immigration and Naturalization Service now known as Citizenship and Immigration Services) had discovered that David had long overstayed his six

Christian and Sibi at the Sundance Film Festival.

month visitor's visa. He had been stalling INS proceedings against him begun in 1999 by claiming medical duress. David steadfastly claimed that he was unable to fly and therefore unable to be deported. He produced two doctor's letters—one wasn't even from a doctor—to keep the INS at bay with claims of medical problems that made it impossible for him to board an airplane. But after overstaying his visitor's visa for almost eight years, the INS finally issued a deportation order. It looked like David's California dreaming had come to an end.

[10]

Post-Psychotic

"Popcorn movie: A Summer action flick, not monumental, a good waste of time."
—**Urban Dictionary**

American Psycho was the breakthrough role that Christian needed. Thanks to his dedication, he transformed himself physically from the lanky boy from Bournemouth with the peaches and cream complexion and the English teeth to a tanned, muscled American hunk in a movie that garnered critical raves and a cult following. Christian was now getting more scripts to look at as he was clearly an actor who was committed to his roles.

Most importantly, Christian was expanding the Balehead fan base. His fans had previously been mostly college or high school girls, but a role like Patrick Bateman invited Bret Easton Ellis fans and others who followed off-the-wall serial killer portrayals. It was the old Hollywood maxim at work again. A Hollywood star needed to attract both men *and* women—men who wanted to be like him and women who wanted to sleep with him.

Thanks to the success of *American Psycho* in its limited release and on video, Lionsgate immediately green-lit two sequels, which were released in 2002. *The Rules of Attraction* starred James Van Der Beek as Patrick Bateman's cousin, Sean. Desperate for Christian to make a cameo in his movie, Van Der Beek wrote a letter to Christian but he was unmoved. He didn't want to revisit the part. *The Rules of Attraction*, like *American Psycho*, was at least based on a Bret Easton Ellis novel but odder still was Lionsgate's second sequel project, which was released straight to video— *American Psycho 2: All American Girl*. Starring Mila Kunis (*The Black Swan, That 70s Show*) and William Shatner (*Star Trek*, of course!), this turkey was Lionsgate's none-too-subtle move from artsy independent films to the studio that would produce the *Saw* franchise.

American Psycho proved that Christian looked good as a killer, particularly in a tuxedo, so it was no surprise that Christian was invited to meet with Barbara Broccoli, the producer of the James Bond movies. Broccoli was looking ahead for the next James Bond after Pierce Brosnan's contract expired. She intimated that the role of 007 would be Christian's for the asking.

The meeting was polite and cordial but Christian was not interested in being committed to a franchise that was very British. He thought that James Bond represented every despicable stereotype about England and British actors. Besides, he quipped: "I've already played a serial killer."

But Christian was still very keenly aware that an actor had to be competitive. The battle with DiCaprio for *American Psycho* taught Christian a lesson. He could not sit back and passively wait for roles to come to him. His father had coddled him so much that Christian sort of expected that roles would be offered to the "greatest actor in the world." And Christian continued to compete for roles against his old nemesis Ethan Hawke. He lost a part in *The Newton Boys* when he was told he looked too English. *Snow Falling on Cedars* was also lost to Hawke. Then came *Training Day*.

Christian was thrilled to announce that he was up for the lead in *Training Day*, the violent police drama directed by Antoine Fuqua and starring Denzel Washington. Originally, word was that the part of Jake, the rookie cop, was supposed to go to Freddie Prinze Jr., who was looking for a gritty comeback role. But Christian auditioned for the part and the producers liked his look and his reading. A few days later, Christian was distraught to hear that they thought he looked too old for the part.

"That," I teased him, "is because you spent too much time on the tanning bed for *American Psycho*!"

Christian was not amused. Worse was when he heard that the part ended up going to Ethan Hawke who was four years his senior! It was a bitter pill to swallow when Hawke earned his first Oscar nomination for his performance in *Training Day*.

Unlike the career lag after *Little Women*, Christian had a lot of opportunities post-*American Psycho*. He signed on for a number of follow-up projects; 2000 and 2001 were going to be very busy for him. Adding to my day job, I wore a number of hats for Christian, including personal assistant. All calls and e-mails had to go through me, even while I was working my full-time job.

First up was *Shaft*, Christian's first big popcorn movie, a $50 million Paramount Pictures movie that he landed in the afterglow of the rave reviews he got from *American Psycho*. The lean years of indie films were over! To Christian's delight, he would play an American *and* a bad guy, Walter Wade Jr., in a reboot of the popular 1970s *Shaft* movies, which had starred Richard Roundtree. This time, Samuel L. Jackson starred as the titular character, a tough-talking New York detective hot on the trail of a racist rich kid (Christian) who had killed a black man at a club. Directed by John Singleton (*Boyz n the Hood*), *Shaft* ended up a moderate summer 2000 box office success, grossing more than $70 million domestically.

The production was not without its problems as Jackson had issues with director Singleton and the script. Jackson told the *New York Daily News* at the time that: "I told him point-blank that I refused to say that white man's [screenwriter Richard Price] lines."

Critics were lukewarm on the movie. The *Shaft* of the 1970s was bold and blatant and defined the blaxploitation movie genre. Roger Ebert summed it up: "Too much of it is on automatic pilot, as it must be, to satisfy the fans of the original *Shaft*."

When he was single, Christian, concerned about being distracted or jarred out of character, barely tolerated set visits from family and friends. Though untrained, Christian's method-like acting required focus and a prickly professionalism. He told a reporter just a year before he got married that he enjoyed staying in character. "I just actually find it enjoyable to do that. And it's part of my pleasure of making films, in a way, that I can go away and pretend to be somebody else, to all these people who don't know any different, you know? Which is why I dislike having family or friends visit the set."

But that was before Christian got married. After they were married on January 29, 2000, Sibi and Christian were inseparable, and she followed him on location everywhere. *Shaft* was shot in New York City, *Reign of Fire* in Ireland, and *Captain Corelli's Mandolin* in Greece. And *Equilibrium* was shot in Germany. Sibi's presence on location was constant and unique.

After *Shaft*, Christian and Sibi packed up to go to the remote Greek island of Kefalonia for *Captain Corelli's Mandolin*. This was the highly anticipated follow-up project for director John Madden after his tremendously successful *Shakespeare in Love*, which had earned Oscars for both Gwyneth Paltrow and Dame Judi Dench.

Based on the novel by Louis de Bernieres, *Captain Corelli's Mandolin* is a tragic love story set on Kefalonia during the Second World War when the island was occupied by Italian and German forces. I was looking forward to this project as I had been following the book since it was brought to me by my former English high school teacher, Jean McKay, back in Toronto as a possible project for Christian. Of course, David and I were hoping for Christian to snag the title role but by the time the book was optioned and a screenplay written, the juicy starring role went to Nicolas Cage. However, Christian wanted the morally corrupt (and more dramatically interesting) part of Mandras, the Greek fisherman.

In typical Hollywood fashion, here was a big $60 million movie set in Greece without any Greek actors in the lead roles. Spaniard Penelope Cruz played Cage's love interest, Pelagia, while Christian's *All the Little Animals* costar, the very English John Hurt, played Dr. Iannis. Christian landed the role of Mandras.

While shooting on Kefalonia in the summer of 2000, Christian and Sibi were overwhelmed by the heat. WENN (The World Entertainment News Network) reported that Christian was having a miserable time during the shoot. WENN noted that a friend of Christian's said: "He hates the food and I get e-mails every day from him saying that he's lost another 5 pounds because he can't eat anything. He says the weather is too hot as well, he's not enjoying it at all."

Of course, WENN was also the news outlet that reported that Christian had a private jet for his use during the *Corelli* shoot!

Christian was furious at the report. He e-mailed me: "It makes me sound like a bitchy, faggot actor!" I had to laugh when I read his e-mail, as Christian often complained about any location that wasn't Italy. He blamed his mother for the possible leak, thinking that she may have shared their correspondence to the press.

The truth of the matter is that Kefalonia is such a remote island, it took a charter plane to get cast and crew to a major airport. I personally organized flights for Christian whenever he had work on a shoot. And Christian was also busy flying around Europe to promote the release of *American Psycho* in those countries.

Christian was disappointed with two omissions in the final film. His character, Mandras, was supposed to swim with the dolphins but budget and timing constraints cut that scene. Also, Mandras attempts to rape Pelagia but that scene was cut, so Mandras oddly disappears halfway through the movie with no explanation.

Captain Corelli's Mandolin was an expensive bomb for Universal Pictures when it was released in August 2001, grossing just $25 million domestically. The critics laughed at the watered-down adaptation of the book and the casting choices.

Perhaps the toughest criticism came from the *Wall Street Journal*'s Joe Morgenstern, who wrote: "I wish I'd brought a pair of peas to the screening. Then I could have taken in the glorious scenery without the dumb dialogue, which is delivered in a jangle of accents that makes a mockery of ethnicity."

Alarmed at the bad reviews, Christian decided to skip the L.A. premiere, breaking with Hollywood tradition where even a poorly reviewed studio movie merited a glamorous red carpet event where the cast could express their solidarity, generate press coverage, and schmooze with filmmakers for their *next* project. Christian didn't like the Hollywood game—particularly publicity and the red carpet walk where one had to spit out all the same answers to the same questions.

The night of the premiere for *Captain Corelli's Mandolin* was memorable for a number of reasons. I had recently moved to an apartment in Marina del Rey, and since Christian had decided not to attend the premiere, he came over to meet my new dog, Dodger, the world's largest dachshund, which I had adopted from a rescue in Canoga Park. As Christian settled on my couch,

Dodger took one look at Christian, jumped up, and bit him right in the crotch. Dodger survived Christian's wrath by being fast, but it definitely added to Christian's unhappy mood for the evening.

Touchstone Pictures' *Reign of Fire* was another popcorn movie. Directed by Rob Bowman (best known for his work on the *X-Files*), this was Christian's first role with the gruff, survivalist beard that would become a familiar sight in his later films.

Shot in Ireland, *Reign of Fire* was supposed to be a modern dragon movie. Budgeted at $60 million, it was *Dragonheart* meets *Dragonslayer* meets *Mad Max*. In a construction site in London, hibernating dragons are accidentally awakened. The dragons lay waste to the earth and the surviving humans are holed up in little communities in a postapocalyptic existence. Christian stars as the leader of one English survival camp. A seventeen-year-old English actor named Scott Moutter played Christian's adopted son, Jared. When an army of Americans show up—led by Matthew McConaughey biting a big cigar—the humans band together to kill the lone male dragon.

When I first read the script, I had added my own flurry of sticky notes to give to Christian. I had done my IMDb research and warned him that no live-action dragon movie had ever done well at the box office, so I was wondering if the script could be changed to be more about pterodactyls in the vein of *Jurassic Park*.

Christian took these concerns to Bowman. He said in an interview: "I had some concerns about the story but what was great is that Rob had the exact same concerns and promised that there were going to be changes. I did a complete 180 degree turn in the meeting. I went in there thinking: 'No, probably not,' and left thinking this is something exciting and different for me to do."

Christian's costar Matthew McConaughey, was a big fan of *Empire of the Sun*. He told *OK! Magazine* in 2008 that he had whistled the theme from *Empire of the Sun* to his son, Levi, while he was still in the womb. McConaughey was thrilled to be doing the project, although in typical McConaughey style, Christian recalled that he kept asking Bowman for a nude scene.

Shooting a special effects movie was a lot of fun for Christian. He told a journalist: "This was more like playing silly buggers in the playground than almost any movie I've ever done before." But Dublin was not his favorite place to live. He complained about Dublin as much as he complained about Greece. "We stayed in a house right in the middle of Temple Bar. We had vomit and vodka bottles on the doorstep each morning and had to stick foam up against the windows if we wanted to sleep at night."

Science fiction fans are very fussy about story line—particularly believability. And one of the many problems of the critically-reviled *Reign of Fire* was that of dragon biology, since the movie's key plot point was that there was only one lone male dragon that presumably flew around the world to mate with the females. With an improbable and unbelievable scenario and a movie that looked as if it were *Waterworld* in flames, *Reign of Fire* opened as the big summer movie for 2002 only to be shot down by the critics.

Reign of Fire ended up as a box office disappointment, grossing just $43 million domestically, far short of its estimated $60 million production costs. However, the movie gave Christian his first opportunity to appear on an American talk show. When he appeared on *The Late Late Show* with Craig Kilborn, he bristled at doing the obligatory station identification, where the celebrity would say, "I'm Christian Bale and you're watching *The Late Late Show* on CBS." Kilborn decided to force the issue by asking Christian to do the station identification live on the air during a segment called "5 Questions for Christian Bale." Christian wittily replied, "I'm Christian Bale and I'm sucking corporate cock right now."

Christian's young costar, Scott Moutter, came to the *Reign of*

Fire premiere with his family to size up the possibility of pursuing a Hollywood career. Interestingly enough, Christian passed on lunching with the Moutters, so David and I took them out for lunch instead. After all that David had been through in America, I was surprised when David bluntly told Moutter's father not to move to Hollywood. "It's too difficult and competitive," David explained. "And your son will never get his childhood back again." The Moutters ended up staying in England.

It was while Christian was shooting *Reign of Fire* in Ireland that *Batman* came up. There were competing Batman projects at Warner Bros. to reboot the franchise and only one would proceed. Warner Bros. had also changed its casting strategy, preferring to look for a good actor it could transform into Batman, rather than a movie star that would distract from the reboot. For my very first use of Amazon.co.uk, I had sent Christian Alan Moore's *Batman: The Killing Joke* and Frank Miller's *The Dark Knight Returns* and *Batman: Year One* so that he could consider pursuing a Batman project that was in the works.

Christian was feeling pretty good about his career at this point. In the 1990s, post-*Little Women*, he was relegated to small British indie films that couldn't find distribution. Now in the 2000s, he was doing major studio work. I remember we had a good laugh at his résumé then.

"What do you think my porno movies would be called?" Christian asked me.

"Your porno movies?"

"You know, if they do porno versions of my movies, what kind of titles would they come up with? Of course, there'd be *Empire of the Bum*."

"Yes," I agreed.

"*Newsies* would be *Nude-sies. A Midsummer Night's Shag*, um, *Poke-Her-Eyes-Out, American Shag-o* . . ."

"Yes."

"*Swing Kids* would be *Swinging Dicks*. But of course, *Shaft* and *Little Women* would keep their existing titles!"

Eventually, there would of course be a couple of actual porn parodies; the most infamous would be *European Psycho*, which starred British porn star Danny Mountain.

One strange thing about living in Los Angeles is that time moves slowly. Maybe it's the near perfect weather without seasons that makes you forget how many years have passed. One day, Christian presented me with a new computer. He wrote:

> *Enjoy the computer. Sorry I've not been able to pay you anything for all of your work, but I hope the computer can suffice until a time not too far in the future when we'll form a huge corporation, take over the world and sell out!*
>
> Love, Christian

He was referring to our family production company that I was eagerly waiting to begin. I had dreams about writing screenplays and producing films, but I was patient because Christian was always getting hit by surprise expenses thanks to his father's financial mismanagement.

There was a lot of debate in the House of Bale about *Equilibrium*. On one hand, Christian liked the script and wanted to work again with his *Metroland* costar Emily Watson. On the other hand, it was a small production ($20 million) and writer/director Kurt Wimmer was green. Though Wimmer would go on to direct other cult sci-fi movies like *Ultraviolet* and have a very successful screenwriting career, it took a lot of convincing before Christian would agree to work again with a first-time director since his experience on *Swing Kids*.

Originally entitled *Librium*, the first sign of trouble was that the drug maker of Librium, an anti-anxiety drug, threatened to sue unless there was a title change. When directorial duties were beginning to overwhelm Wimmer, there was talk that one of *Equilibrium's* producers, Jan de Bont, might direct. De Bont had directed *Speed*, *Twister*, and *Lara Croft: Tomb Raider*. But Wimmer ended up helming the project, which was primarily shot in Berlin, Germany, with an impressive cast that included Emily Watson, Angus McFayden, Taye Diggs, Sean Bean, Sean Pertwee, and William Fichtner.

De Bont was one of the main reasons why Christian decided to do *Equilibrium*. His 1994 action hit, *Speed*, turned Keanu Reeves into an action hero. Reeves was one of Christian's favorite actors. But before *Speed*, Reeves was best known for playing dufus roles like *Bill & Ted*. After *Speed*, Reeves's career shifted into high gear, paving the way for *The Matrix* trilogy. Would *Equilibrium* do the same for Christian?

Christian and I both saw *Equilibrium* as a good stepping-stone. He would look good as an action hero, had a couple of shirtless scenes to show off his buff body, and he was sold on the film as a low-budget version of *The Matrix*. Christian would be trained in martial arts. Wimmer envisioned a gun-based martial art called gun-kata or gun-fu. Unfortunately, by the time production began, Christian did not get along with Wimmer and there was a lot of tension on the set. To say that he was happy when production finally wrapped in December 2000 would be an understatement.

"This movie is finally fucking over!!!" Christian e-mailed me. "Director didn't even say goodbye. He ran out with his tail between his legs."

The shoot in Berlin wasn't all moviemaking pain. Christian recorded vocals for a now defunct German breakcore band called The Thunderinas which was headed by Austrian musician, Rachael Kozak (aka "Bloody Knuckles"). On the song "1-800-INNO-CENT," Christian calls a suicide help line and says, "It's very hard for me to talk about this, to know if I really have a problem or

not. I need to come to terms with myself. Christian was very disappointed that the original ending of the film had been cut back
because of the budget. In the original ending, the climactic battle
between Christian's character, Preston, and MacFayden's character, Dupont, was supposed to be a stylized gun battle where
the two men would be shooting at each other, but the bullets
would hit in midair because both men had been trained identi-
cally. It would have been a more elaborate version of *The Matrix's* bullet-time fighting. What actually ended up on the screen,
Christian laughed, "looked like the two of us were trying to bitch
slap each other with guns."

Equilibrium was ravaged by critics and it bombed at the box
office.

Washington Post noted: "*Equilibrium* is like a remake of *1984*
by someone who's seen *The Matrix* 25 times while eating
Twinkies and doing methamphetamines."

Dennis Harvey at *Variety* wrote: "Misses with its blowhard
treatment of a silly, obvious script. Results might hazard *Battle-
field Earth* comparison if new pic were a tad more fun."

And the *San Francisco Chronicle* lashed out with: "Super-
violent, super-serious and super-stupid."

But the film served an important part of Christian's campaign
to win *Batman*. He demonstrated vividly that he was not just an
actor, but that he could be an action hero.

At the time, I remember a series of journalists in a hotel
room asking Christian which of his characters he identified
with the most.

"I'm not going to answer that," he'd say to each one.

After the last journalist had left, I turned to Christian and said, "I bet I know which character you identify with the most."

He looked back at me, eyebrows raised, a slightly amused look on his face.

"Patrick Bateman," I said.

Christian laughed. "That's right!"

It's not that I thought Christian was a serial killer, but the curious torment Bateman has with himself was very much Christian. I thought back to a line from the movie: "I have all the characteristics of a human being: blood, flesh, skin, hair; but not a single, clear, identifiable emotion."

Back to the Hollywood maxim—one for the studio, one for yourself. After doing a string of big studio films and earning big studio dollars, Christian returned to small drama in *Laurel Canyon*. It would reunite Christian with his *Prince of Jutland* costar Kate Beckinsale. Indie queen Frances McDormand starred as a veteran rock producer, while Christian played her uptight, conservative son, a theme Christian had explored earlier in *Metroland*.

I remember Christian decided not to attend the cast screening of *Laurel Canyon*. I was sitting beside Frances McDormand when she turned to me, got in my face, and asked, "Where's your boss? Why isn't he here?" She was so direct and unexpectedly blunt that I babbled some excuse, but it was clear that she wasn't pleased that Christian was absent.

Laurel Canyon fared poorly at the box office, grossing less than $5 million worldwide, and garnered mixed reviews. Todd McCarthy, *Variety*, wrote: "The dramatic trajectory is frightfully obvious, the characters tediously one-dimensional, the dialogue banal."

Shaft, Captain Corelli's Mandolin, Laurel Canyon, Reign of Fire, and *Equilibrium*—there wasn't a box office hit among them. Whispers of "box office poison" resurfaced, and Christian "Fail"

realized that his next major studio film had to be chosen carefully. Though every one of Christian's films had found an audience on video thanks to his very strong Balehead fan following
on the Internet, he needed bigger theatrical box office appeal to
secure the A-list, leading-man status he craved.

While the post-*Psycho* years were busy for Christian professionally, at home, he was in a personal hell with his father. Christian and Sibi's marriage was a surprise start to a year that would
be full of challenges for father and son. The newlyweds initially
moved in with David in the Manhattan Beach house and there
was immediate friction.

David was spooked by Sibi's legal name, Sandra. The mail that
came in for her was addressed to Sandra Bale, the name of David's first wife in South Africa. David complained that he got a
heart attack every time he saw a letter for her. And while David,
as Christian's manager and father, had held onto the purse strings,
Sibi was put in the position of being forced to deal with a father-
in-law who was immediately paranoid of her every move. If Sibi
needed to buy a household item like a mattress, she had to ask
David for the money, which would immediately trigger David's
scrutiny and criticism. And of course, I'd get an earful later that
evening when David would vent.

David had been fighting deportation as he had long overstayed
his 1991 visitor's visa, which was only good for six months. David
claimed he was too ill to board an airplane and therefore too ill
to be deported back to England. On April 12, 2000, David waved
around a letter from his cardiologist, which stated in part:

> *Mr. Bale's departure from the United States carries significant life-
> threatening risks which include but not limited to the following:*
> *Physical and mental stress of flying*
> *Stresses placed on him by virtual of separation from his chil-
> dren and his home.*

The INS was not sympathetic. In one meeting with David, an INS officer bluntly told him that there was an illegal immigrant with spina bifida that they were deporting, so his claims of medical duress weren't enough to stop the proceedings.

Christian's relationship with his father had started to deteriorate after he discovered back in 1998 that his father had badly mismanaged his finances. He had paid off a big chunk of debt by doing *Mary, Mother of Jesus*, and the flurry of movie shoots in 2000 and 2001 put Christian back in black. In fact, Christian was so pleased that he was making good money again as an actor, he turned down two commercial endorsements I had negotiated in 2000—Cerruti, the fashion designer behind *American Psycho*, had wanted Christian to be The Cerruti Man, and The GAP had also offered Christian a series of TV commercials. To torment the Cerruti people, Christian offered to be their spokesman only on the condition that they renounce leather from their entire fashion line. Cerruti politely declined.

But David's parenting strategy of keeping financial secrets from his son was backfiring.

The bungled production deal with Santa Monica Studios, the debts, the two liens filed against him, taxes owed to both the U.S. and U.K. governments? *Jungle Croquet?* Christian felt betrayed and retreated to the sanity and calm of his wife's family, the Blazics.

Embattled with his immigration problems, David had little time to smooth things over with his son. David was up against the wall. How could he stay in the country? He began to plead and lobby all their Hollywood contacts to write to California senator Diane Feinstein to introduce a private bill to grant him a green card. The lobbying worked. Feinstein, without even doing a background check on David Bale, introduced the bill (S.2945) on July 27, 2000. The full text of the bill is in the Appendix—enjoy!

Sadly for David, time ran out. The bill was introduced and read but that session of Congress ended before it could be voted on.

It seemed that maybe true love saved the day for David. Standing in the kitchen, David told me he had three women eager to marry him, and he just had to make a decision. He carefully analyzed each woman's prospects—one woman, Charlotte Cornwell, a drama teacher at the University of Southern California and sister to spy novelist John le Carré, loved him but had no money or fame to go with her green card potential; another woman, Luanne Wells, was the multimillionaire-widow of Disney chief Frank Wells, but she had no fame and had several highly suspicious sons who threatened a background check and a prenuptial agreement; the third was legendary American feminist Gloria Steinem. David had met the New Yorker Steinem on

Christian shows off his knife skills (and his new veneers specially made for *American Psycho*).

one of her many visits to California at a charity fund-raiser. After careful consideration, Bale decided to marry Steinem, who was seven years his senior, as he assumed she had both the wealth and the fame he so craved.

She is, of course, the American feminist who had preached against the institution of marriage as outdated and patriarchal. She had led campaigns against the book and the film *American Psycho*. Incorrectly but widely attributed to Gloria: "A woman needs a man like a fish needs a bicycle." Yes, *that* Gloria Steinem.

On August 31, 2000, just three days before David married Gloria in Oklahoma, Christian was hit with another surprise courtesy of his father's mismanagement—yet another lien, this one for $50,269—for back taxes owing to the state of California. Christian and David were done professionally.

On September 3, 2000, a day after David's fifty-ninth birthday, David and Gloria wed on a secluded Oklahoma Indian reservation. Conducting the nuptials ceremony was Gloria's friend Wilma Mankiller, a former chief of the Cherokee Nation. Although Louise attended the ceremony, Christian was not invited. Gloria had chosen private and secluded Oklahoma away from her family and friends, rather than New York or California, because she knew that her marriage would stir much press coverage and criticism thanks to her longtime stance against the institution of marriage. But David had already given instructions to me as Christian's publicist to leak the news to my contact at *People*. Perhaps out of a force of habit, David lied to the press at the time about his age, narrowing their age difference to three years. Steinem's marriage was headline news around the world.

Oddly enough, David Bale, who had told the INS that he was too sick to fly, began commuting regularly between New York and Los Angeles with his new wife. The deportation order was dropped and he was granted "conditional residency," which allowed him to stay in the U.S. for two years. Gloria's home base remained in New York, although the Manhattan Beach house was now well-stocked with almonds, her favorite snack food.

After David was married, he was depressed about the damage to his relationship with his son. "I've failed him! I've failed my own son!" David would weep into his beer. Although David was thrilled to be married to a celebrity, he was still very hurt that he was no longer close to his son. When David and Gloria were interviewed by Barbara Walters on *20/20*, Christian instructed me not to provide any clips or photos of him for Walters' show to use. Everything David had hoped for—the family production company, the family business—was through. He now had to turn his attention to making Gloria happy. They had to prepare for an interview with INS to prove that their marriage was legitimate.

Within a week of their marriage, the press had discovered David's deportation woes. Gloria quickly went on the defensive, telling the *New York Daily News*, "Apparently, there is a need to look for ulterior motives when a feminist marries." But eleven years later, on August 9, 2011, Steinem would finally admit on the *Joy Behar Show* that the reason they married was because David "needed a green card."

I confess I had no sympathy for David's predicament. He had brought this on himself by raising Christian to be blissfully unaware of his financial status. It seemed to me as if David had been happy to keep Christian childlike. It was his way of keeping control over his son.

For his part, Christian spent the rest of 2000 arguing with his father to turn over all of his accounting files to a new accountant. By the end of 2000, Christian had asked me to intercede and I worked with Christian's new accountant, Mark, to repair the House of Bale. To say that David was furious was an understatement. Here was Christian's new accountant prying into David's mysterious years of money-juggling.

Christian e-mailed me, "Dad is speaking with Mark. My

ultimate point is for him not to have to deal with taxes, but right now it is essential for the transition as I do not know enough about past years. Please help him in any way you can, and keep him from strangling Mark." I remember my first face-to-face meeting with Mark the Accountant, as I told him to be patient and prepared for an avalanche of David's mystery files.

Christian himself was in a darker place. He was no longer the young man with the easy laughter. He had become much more insular and somehow humorless. Understandably, he was taking his career much more seriously, but he had also felt betrayed by his father. And since David had spent the past decade painting his mother, Jenny, as a money-hungry shrew, Christian trusted very few people. Conversations became confrontational, as he took the tactic that he would deny the premise and validity of any question.

"Why do you look so down, Christian?" I would ask.

"What makes you think I look 'down'?" he'd fire back sarcastically. "Who do you think you are to ask me that? You have no idea how difficult it is to be an actor!"

To me, my former adopted kid brother was becoming increasingly bossy and angry. I was tethered to his whim by cell phone, so at any time of the day or night, I could receive a call asking me to buy him socks (easier than doing laundry) or to restock his fridge with Guinness. Even while he was beginning to make good money, he had me take the photos to be his headshots.

"Why," I asked him, "don't you go to a professional photographer? It's like $150 and you'll get your headshot." I was complaining as we snapped photos outdoors in the heat since we didn't have a studio or lights for a photo shoot.

Christian gave me an icy stare and replied, "Because you'll do what I say." This shift in his personality was unsettling and somewhat frightening.

By the time I had mustered the courage to ask Christian again

about a salary for me, he had begrudgingly agreed to add me
to his film contracts—so that for the couple months he was
shooting a film, I'd be paid a small wage from the production
company itself. Outside of the shooting period, we would still
need to figure out a fair salary that he would pay me directly.

When a fan letter showed up at Christian's Manhattan Beach
home address, he was livid and blasted a scathing fax to me.

*This letter was sent to 3101—something that makes me uncom-
fortable for obvious reasons—especially when it's someone who is
on the Internet regularly.*

*We've got her address. I think we should eliminate her. Better to be
safe than sorry. A screwdriver thrust thru the eyeball into the brain
prevents any screaming.*

Let me know how it goes.

Yours,
Christian

Clearly, Christian's relationship with his fans was changing, and
not for the better. When he had first moved to America, at the rare
times he was recognized, it was for high praise for his performance
in *Empire of the Sun*. But the *Newsies* phenomenon meant that
Christian had become a teen idol and the object of the Internet.
It was his first taste of American-style celebrity and he alternated
between enjoying its benefits and chafing at its burden.

Pity the fan who recognized Christian at a restaurant. He refused to sign autographs while he was seated. He would lecture
little girls about being rude and intrusive until tears streamed
down their faces, and their parents tugged them away from our
table.

On June 22, 2001, after much mulling over the graphic novels I had sent him back when he was in Ireland, Christian decided he wanted to pursue *Batman*. He e-mailed me the go-ahead to launch an Internet campaign to convince the important and opinionated Batman fandom that Christian would be a great choice for the Caped Crusader. We ignited the powerful Balehead community with leaked photos of Christian from *Equilibrium*, which would not be theatrically released until December 2002. Bruce Wayne? Here's Christian in a tuxedo from *American Psycho*. Action hero? Here's Christian in various martial arts poses from *Equilibrium*. Conversations were seeded and started in Batman-related chat rooms and message boards, and soon there were fan-generated posters of Batman with Christian's face superimposed all over the Internet.

Christian's Balehead fan base had grown to encompass sci-fi fans who had enjoyed Christian's work in *Reign of Fire* and *Equilibrium* as well as longtime fans from the days of *Newsies, Little Women,* and *Empire of the Sun*. In 2002 we aggressively built a sci-fi fan base. By the summer of 2002, media outlets around the world were covering the Internet buzz that Christian was in the lead to be considered for Batman.

He and Sibi moved out of the Manhattan Beach house on August 31, 2001, leaving 3101 Oak Avenue to David as his financial responsibility. They bought a little house in Santa Monica, near the Santa Monica Stairs. He was thrilled to have his own place.

"You know," he told me, "this is the first time I'll have a house of my own. Without Dad living off me." A biting remark that highlighted just how far the two Bale men had fallen out.

In March 2002, when Christian's mother, Jenny, brought his grandmother over from Bournemouth to Los Angeles for her very first trip abroad, he refused to see them. During their stay, I gave Jenny and her mother the VIP treatment with a tour of Paramount Pictures. They were all thrilled to meet Christian Bale's mother and grandmother and Jenny was delighted to be treated with such respect, as if she were a visiting dignitary.

But the visit turned sour very quickly. David and Gloria were in New York at the time and naturally did not want Jenny and her mother entering the vacant Manhattan Beach house. Christian and Sibi had just moved into their new home in Santa Monica, so Jenny was surprised to find herself staying with Louise and her husband in their tiny little house in Culver City.

After days turned into weeks, Jenny and her mother were about to return to England with no word from Jenny's son. As luck would have it, I arrived at Louise's house when Jenny was crying on the phone, asking Christian to see them—if not for her sake, then for his grandmother's first visit to the U.S. He refused.

It was around this time that Christian's temper was becoming well known throughout the industry. His dislike of publicity, his avoidance of Hollywood scenes—all would come together when he was invited to appear on the cornerstone TV show of the entertainment industry, *The Tonight Show*. *Reign of Fire*'s opening weekend was set for July 12, 2002, and Touchstone's publicity department had scored a major coup: Christian was set to be a guest on *The Tonight Show with Jay Leno* in the prestigious and highly rated Friday-night slot.

Ever since it debuted on NBC in 1954, *The Tonight Show* has been *the* launching pad for many an actor, comic, and musician's livelihood. For Christian, who had done precious few American talk shows in the past, to land a lead guest spot on a Friday night was very important to his career.

Christian's new stepmother, Gloria Steinem, insinuated that it was she who had helped get Christian the Friday guest slot. She was friends with Leno's wife, Mavis.

Christian and Sibi were in New York at the time when I told him the good news. I impressed on him how important *The Tonight Show* would be to his career.

Like most major American network talk shows, Christian would be pre-interviewed by a producer so that the host could develop his talking points. Christian was annoyed at this concept.

"I've done chat shows in England and there's no such thing as a *pre*-interview," he seethed.

On Monday, July 8, Christian had his first phone interview with *The Tonight Show* producer. Christian called me immediately afterward and complained that the producer was rude to him.

"I'm sure it was a misunderstanding. Don't worry about it. Just think about chatting with Jay Leno," I tried to assure him.

Meanwhile, the folks at NBC were trying to arrange Christian's flight from New York to Los Angeles. It was standard *Tonight Show* policy to fly guests in at least the day before, just in case of flight delays. For some reason, this, too, offended Christian.

"I have no intention of cutting short my New York trip. I'm flying back Thursday night," he snapped.

During the week, *The Tonight Show* producers asked for clips from *Reign of Fire* and sent me additional questionnaires to prepare Leno for Friday night. Christian, the producers were telling me, was being very difficult. Touchstone was eager for Christian to promote the movie as poor advanced reviews for *Reign of Fire* started coming in the same week. As a summer popcorn movie, *Reign of Fire* needed to open at the top of the box office.

On Thursday night, Christian called and told me he was not going to appear on *The Tonight Show*. To make matters worse, he instructed me not to notify NBC until Friday morning—well past their point of last return to be able to schedule another guest. Christian figured that the producer who had interviewed him would be blamed and fired.

I warned Christian that he could be banned from *The Tonight Show*, but he didn't care. He wanted to punish this producer and figured his absence would do just that.

I contacted Christian's agent immediately, hoping that he

could talk some sense in him. But neither of us could change his mind. Friday morning, the conversations with *The Tonight Show* producers were terse but professional. They were not going to beg or plead. Throughout Friday, NBC stations were running promotions for *The Tonight Show*, announcing that the guests would be Christian Bale and Kylie Minogue. Christian's fans were abuzz on the Internet, talking about Christian's first appearance on a major U.S. talk show. They wanted to know what his real accent sounded like and what he'd wear and if he'd give a shout-out to anyone.

But the fans never got the chance to see him, and Christian's stubborn move didn't help *Reign of Fire*'s fortunes.

Reign of Fire opened in third place that weekend, behind *Men in Black II* and *Road to Perdition* and became the latest in Christian's string of box office misfires.

To cap off a year of mood swings, I got the weirdest Christmas card from Christian. He wrote:

Harrison

With eternal gratitude for all you've done.

Remember Jesus died for all of us.

Except for you.

You're a cunt.

Christian

11

An Apple a Day Keeps the Doctor Away

"I always like to immerse myself as deeply as possible in the characters I play but I probably didn't need to go to such extremes with the whole weight loss thing."
—Christian Bale

Christian was depressed. Not "regular human being" depressed, but Christian Bale depressed, which meant that he was barricaded in his fortress of solitude (yes, I know, wrong superhero). He was sitting at home staring at the four walls day in, day out. His last three movies—*Reign of Fire, Captain Corelli's Mandolin,* and *Equilibrium*—had failed to set the box office alight and he hadn't been on a movie set in nearly eighteen months. Even though Christian Bale was not a box office name, at least he used to merit good reviews from the film critics, but those kinds of accolades were few and far between for his last films.

Deep down, he honestly believed he was an actor who was washed up at the age of twenty-eight because of the bad choices he had made. Both Christian and David had fully expected him to be the next big thing in Hollywood after *American Psycho* but it just hadn't happened. Of course, David blamed Christian's new agent at CAA for choosing the bad projects. He would never criticize Christian directly.

"Why," David asked, "is my son getting scripts that have been wisely turned down by everyone else?" Naturally, David thought Christian was irreproachable.

Christian's proclivity to shun the limelight and pick smaller, edgier roles had paid off—but not in the way he wanted.

He wasn't splashed all over the pages of the latest celebrity magazines nor was he a household name like DiCaprio or Nicolas Cage. Instead he was known in Hollywood as a risk taker but not someone who could open a blockbuster movie. Christian saw himself differently—as someone who wasn't a sellout for his art—but it was all starting to catch up with him.

Unlike many stars who team up with directors again and again—Johnny Depp and Tim Burton, Leonardo DiCaprio and Martin Scorsese, and Russell Crowe and Ridley Scott—at this point in his career, Christian had never worked with the same director twice. Ever since *Empire of the Sun* back in 1987, there was a logical expectation that Christian would reteam with the legendary Steven Spielberg, but Christian's odd speech at the AFI Tribute to Spielberg back in 1995 was rumored to have damaged their relationship. David's heavy-handed Spielberg name-dropping around town didn't help.

A few years earlier, David revealed to me that Spielberg had asked Christian to do a cameo in *Schindler's List*. Christian refused. It was the scene where a young German soldier stops to play the piano while the Jewish Ghetto in Krakow is being raided. Spielberg had wanted Christian as the German soldier. "Not only was it a request from Steven," David sighed at the time, "but Steven's people thought it would be a wonderful reference to *Swing Kids*. What happened to Christian's character, Thomas, once the War started? Of course he'd be old enough to join the army."

It looked like 2002 would be another rough year for Christian; he was having trouble getting anyone interested in having him in their movie. It seemed that the momentum Christian had built after *American Psycho* was petering out with each successive failure. But his passion and interest in moviemaking came back when a little script called *The Machinist* dropped in his lap. Christian loved the script and immediately knew he wanted to play the role of insomniac Trevor Reznik.

A few years earlier, I had seen an incredible horror movie called *Session 9* and begged Christian to watch it. But he refused to see it at first because it starred Josh Lucas. Handsome Lucas had previously costarred in *American Psycho* with Christian; Christian had instantly disliked him, mostly for his ambition. Lucas remained friendly with me after the movie, but when we bumped into each other at the Sundance Film Festival for the premiere, Christian lost his temper and warned me not to talk to Lucas. It would not be the first time Christian would get incredibly possessive, but this was a particularly volatile exchange. Before *American Psycho*, we could argue as friends, as equals. But Christian's attitude toward me was becoming more "master and servant." I was looking for new paying Internet marketing clients, while Christian expected utter and complete loyalty to him even though he was still not paying me for my work as his publicist, assistant, and Internet marketer.

American Psycho's premiere at Sundance was Christian's opportunity in the limelight and he was very annoyed that Lucas had even showed up. In Christian's mind, Lucas was stealing his thunder as he hung around our hotel suite to participate in press interviews. I thought the more the merrier. If reporters knew they could talk to a couple stars from the movie, it'd make our suite a better prospect to get editorial coverage. But Christian was so upset with Lucas that he made him sit out in the hallway.

For this simple reason, Christian initially refused to watch *Session 9*—until he realized its director was Brad Anderson, whom he needed to win over to get the part in *The Machinist*. Christian quickly put all his reservations behind him and we rented *Session 9* for movie night. (If you've never seen *Session 9*, watch this movie with all the lights out. I'm very jumpy when it comes to horror movies, and to Christian's amusement, I jumped into the air when he let out a fart during the movie.) He soon decided to meet with Anderson after agreeing the movie was great.

Written by Scott Kosar, *The Machinist* is the story of Trevor Reznik, a factory worker who hasn't slept in a year. He thinks he is losing his mind when he begins seeing hallucinations and his perception of reality becomes twisted. He's haunted by a co-worker who no one else can see, and he keeps finding Post-it notes with secret messages on his fridge, which could be a mysterious plot against him—eerily similar to the way Christian's dad used to communicate with him.

The character's name was an homage to Trent Reznor, lead singer of the industrial rock band Nine Inch Nails. Brad Anderson told a reporter: "The original script had a quote from some Trent Reznor song at the beginning. I think Scott always envisioned the film as more industrial and maybe Nine Inch Nails would actually do the soundtrack."

Christian knew immediately he wanted the part. He became obsessed with Reznik and even began having strange dreams about the character.

Christian revealed: "I spent weeks staring at the wall in my house out of depression because of things that had gone wrong and the choices I had made. When I read *The Machinist*, I just went: 'Wow! This is perfect.' I was having dreams about the character and I couldn't stop thinking about it. I felt like this one was going to save my arse and pull me out of the depressed state I had got into."

But despite wanting the role there was no guarantee that Christian would get it. He would have to work hard to impress director Brad Anderson—someone whose movies he had previously refused to watch.

Christian faced a huge challenge. Because the character Reznik had not slept for a year, he looked ill and underweight, his every waking minute an unremitting nightmare of confusion, paranoia, guilt, and anxiety. Christian needed to lose weight for the role. Not a problem. From as early as 1987's *Empire of the Sun* when he lost weight for Spielberg to portray a concentration camp prisoner, Christian was renowned in Hollywood for being able to transform himself for any role.

But this time he took things to extremes. He lost a staggering 65 lbs., existing on just water, an apple, and a cup of coffee a day with a glass of whiskey sometimes in the evening. He explained: "Firstly you just drink a lot of water because it makes you feel full. Then you do substitution when you feel hungry—go and read instead. Or draw. Things that kill time."

But Christian still found it tough being around food or watching anyone else eating. He revealed: "There's an initial irritability because of the restraint you are putting on yourself. That's very difficult because you're still used to seeing friends for dinner and going out and everything being about food and drink. In the end I had to stop going out. I realized that wasn't going to work. I'd do a bit of eating hardly anything and losing 5lbs and then I'd put on 7lbs bingeing one night because I'd have a couple of drinks. So I decided no more social life, no more friends, no more dinners, no more drinks. It got very hard so I just avoided everything. In fact, every time I smelled some great dish, I became this drooling beast that just wanted to eat everything I could get my hands on.

So I couldn't go out at all. My life was like that, pretty much, except for the smoking and some whiskey I had each night."

As Christian withdrew from the world and became more and more like his character Reznik, the process became easier for him. He added: "I guess it's the stomach shrinking. Once I stopped running to lose weight, my legs got feeble—I just sat for hours without moving. I began to enjoy the mental state I was in because as my weight got lower the moods just disappeared. It does change you mentally and it did give me a noticeably different mental outlook on the world. I became very calm because you have no energy to deal with anything else except the basic necessities of life. Nothing made me anxious or upset. You couldn't get me angry at all. I could just sit still for hours without moving a muscle. It did feel like some spiritual mission I was on."

Christian also refused pleas from Sibi, David, and me to let a doctor monitor his crash diet, choosing instead to dose himself with vitamins. "I always felt in control. Anyway, what doctor's going to tell me to keep going? I knew if I went to see one I would be scared into not going as far as I wanted. I knew I looked skinny and it was a weird feeling because you're disconnecting from this thing down below you. But I knew I could stop whenever I wanted."

David was not convinced. Both he and Louise were worrying about possible organ failure. "You must say something to him! It's a source of extreme worry and concern to everybody as to why Christian is so angry all the time." David would beg me, but we both knew how stubborn Christian could be. If his own wife and father couldn't talk him out of this, nobody would. Again, it seemed that David's unique parenting skills had led to Christian's single-mindedness.

Christian admitted after the movie was released that director Anderson never actually asked him to lose all that weight and get down to 120 lbs.—a shockingly low weight for someone 6'1". It was his decision to make himself look anorexic for the role.

He revealed: "It was simply the best thing I'd read in a long time and I hadn't worked in a year and a half. But I knew it'd be tough and it was. The director certainly never asked me to do it but I just felt the physical side was very important. After all, this guy is meant to look like he is on the brink of death and that really is a challenge in itself. I started doing it gradually, then I did become obsessed with it and thought: 'Maybe I can actually hit the weight which is mentioned in the screenplay.' I did it and on the very day I was supposed to be that weight, so I was very pleased about that."

Christian might've been pleased with himself about hitting his target weight but to everyone else the transformation was shocking, even to costar Jennifer Jason Leigh. Although she later admitted she was even more horrified when he started to put the weight back on by eating donuts! She revealed: "When he started to eat again we warned him: 'Start slow, eat poached eggs and raw foods.' Then we watched in horror as he started with donuts!"

Even Christian later admitted in interviews that he would probably never again go to such extremes for a movie role. He seemed to realize the strain he was putting his body under and admitted he also did not want to be seen as an actor who tried to get attention through gimmicks.

He confessed: "I seriously doubt I would do what I did for *The Machinist* ever again. Certainly not to that degree. I would lose weight for a part but I wouldn't take it that far again because I think I would be really asking for trouble although I think a second time would also be less of a challenge because I know I can do it. There was that challenge of: 'Am I actually able to do this?' Now I've answered that question. And I would be worried if I did it a second time it would turn into a gimmicky thing, people would say: 'Oh, he's the guy who loses a lot of weight for

movies.' I can't envision there being an awful lot of other parts
where it would be so essential. But you know, on *The Machinist,*
my wife did get to witness what my ass is going to look like when
I'm 90! Not a pretty sight."

But while things were once again beginning to work out on
the professional front, personally Christian was still struggling.
After years of working on Christian's career, we were done professionally. From my point of view, I had faithfully worked on
Christian's career for many years. Promises were made. Promises were broken. I could see how he was treating his father, his
mother, his family, and I thought to myself, "If he could treat his
own family like that, what chance do I have that he'd treat me
fairly?"

To add insult to injury, Christian demanded that I sign a Non-
Disclosure Agreement (NDA). An NDA is a document that
celebrities often make their employees sign to secure confiden-
tiality. However, it was part of Christian's odd sense of entitlement that he'd think I would sign an NDA while we were still
figuring out what he was going to pay me, and what my role
would be in his production company. The NDA was, in effect, a
gag order. If I didn't like the results, I could never complain—
to my family, my friends, to the press, or to a court. On one of
Christian's many calls to me about the NDA, he bellowed, "Sign
it! I deserve this!"

That was the end. He *deserved* it? After I had launched his
career to become the biggest star on the Internet? To put him in
an orbit where he could seize *Batman?* What did I deserve? I had
been his friend for so many years, but he didn't stop to think or
ask why I'd be reluctant to sign such a draconian document. His
sense of entitlement was extreme.

David begged me to sign the NDA. Christian had actually demanded that everyone in his family sign such a document—again,
something particularly outrageous to require of a family member.

But David had raised his son to think he could do no wrong. The end result was the unraveling of many of his family ties. "Between true friends, words are not needed." That card from Christian seemed like it was a long time ago.

I didn't realize I had built a reputation in Hollywood over the years. But many industry people asked me how I could bear to work for Christian for so long. His temper had become well known, his demanding nature notorious. Whenever people asked me, I always thought back to a line from *Macbeth*:

I am in blood, Stepp'd in so far that, should I wade no more,
Returning were as tedious as go o'er.

I suppose David's flair for Shakespeare and the melodramatic had rubbed off on me a little.

A couple years ago, a friend of mine in L.A. asked me if I had seen the HBO show *Entourage*. I had not, and in fact, I had made a point of avoiding it. Something about a rising young actor being loyal to his inner circle of friends rang particularly false to me.

"You have to see it," she said. "Don't you know the character Lloyd was based on you?"

I don't know if that was the case or not. *Entourage* is one of those slices of Hollywood life where everyone can see a piece of reality in it. But I had to snicker when I read about Lloyd Lee, a "Chinese American assistant who has a demanding and verbally abusive boss." That definitely sounded familiar . . .

It was a tough choice, but after nearly ten years working for Christian and taking care of his family—first as his Web designer and then as his personal assistant and publicist—I wasn't having fun anymore. After Christian pointedly turned down *The Tonight Show*, there just wasn't any joy in his accomplishments. I was tired of dealing with the Bale family dramas and Christian's tantrums, which had become the soundtrack to our lives. It was no longer rewarding. I had been offered work with another rising star, Jake Gyllenhaal, and decided to practice my Internet marketing outside of the House of Bale.

Surprisingly, Christian gave me a nicely worded reference letter, which read in part:

> *I am happy to have this opportunity to recommend Harrison Cheung for any Web marketing project you may be considering. Harrison has been instrumental in building my profile on the Internet and leveraging this Internet presence into strategic publicity. Providing more than simply Web design, Harrison has adeptly created—either singularly or in conjunction with the studios—marketing campaigns custom-tailored to grow my audience.*

It only took me five years of therapy to get past my Bale years. My therapist would describe my condition as post-traumatic stress disorder.

It was very bad timing. Christian was furious at my departure as I was one of the few people who understood him and helped buffer his way in Hollywood. Ironically, Christian couldn't even exert any financial pressure on me since I was still patiently waiting for his "deferred payment" arrangements to kick in. You could say that his family circle was bullied into obedience—the rich relation and all. But I could part ways without signing the NDA, which represented my freedom.

The timing was also bad because David had fallen ill and had been diagnosed with brain lymphoma, a type of cancer that begins in the lymphocytes of the immune system.

With all the turmoil going on in his life at the time, Christian found it easier to withdraw into himself and lose the weight needed for the role in such a short amount of time. As he got skinnier and skinnier and more withdrawn, it was easier for him to cut himself off from the outside world, like Reznik, and ignore the problems around him.

He refused to take my calls and found it hard to accept that his father was dying, even when he was admitted to the leading cancer care center in New York because the cancer was spreading so quickly. Instead, he immersed himself completely in the role as preproduction on the movie began in early April 2003.

With Christian completely immersed in his roles and focusing on his own marriage, he now didn't have as much time for his father, the man who had once controlled every aspect of his life. Christian was now his own man, picking his own projects and living in his own house with his own family. So David began spending more and more time on the East Coast to be with his wife, Gloria. He would still check in with his son regularly. But Christian admits that while he was filming *The Machinist*, he had so little energy he rarely spoke or interacted with anyone off the movie set apart from his Sibi. The movie was also shot more than 6,000 miles away from David, in Spain in May and June.

As David became sicker after being diagnosed in April, the calls became less frequent. David complained to friends about not being in close contact with his famous son. He called me one evening as woeful as King Lear. "I miss the laughter," he said.

He also missed having his family by his side as his doctor and hospital visits became more and more frequent. He still kept his spirits up though, joking with the doctors and nurses. In one of my last conversations with David, he told me that he wanted to be buried back in South Africa. He wanted Nelson Mandela to speak at his funeral to tell the world what a humanitarian he was. David's illusions of grandeur remained intact, it seemed.

Before long he was too sick to stay at the New York home he shared with Gloria Steinem, and in July he was admitted to New York's Memorial Sloan-Kettering Cancer Center. Steinem visited him every day. However, his condition worsened and in

November 2003, Gloria and the doctors made the decision to transfer David back to Los Angeles to be nearer to his family. He was admitted to the Santa Monica Health Care Center, where he remained until his death on December 30, 2003, at the age of sixty-two. His ashes were scattered in the Pacific.

Following David's death, Gloria wrote a moving tribute to her husband. In fact the memorial was so glowing that anyone reading it would've thought David was on the verge of sainthood. It was in sharp contrast to the David Bale other people knew over the years—a confidence trickster who had left behind two broken families as he pushed and pushed his only son toward the fame and fortune he himself had always aspired to.

Gloria wrote:

In 1991, he moved with his two younger children, Christian and Louise, then teenagers, to Los Angeles where they could continue their careers in film and theater. Soon, animal rights activists in the South Bay became aware of a tall man in a black shirt and black sneakers who brought injured animals into clinics, found homes for strays, and stopped on freeways to rescue hurt animals or set their bodies aside with words of respect. Indeed, he tried never to pass a living thing in need, whether this meant driving a homeless person to a shelter, helping over-burdened single mothers in the street, or fighting against developers to save wetlands for mi-grating birds. As an activist, he also lobbied for such issues at the upper levels of politics and society. As an individual, he took loving care and gave a home to many stray cats, any birds or migrating ducks who visited the backyard, and a series of dogs, including an L.A. street dog named Mojo who soon was traveling back and forth by plane to New York when David also began to live there. David Bale walked lightly on this earth, with few possessions, a great heart, and a rare ability to cross boundaries between people, countries, even species. He had a gift for living in the present, and for giving others the love and self-belief that he had missed as a child. If each of us who loved him nurtures these qualities in ourselves, he will be with us still.

Even though Gloria had written her glowing memorial of David, Christian has never made any comment about his father's passing. It was Gloria who made the announcement of David's death to the press and while Christian was mentioned in all of the obituaries in newspapers around the world, he remained silent.

The intensely private star instead threw himself into his next movie role—*Batman Begins*. In September 2003, just three months before he died, David was told that Christian had been cast as one of the world's greatest superheroes. He told Christian he was "achingly proud" of him, but they both knew deep down he wouldn't be around to see the movie.

The Machinist opened in limited release on October 22, 2004, to mixed reviews and minimal box office success, grossing just over $1 million domestically. It was also Christian's first movie that wasn't particularly popular on video. This was not the kind of movie that people happily went to see after dinner or watched at home with a big bowl of popcorn. Christian's fans, by then aware that he was going to be the next Batman, seemed both horrified and impressed by his skeletal appearance. Here was an actor clearly committed to the cause of really living a role.

Robert De Niro had won an Oscar for his weight-fluctuating turn in *Raging Bull*. Tom Hanks had been nominated for an Oscar for his food-deprived turn in *Cast Away*. But if Christian expected any awards, he would be disappointed. He did not win any major acting award for *The Machinist*, even though it was a very showy role.

Meghan Lehmann of the *New York Post* wrote: "Anderson gives *The Machinist* a sickly noirish look that contributes to the creeping horror—but it's the emaciated Bale's spectral presence that leaves the imprint."

Rolling Stone's Peter Travers noted: "Director Brad Anderson tightens the screws of suspense but it's Bale's gripping, beyond-the-call-of-duty performance that holds you in thrall."

Lisa Schwarzbaum of *Entertainment Weekly* seemed to take offense: "Bale exists all too large under the circumstances, a well-fed actor playing at emaciation for the sake of a fiction about a character whose torment is as unreadable as his vertebrae are countable."

Filming for *Batman Begins* was scheduled to start on March 7, 2004, and Christian began preparing himself both physically and mentally for the role. And while Christian had not been so close to his father in recent months, he vowed to make Batman his best performance ever—in memory of his dad.

Christian hamming it up, with his "Blue Steel" look.

12

A Balance of Darkness and Light

"What I see in Christian is the ultimate embodiment of Bruce Wayne. He has exactly the balance of darkness and light that we were looking for."
—Christopher Nolan, Director, *Batman Begins*

"It makes absolutely no difference who plays Batman, there's nobody at home. The character is the ultimate suit. Garb him in leather or rubber, he's an action hero. Put him in civilian clothes, he's a nowhere man."
—Roger Ebert, *Chicago Sun-Times*

On Thursday, September 11, 2003, Warner Bros. made the announcement that Christian Bale was next in line to play the ultimate American antihero, Batman, in the upcoming movie *Batman Begins*. It was the climactic moment to years of excitement and speculation, with names as diverse and unexpected as Jude Law, Ashton Kutcher, Guy Pearce, and Ben Affleck originally bandied about within the studio, leaking out to excite the worldwide rumor mill better known as the Internet.

How important was the choice of the next Batman? It may not have been as historic as a puff of white smoke from the Vatican or as earth-shattering as Barack Obama's being elected the first black president of the United States, but the fact that it had taken Warner Bros. six years to get the fifth Batman movie off the ground was proof of how much activity was going on behind the scenes in reviving the studio's "largest asset," one of its most profitable movie franchises.

In the world according to Hollywood, one could forgive Warner Bros. for generating the kind of fever and excitement over a casting decision not seen since the selection of Scarlett O'Hara in *Gone with the Wind*. Back then, it was scandal when the British actress Vivien Leigh was cast as all-out Southern Belle Scarlett, beating such well-known names as Norma Shearer, Katherine Hepburn, and Paulette Goddard to the coveted role.

Now it was another Brit, Christian Bale, with his uncanny knack of mimicking American accents, who shocked Hollywood when it was announced that he would be donning the Batsuit, following a long line of U.S. stars from TV show actor Adam West to the big-screen incarnations of Michael Keaton, Val Kilmer, and George Clooney, who had all tried to make Batman their own.

Weeks before Warner Bros. made its choice, *The Hollywood Reporter* had discovered that the studio would be holding test readings with several contenders for the role of the Dark Knight. The short list of young men competing to fill Batman's codpiece included: Hugh Dancy (*Black Hawk Down*), Eion Bailey (*Fight Club*), Henry Cavill (*The Tudors* and finally, *Superman!*), Billy Crudup (*Almost Famous*), Jake Gyllenhaal (*Donnie Darko, Prince of Persia*), Joshua Jackson (*Dawson's Creek*), Cillian Murphy (*28 Days Later*), and, of course, Christian Bale.

Directing this new Batman project would be acclaimed English director Christopher Nolan, who scored both a critical and commercial hit in 2000 with his sophisticated indie murder mystery, *Memento*. In 2002, Nolan followed up with another hit,

Insomnia, proving to Hollywood that he could handle a big star like Al Pacino in a big studio production. Nolan had originally wanted his *Memento* star, Guy Pearce, as his Batman but, when Pearce declined, the hunt for the Caped Crusader was on.

Of the eight contenders for Batman, Christian already had a huge advantage. He was the biggest star on the Internet thanks to our years of campaigning, powered by the Baleheads, and we had been actively pushing for the role for the past two years. *Entertainment Weekly* had crowned him King of the World Wide Web in their October 11, 1996, issue and from that point on every major entertainment trade magazine annually sang odes to the mystery of Christian Bale—the Welsh-born actor who was enigmatically popular on the newest entertainment medium in spite of not having a single box office hit.

This disparity puzzled the studios. Who was Christian Bale—the little known indie actor who could get his face on the cover of a magazine but did not have the clout to open a movie? Why was he so popular on the Internet? Studios often look to other mediums for signs of the next crossover star. That's why singers try to get on TV shows while TV actors try to get in movies. To actors, movie fame is still the Holy Grail of celebrity.

Christian's unusual fame was built on a new and untried medium. The Internet was unlike radio, television, or the movies because the audience could be interactive. This new audience could make their likes and dislikes known immediately and it was this interactivity that gave power to grassroots campaigns.

> "Is Christian Bale too good to be true? Perhaps he's some sort of spiritual messiah, or a synthetic android simulation of the ideal human, but something has made Bale one of the most popular stars in the Internet firmament—and it's not just his cheekbones."   —Marc Mohan, *The Oregonian*

Yet when I first told him about Batman, the role that would eventually catapult him to superstardom, Christian's initial reaction was far from enthusiastic. He despised American comics and he hated movie adaptations of comic books. He didn't want to be a movie star, and he thought even less of movie franchises. He physically pretended to gag whenever anyone would mention superheroes to him and it took months of convincing before he came to see that playing Batman made sense.

But while Christian was initially reluctant to being a superhero and trying to find less boring things elsewhere in his life, Hollywood knew it was time to resurrect one of their biggest money-making franchises of all time.

Three years before Warner Bros. even made their Batman casting decision, three Batman movie projects simmered in development. One project, tentatively titled *The Dark Knight*, was to be directed by indie director Darren Aronosky (*Requiem for a Dream*); *Batman Begins* by another highly praised indie director, Christopher Nolan (*Memento*); and the third was *Superman vs. Batman* to be directed by Wolfgang Peterson, who had had both critical and box office success with *The Perfect Storm* and *Air Force One*.

Mating a comic book project with an acclaimed, proven director seemed to be a smart move to revitalize the franchise, though in reality, for every success like a Sam Raimi-helmed *Spiderman*, there's a bomb like Ang Lee's *Hulk*. But all these projects looked perfect for Christian.

For Christian, hot off the critical acclaim of *American Psycho*, he was looking for meatier American roles. His villainous turn in *Shaft* had opened 2000 to mixed reviews and lackluster box office ratings. If he had a dream role, it was to play Anakin Skywalker in the next *Star Wars* movie. Christian had grown up as a huge *Star Wars* fan and he was extremely disappointed when he lost the role of Obi Wan Kenobi to Ewan McGregor. So he desperately wanted the role of a grown-up Anakin Skywalker because of the dramatic challenges of playing someone seduced by the Dark Side of the Force, transforming from Anakin to Darth Vader. For an actor like Christian, there could be no better mainstream role.

But from the start the prospects didn't look good for Christian to land the part of Skywalker. First of all, he was too old. Anakin Skywalker was supposed to be a couple of years younger than his future wife, Princess Amidala, played by Natalie Portman, who was seven years younger than Christian. Secondly, George Lucas was looking for an actor who would physically look like a grown-up version of Jake Lloyd, the child actor who had played Anakin in *Star Wars: Phantom Menace.* For a number of months, it was rumored that Christian's old nemesis Leonardo DiCaprio would be the one to strap on the lightsaber.

With that pivotal seduction to the Dark Side in mind, I thought the role of Batman looked like it would suit Christian perfectly, especially as one of the projects was to be a prequel that would be the origin story of how and why a young Bruce Wayne became the Dark Knight.

As mentioned before, I began pitching the *Batman* projects to Christian when he was on location in Ireland. Initially he resisted whenever I brought up the subject. When I called him on set to pitch the idea, the first response I got was: "Are you mad?"

It seemed Christian would never come round to the idea, despite repeated e-mails and calls from me over several months. Christian's reaction was always the same—a vehement: "No, no no!" He frowned on comic book movies and he had a British actor's sensibility that taking on a role like Batman would be selling out for a crass, American, hyper-merchandised commercial "product."

So to convince him that Batman could be written seriously and darkly, I sent Christian his very first Batman graphic novels: Alan Moore's *Batman: The Killing Joke* and Frank Miller's *The*

Dark Knight Returns and *Batman: Year One.* These two authors (Moore is from Northampton in the U.K., Miller is from Vermont in the U.S.) had revitalized the Batman name with dark, serious and moody graphic novels that had less to do with Batman's pre–World War II American origins and more to do with the anime style coming out of Japan and Hong Kong. With these critically acclaimed Batman interpretations in hand, Christian had a chance to see how this comic book legend could be treated as a serious, dramatic subject.

After a ton of cajoling, I finally managed to convince Christian to at least consider Batman. More to the point, he had also been convinced that he needed to do bigger movies with bigger paychecks. He sent me an e-mail to launch an Internet campaign and to prepare pitch packages for directors Christopher Nolan and Darren Aronofsky. Soon, every major Batman, sci-fi, and comic book Web site was seeded with the suggestion to rent *American Psycho* and imagine Christian in the dual role of millionaire Bruce Wayne and his alter ego, Batman. This seeding was crucial because the highly opinionated and often protective sci-fi and comic fans had to be convinced that *British* Christian could play Batman, a legendary *American* character. At the time, the only other name being floated was Ben Affleck—someone the sci-fi fans scoffed at, thinking he lacked the intensity or gravitas to play Batman.

Like all of Christian's previous Web campaigns, it didn't take long for Internet buzz to convert into mainstream editorial. Almost two years before Warner Bros. made a casting decision, we had key Web sites like FilmForce, Superhero Hype, Batman On Film, and MovieHole reporting that Christian was rumored to be the next Batman. On Comics2Film.com, Baleheads and Batman fans were showing off their Photoshop skills, digitally mocking up *Batman: Year One* posters with Christian. And newspapers around the world soon picked up the scent.

"The buzz in Hollywood is that Bale is the front runner to play Bruce Wayne."   —*The Sun*, July 17, 2002

"Welsh actor Christian Bale is being hotly tipped to play the caped crusader in the new Batman movie."
                                —*Wales on Sunday*, August 11, 2002

"The Internet was buzzing with rumours linking him to the role of Batman. It says something about Bale's current stock that the concept of the Welsh-born actor as the caped crusader is not only enthusiastically received by the notoriously unforgiving comics community, it also appears somewhat credible in industry circles."   —*The Irish Times*, August 17, 2002

Once he decided to pursue the role, Christian wisely leveraged his Web popularity. Internet fandom for Christian translated into clout at the polls, specifically, the many online opinion polls that gave voice to fan speculation on which actor should play the next Superman or the next Batman or the next James Bond. Like an invisible hand moving through cyberspace, the idea of "Christian Bale as the Dark Knight" was intentionally planted on every major Batman fan site. The Baleheads were legion and they had done their job. Soon, every Batman pundit was renting Christian's starring turn in *American Psycho* and *Equilibrium* to check out his muscled body, nude or tuxedo-clad, to see if he was Bruce Wayne material.

Though the major studios were loath to acknowledge that any other medium could influence their casting decisions, the Internet was an easy way to conduct quick and dirty market research to test brands, colors, flavors, and actors. "You don't want to draw too much out of a small group of people talking, but if you look cumulatively across sites, it can start to mean something," admitted Warner Bros. Vice President of Interactive Marketing.

And while the studios like to think that they dictate popular culture, to make a movie based on a graphic novel they had to test fandom opinion constantly, using the Internet and attending key conventions like Comic-Con to discover trends and to portend the next possible blockbuster franchise.

In the indie film world, Christian's Internet clout was renowned. By 2001, the tenth anniversary issue of *Entertainment Weekly* crowned Christian "One of the Top 8 Most Powerful Cult Figures of the Past Decade," citing his incredible and legendary cult status on the Internet as the unknown British guy who had wrestled the lead role in *American Psycho* away from none other than *Titanic* star Leonardo DiCaprio.

Winning the role of Batman was the ultimate achievement for Christian. He constantly worried about ending up trapped, like so many of his compatriots in England, in sort of a Merchant-Ivory-BBC-costume-drama hell. Ever since he had moved to L.A. in 1991, he actively pursued contemporary American roles, anxious to demonstrate his versatility and to avoid being pigeonholed.

Put this casting triumph in perspective. Christian had won a quintessentially *American* role—the antisuperhero, Batman. Imagine the reaction if an American was cast as James Bond? This was years before Brits like Andrew Garfield could win the part of *Spiderman*, Henry Cavill could finally land *Superman*, or Aaron Johnson could *Kick Ass*.

On September 3, 2003, just eight days before Warner Bros. would make its announcement, Yahoo, then the second most popular Web site on the Internet according to Nielsen Netratings, ran an online poll asking who should be the next Batman. Christian won 47 percent of the 10,420 votes, triple the number two choice, Joshua Jackson.

So not only was Christian the first non-American and the seventh actor to play the revered role (including Lewis Wilson and Robert Lowery from the 1940s serials, and Adam West from the 1966 movie and TV series), he also became the youngest to don the cape and cowl at the age of thirty-one. Bale would be perfect for Batman, the fans had overwhelmingly decided. But would Batman be good for Bale?

> "Forget the Superman curse: it's playing his pal Batman that may be hazardous to an actor's career health. Michael Keaton and Val Kilmer saw their stars fade like a broken Bat-Signal after donning the winged-mammal suit. George Clooney escaped that fate but only because 1997's *Batman and Robin* was so bad that viewers blocked it from their memories."
> —*Entertainment Weekly*, September 9, 2003

It was a bittersweet casting victory for Christian. Just a few months after the Warner Bros. announcement, his father, David, would be dead. David, the man who had so desperately wanted Christian to be successful and famous, would not live to see his son starring in his first real blockbuster film.

Similar to Lionsgate's strategy with *American Psycho*, Warner Bros. beefed up the *Batman Begins* cast to surround Christian with talent that had both box office clout and indie credibility. Michael Caine stepped into the role of Alfred Pennyworth, Bruce Wayne's trusted butler. Liam Neeson was cast as villain Henri Ducard. One of Christian's personal favorites, Gary Oldman, was Sgt. James Gordon, an uncorrupted cop who had been there the night Bruce Wayne's parents were murdered. Morgan Freeman was Lucius Fox, a Wayne Enterprises employee who provides Bruce with all the gadgets and vehicles that Batman needs. Cillian Murphy was cast as the villain, The Scarecrow, while Katie

Holmes was Bruce's love interest, Rachel Dawes. All Christian had to do now was convince everyone that he was Batman, one of the longest running superheroes ever created.

In 1989, the Batman movie helmed by eccentrically goth Tim Burton (*Heathers, Edward Scissorhands*) grossed over $251 million. A new franchise was born. If Warner Bros. had wanted a dark movie, they got it. Michael Keaton, hot off a string of hits (*Mr. Mom, Gung Ho, Clean and Sober,* and *Beetlejuice*), played the first Batman. Keaton returned in *Batman Returns* (1992), which pulled in $163 million. But Keaton wasn't interested in donning the cape for a third time. "I wasn't very inspired when I read the third installment," he admitted.

Though the first two *Batman* episodes were box office hits, the critics derided the movies as product merchandising over substance. Still, Batman soldiered on, seemingly flop-proof. For the third movie, Warner Bros. revamped the franchise with a new Batman and a new Batman director. Val Kilmer was paid a reported $7 million paycheck to star as the next Batman. But *Batman Forever* was not a happy experience for Kilmer. Disaster loomed even during filming, when he kept searching for deeper motivation to Batman's scenes, prompting director Joel Schumacher to brand him "childish and impossible" and snap: "Well, you're Batman. Just you do it."

Next up to bat was George Clooney. The fourth film, *Batman & Robin*, brought back Chris O'Donnell (who also appeared alongside Kilmer) as the Boy Wonder and starred Alicia Silverstone as Batgirl. This time, Uma Thurman and Arnold Schwarzenegger played the villains. Though Clooney was *People's* Sexiest Man Alive that same year, *Batman & Robin* was a major box office disappointment, grossing only $107 million, less than any of the previous Batman movies. Adding insult to injury, this Batman earned an unprecedented ten Razzie Award nominations, including one for Worst Remake or Sequel, while Alicia

Silverstone won her Razzie for Worst Supporting Actress. Razzie Awards dishonor the worst achievements in film for the year. His Batman experience prompted Clooney to quip: "I am single-handedly responsible for killing Batman!"

In all seriousness, Clooney was thoughtful in his postmortem over the *Batman & Robin* disaster: "It was just too big. By the time we made our Batman movie, they were just about selling toys. They got $25 million from Taco Bell before we started shooting. It's a moneymaking machine. They say I was a bad Batman, that it was my fault. They say I buried the franchise. But the truth is, it was a $150 million film and they paid me $10 million. I was pretty intimidated in that world."

Like Kilmer, Clooney did feel that Batman was a smart career move to shore up an actor's profile and bankability, adding: "I've now got money in the bank and there's no reason to do any movie unless it's one that I really want to do. With money in the bank, it is easy to be more selective, to make smarter decisions."

As for advice for Christian, Clooney joked: "Hopefully he won't tank the franchise the way I did. I set the bar so low he shouldn't have a problem."

Christian might've been ready for the movie after his months of Internet campaigning to get the role, but was this private actor really ready to deal with his face splashed all over the Batman merchandise? Was he ready for his Balehead army to grow dramatically to include the Batman fan boys who had very high expectations? Christian had his own philosophy about acting: "If you're an actor, there have to be times when you're ready to step up to the plate and make a fool of yourself and possibly embarrass yourself."

However, at Comic-Con 2004, Warner Bros. promised a sneak peek at *Batman Begins* to the eager fan community. They would be disappointed as the promised trailer was not available and there was only "a half-hearted videotaped greeting from

Chris Nolan and a distracted/annoyed Christian Bale." Although Warner Bros. told Comic-Con attendees that a trailer was not available, just five days later, it appeared online. Not the nicest way to treat the hard-core fans! When Christian won the role of Batman, he had just five months to prepare himself for the role and threw himself into pumping up his body and getting it into superhero shape.

Christian had to look good for the part of Batman—a man who has no superpowers but a man who can fight crime with martial arts and weapons skills and an unlimited fortune to fund his gadgetry. But once again he went overboard.

This time he went completely the opposite, bulking up too much. Christian revealed: "I was in a really pathetic state after *The Machinist*. But Batman has no superpowers so we couldn't get away with him looking like some Joe Schmo who never works out. Losing the weight was more of a mental discipline, which actually leads to a place of great calm. It was far less healthy putting on the weight because I was just stuffing myself. A doctor actually said to me: 'You're nuts, you're going to do some real damage.' I went from 120 lbs. to 220 lbs. within five months. I turned up in England, bearded, long hair and I was walking toward Chris Nolan. I was like: 'Hi Chris,' and he had absolutely no idea who I was. When I got closer he went: 'Holy, f * * * ! You look like Grizzly Adams what's going on?' Then he was like: 'Ok, you did a good job, you got really big like I asked you to but maybe we should try slimming you down a little." Some crew members were somewhat more candid. They came in and were like: 'What movie are we doing here? Fatman?!'"

So Christian worked out and got the toned, perfect body by the time filming began in March 2004 in the Vatnajökull glacier in Iceland before the production moved to London and then Chicago. Despite now looking the part, Christian still wasn't comfortable on set inside the Batsuit. He would sometimes have to wear the specially designed costume for up to fifteen hours a day. Unlike previous incarnations of the suit, which had been stiff and restricted full head movement, the new Batsuit was made of a special material, neoprene, to make it more lightweight and move more easily when Batman was fighting.

Costume designer Lindy Hemming and her team worked on the Batsuit at an FX workshop code-named Cape Town in a secure compound located at Shepperton Studios in London, where scenes from the movie were also shot. The suit's basic design was a neoprene undersuit, which was shaped by attaching molded cream latex sections. Christian was molded and sculpted prior to his physical training so that the team could work on a full body case. To avoid imperfections picked up with sculpting clay, plastiline was used to smooth the surface while the team also brewed different mixtures of foam to find the one that would be most flexible, light, durable, and black.

But despite the hard work and the flexibility of the Batsuit, Christian revealed it still wasn't the most comfortable costume to wear. The suit heated up regularly, which reportedly put Christian in a foul mood—a mood he later claimed helped give Batman his dark and brooding persona: "The truth is, it's just a lot of fun to put on the Batsuit and jump into the Batmobile and just roar around. That was a huge thrill for me, one hell of a kick. I've never been that much into cars but you get in the Batmobile and you can't help but love it. The engine's screaming and it's just like a bat out of hell! The Batsuit ain't so great! But I think they've honed it and refined it and mine is probably the most comfortable made yet. That's not to say it was comfortable. It is a big pain putting it on and I was in it for seven months. But Batman's meant to be fierce and you become a beast in that suit, as Batman should be—not a man in a suit but a different creature."

The Batsuit and the movie were a huge hit with moviegoers, who flocked to cinemas to see Christian resurrect the role.

The film opened on June 15, 2005, and grossed $48 million its opening weekend in the U.S. and ended up grossing over $370 million worldwide.

More importantly to the devoted fans, *Batman Begins* had restored critical respectability to the franchise. It was a vindication that the Baleheads—which had now grown to encompass Batfans—had helped Warner Bros. choose wisely.

Batman Begins was deemed a huge hit and Christian had suddenly become a worldwide superstar. The days of box office poison, Christian Fail seemed over. The question now was not whether there would be a sequel, but whether Christian would be able to handle his newfound fame?

13

Harsh Times

"I don't think I would ever act in a movie with Christian."
    —Louise Bale, sister

Batman Begins was both a box office and critical success and Christian had finally become an A-list star, an actor who could open a movie. But that fame came at a heavy price both personally and professionally. He was now a household name for the first time in his twenty-year career. Moviegoers, not just fans, recognized him on the street, something he'd never really encountered before.

Because Christian hated interacting with fans almost as much as he despised dealing with the press, it was almost unbearable for the intensely private star to be recognized in public. Until *Batman*, he never really had to deal with fans on a personal level, preferring to keep his army of Baleheads at arm's length on the Internet. But now he realized he would have to bite the bullet, try to put a smile on his face, and turn on the charm when confronted with the *Batman* fan boys who were rapidly swelling the ranks of the Balehead community.

He told one reporter: "I'd love to remain a secret and still work but I also want people to see the movies I'm in and get a higher profile because of that. But I don't want to know about the lives of other actors and I don't want people to know too much about me. If we don't know about the private lives of other actors that leaves us as clean slates when it comes to playing characters."

That, of course, is Christian's standard rationalization for keeping the public away. It's the evolution of his upbringing. David fostered Christian's sense of entitlement and his belief that no one had the right to tell him what he "should" or "must" do.

Christian admitted in an interview with GQ magazine that he preferred his pre-blockbuster days when he could be completely anonymous. Christian told GQ: "I used to think about it way more when I wasn't being recognized. For ages I used to think people were staring at me and I'd think: 'Oh no, I've been spotted by some deranged fan.' But of course, they hadn't really recognized me at all, I just had something unsightly coming out of my nose. But anonymity back then was a lovely thing."

Anonymity was now a thing of the past. *Batman Begins*, which cost $150 million to make, had taken in a respectable $48 million in the U.S. in its opening weekend of June 15, 2005, making it the number-one movie in the country. The film finally went on to earn a staggering $372 million worldwide—more than anyone had dared hope for.

There had been worries while filming that not even director Christopher Nolan could resurrect the failing franchise. But then the reviews started rolling in and studio bosses breathed a sigh of relief as nearly every review threw praise at the film. There were the odd reviewers who called the film "passable" or a "nonstarter" but overall critics seemed to love it. Respected film critic Roger Ebert proclaimed: "This is at last the Batman movie that I've been waiting for. Bale is just right for this emerging version of Batman. It's strange to see him muscular and toned, after his cadaverous appearance in *The Machinist* but he suggests an inward quality that suits the character. I said this is the Batman movie I've been waiting for, more correctly this is the movie I did not realize I was waiting for because I didn't realize that more emphasis on story and character and less emphasis on high tech action was just what was needed. The movie works dramatically in addition to being an entertainment. There's something to it."

Before opening weekend was even over, studio bosses had green-lit a sequel, eager to cash in on the surprising success of the movie. They also launched a whole range of merchandising to tie in to the film, including the *Batman Begins* action figures based on Christian's newly toned physique.

But it wasn't only the movie studio that was cashing in thanks to the success of *Batman*. Around the time Christian was named as Batman in 2003, his own sister Louise was the executive producer of a bizarre "fan" film called *The Death of Batman*, which involved shocking scenes of rape and torture.

Louise herself appeared as Bruce Wayne's mother in the twenty-eight-minute short film. Close friends found the movie more than a little peculiar, especially Louise's role, since for years she had been a pseudo mother to Christian as they grew up 6,000 miles away from their own mother, Jenny.

The Death of Batman was written and directed by Donnie Flaherty, the former surfer dude who had befriended the Bales years earlier when they had first relocated to California. He had tracked Christian down in Bournemouth from America and visited him there. Still, the family welcomed him with open arms and when David told him they were planning to move to Los

Angeles, Donnie kept in touch. When David was looking at places to live in L.A., it was Donnie who introduced them to Manhattan Beach as he lived in nearby Hermosa Beach. After the Bales moved to the U.S., Donnie and Christian became friends; Donnie even taught Christian how to surf.

But all too soon David decided that Donnie was turning more from a fan into a stalker and began to keep him away from Christian. He would tell Christian that Donnie wasn't a good influence and would detract from his career. Over time David managed to shunt Donnie aside but Donnie stayed in close contact with Louise, especially after Christian and David both married and moved away. When *The Death of Batman* was gestating, Louise happily jumped on board and appeared to have no qualms about taking on the role of Mrs. Wayne.

The film starts with Batman, played by Christopher Stapleton, cleaning up the drug problem in Gotham City, but when he comes across a petty thief and druggie, it all goes horribly wrong. The thief first Tasers Batman in the groin, causing him to fall unconscious. When Batman wakes up, he is chained up in an abandoned warehouse but still threatens to kill the thief when he gets free. From there the movie turns from a little weird to just downright bizarre, with the thief injecting drugs into the Caped Crusader's neck and then raping him. He then puts a gun to Batman's head and pulls the trigger, although it turns out there are no bullets in the gun.

The thief then lectures Batman, telling him: "I want you to know pain. I want you to suffer like I've suffered. I want you to realize that what you do is wrong. And I want you to want to die."

He then continues to beat him before giving him a dog bowl to drink water from and then after telling Batman how he had spent five years in prison after being wrongly arrested by Batman, the thief shoots himself in the head. Batman is then seen taking a syringe of heroin from a table nearby. The film then cuts to

Batman's body floating facedown in a river, apparently dead from a massive drug overdose. But the movie ends ambiguously not revealing if the body really is Batman or if Batman has instead put the thief inside the Batsuit and disappeared because he is so distraught over the suicide.

The movie was shot in Sherman Oaks, California, in 2003— the year Christian was named as the new Batman. *The Death of Batman* was posted online and can be viewed on YouTube.

It's a difficult movie to watch, but all the more intriguing when one wonders if the script was written with Louise or Donnie in mind.

Christian has never made any comment about the movie or his sister's involvement in it. But the rift between them, which had been growing wider and wider since the family stopped living together in Manhattan Beach, was almost at breaking point. Up to now, Louise had still been involved in many areas of Christian's life, though she did stay out of the limelight as Christian became a bigger and bigger star, even though she started off as the actor in the family. She preferred theater acting to movie acting and had been left with a bitter taste in her mouth from years earlier when casting agents had gone mad for Christian at the age of nine, spotting him hanging around backstage during a West End production of *Bugsy Malone* that Louise had scored a part in.

Louise revealed in a rare interview in 1997: "The movie business is very, very different to the theatre business. Theatre is my first passion and the path I want to take."

In the same interview she admitted that while she had in the past visited her brother on his movie sets, she didn't any longer because she didn't want to cause trouble and be a distraction for him.

She added: "I have visited Christian on many of his film sets. It is always a weird but exciting experience. On set there are a lot of people all with important jobs to do and I often feel in the way as a spectator. I don't hang around too much because, if you're not working, it's not all that interesting and I always disappear when it is Christian's time in front of the camera. I think having me in the background, behind the camera would be a big distraction."

So over the years, Louise distanced herself from Christian's career, even though she was on hand to look out for him off set. But as home life became unbearable, with David seemingly favoring his only son over everything else, Louise broke out on her own and moved out. Still living nearby, Louise played peacemaker in the family. Whenever mum Jenny wanted to visit Los Angeles and see Christian, she would always stay with Louise, not wanting to be under the same roof as David. Louise would then facilitate meetings between Christian and his mother in a bid to keep everyone happy. Soon Louise was living her own life and had found her own happiness when she met and married actor Shea Kline.

But after *Death of Batman*, Christian began to keep her at arm's length and instead turned to wife Sibi even more for advice and help where his career was concerned. By then, both David and I were out of the picture.

So in an effort to put his personal problems behind him, Christian began earnestly looking for his next role. Even though there was a Batman sequel on the horizon, the script still had to be written and shooting was not scheduled to begin until April 2007, almost two years away.

But with a bumper paycheck guaranteed for the next Batman movie—believed to be a salary of $13 million with back-end profits—Christian knew he could go back to taking risks with indie films.

Tom Cruise had been the first actor to demand back-end profits for *Mission Impossible II* in 2000. This meant taking a lower salary but earning a percentage of the profits made from a movie once the budget and marketing money had been paid back. It can be a huge gamble taking a profit incentive payment instead of a $20 million salary. But for Cruise it paid off as he raked in close to $75 million in the end. After that, other actors began demanding the same deal and by the time Christian came to sign his deal for *The Dark Knight*, it was a standard industry practice.

So he began looking around for scripts that would excite him, rather than movies that would simply be money makers. As Edward Jay Epstein says in his book, *The Hollywood Economist*, "Movie stars come in two flavors: $20 million and free."

And now he could have his pick. With the success of *Batman*, Hollywood finally opened its doors wide to Christian. Before he would have been up against a whole host of other young Hollywood stars vying for the same role but now he could practically pick and choose whatever he wanted to do.

In the end, he made six films in the two years between the two *Batman* movies. Fresh off the set of *Batman Begins*, Christian undertook the role of John Rolfe in the Terence Malick movie *The New World*, a drama about explorer John Smith and the clash between Native Americans and English settlers in the seventeenth century.

However, Christian was not the lead. The lead part went to Colin Farrell, who played Captain John Smith, while Hollywood veteran Christopher Plummer was cast as Captain Newport. Newcomer Q'orianka Kilcher was Native American beauty Pocahontas, who saves Captain Smith from execution.

The movie was another flop for Christian. With a budget of $30 million, the film failed to make back even half of that figure during its theatrical release, taking in just $12.7 million worldwide.

But once again he got glowing reviews for the role, with *Rolling Stone* magazine stating: "Farrell's laddie-boy vigor sometimes feels at odds with the delicacy of the material. Christian Bale is far more persuasively in thrall as tobacco farmer John Rolfe, the widower who marries Pocahontas and sweeps her off to London when Smith deserts her."

By the time the movie was released in December 2005, Christian had already filmed his next two movies, *Harsh Times* and *Rescue Dawn*.

Harsh Times was a tough drama about two friends living in South Central Los Angeles and the violence that comes between them. A small indie film with a budget of just $2 million, it was a movie Christian had wanted to do since 2001, and thanks to *Batman* the studio was happy to cast him.

He revealed in an interview: "I wanted to do something that wasn't a big juggernaut of a movie and this was one that I'd wanted to do for a few years. I'd met Dave [director David Ayers]—I can't remember exactly when but it might have been as early as 2001 and we met at a bar and ended up being there something like five hours arguing about things. He's an engaging guy, he doesn't mince his words and I just loved the character, the momentum of the whole thing. At the time it was a studio piece and nobody wanted me to do it but with *Batman*, I thought, maybe now they'll cast me."

The movie was a modest success, earning $3.5 million—only $1.5 million more than its budget but still a profit, which is always good news for the studio.

Just three months after filming *Harsh Times* on the streets of L.A., Christian was in the jungles of Thailand for his next movie, *Rescue Dawn*. This time Christian was the lead as Lieutenant Dieter Dengler in a fictionalized account of his bravery and comradeship in the early days of the Vietnam War. Lt. Dengler's plane was shot down over Laos and he was taken prisoner by the North Vietnamese.

The film was being directed by Werner Herzog, a director with a reputation for recklessly endangering actors during filming; however, the German director spoke out in 2007 to claim:

"Contrary to the rumors that are going around, I'm very professional, very safety orientated."

Rescue Dawn's producer, Harry Knapp, told Salon.com that Christian had scolded Herzog about a safety issue with a helicopter, telling him: "I'm not going to fucking die here!"

Christian also rebuked Herzog when he broke with director's tradition, yelling "stop" instead of "cut" to end a take. Recalled Knapp: "Out of nowhere, Herzog starts calling 'stop' to end a take instead of 'cut' and it set Christian off. He said: 'Look we don't know what stop is and we won't stop if you say stop . . . say cut.' Very next take Werner yells: 'STOP.' Christian now vomiting says: 'If you say stop one more time I'm done for the day.'"

Despite the friction, Christian really was delighted to be working with Herzog and admitted he took the role because: "I like going to hell and back!" He added: "I knew that Werner would be a good guy to take us there. How many times in life do you get to do this crazy shit? It's something that I was going to take advantage of. That was the big appeal to me for doing it. I like that, just testing yourself and seeing how far you can go. Even though the finished movie is not real life, when you are actually swimming in the snake infested rivers, you're not *acting* swimming in snake infested rivers. You are swimming in snake infested rivers! When you are wrestling with a snake, it's not a pretend snake. You are wrestling with a wild snake. The snake was not venomous but he had some pretty good fangs on him and I got them in the shoulder. So to me that's real life. That is what has become my real life. I really did do that."

Christian also ate maggots for the role and lost weight as the character Lt. Dengler was kept and tortured in a POW concentration camp. Recalled Christian in an interview with *Movies Online*, "Oh, yeah, those were real maggots. They were very real. I didn't mind eating the maggots, but I just wanted to make sure about where the maggots had come from. Where did they find those maggots?" This time, however, he didn't go to the extremes he did for *The Machinist*. He said: "I really actually didn't lose a whole lot of weight for this one. I was thin but there's a lot of good makeup and I just wanted enough to give kind of an indication of time and everything for it but it really wasn't anything on the scale of *The Machinist*. I wouldn't do that again. I've kind of conquered that in my mind and don't need to prove that to myself again."

Rescue Dawn ended up grossing $5.5 million in the U.S., well short of its estimated $10 million budget, but reviews were generally favorable.

With *Rescue Dawn* winding up filming in November 2005, Christian just had enough time to pack on a few pounds and begin rehearsing for his next project, *The Prestige*. The movie would reunite him with *Batman* director Christopher Nolan. With a budget of $40 million—the total of Christian's last three movies combined—the movie was based on the novel by Christopher Priest. It follows a rivalry between two magicians—Christian and Hugh Jackman—which intensifies when one of them performs the ultimate illusion.

Yet when he was first given the script by Nolan during the filming of *Batman*, he didn't bother even reading it since Nolan was already auditioning other actors for the part. He revealed in an interview: "I didn't actually read it during *Batman*. I had spoken with Chris about it before we started shooting *Batman* but just a casual conversation. Nothing to do with me doing it, whatsoever. He was talking to other actors at the time. But then we worked very well. I read *The Prestige* again after I finished *Batman* and I wasn't sure if Chris just wanted to keep me as Bruce Wayne in his eyes and that was it and he wouldn't want to work on anything else. So I contacted him and raised that question. I really liked the character of Borden and just told him: 'Hey, look, this would be great, I could really do this very well.' And he believed me, so we got crackin'."

Christian threw himself in the role, delighted to be working with Nolan again but also eager to learn some magic tricks from pros Ricky Jay and Michael Weber. He was especially excited to learn because of his grandfather's interest in magic.

Christian told a reporter: "My grandfather was a magician. I never saw him perform or anything but he always remembers the Magic Circle in London. By the time I kind of knew that, he had a few old tricks in a chest up in the attic and he would pull it down now and then but most of them were busted so he'd describe how they were done. But certainly, he very much enjoyed that."

But Christian admitted his own attempts at magic were not great and often he would fail in front of dozens of extras during a scene. He added: "There were an awful lot of disastrous attempts at magic that ended very badly but to be honest those were just as enjoyable as when you succeeded and nailed it. It's kind of nice to be making a fool of yourself in front of hundreds of extras who are all there snickering when you get it wrong."

Despite Christian's terrible attempts to perform tricks, the magic formula of Nolan and Christian was a winner again with a well-reviewed movie grossing almost $100 million.

Once again the pair had made a profitable movie, making the studios sit up and take note, especially Warner Bros., who agreed to increase the budget on the upcoming *Dark Knight*. *Batman Begins* had cost $150 million to make but now the studio was happy to let Nolan have another $35 million, pushing the budget on the sequel up to $185 million. While that seems an extraordinary amount, most blockbuster movies cost in the region of $200 to $300 million.

But before Christian could don the Batsuit once more he had two more movie projects to complete. The first one was a small part in the indie film *I'm Not There*. With a budget of just $730,000, Todd Haynes, who had directed Christian in *Velvet Goldmine*, filmed the movie in less than a month with such stars as Cate Blanchett, Richard Gere, Christian, and his future *Dark Knight* costar Heath Ledger, all embodying different aspects of musician Bob Dylan's life.

For Christian it meant he could retain his indie cred while still pumping out the big blockbusters, although his next movie, *3:10 to Yuma*, fell somewhere in between.

> "Here's an idea. Take two of Hollywood's angriest actors. Get them good and mad at each other. Then drop them in the most violent time of American history. What could possibly go wrong?"   —USA Network promo for *3:10 to Yuma*

A remake of the 1957 movie of the same name, the film sees Christian in the role of Dan Evans, a small-time rancher who agrees to hold captured outlaw Ben Wades, who's awaiting a train to go to court in Yuma. Wade is played by former Hollywood bad boy Russell Crowe, and the two got along great while filming in the desert of New Mexico.

Crowe told a reporter: "Right from the first time we did a reading I could see that he had a sense of humor and was very balanced about what the job was all that sort of stuff. Once you've worn that cape it must be hard keeping your feet on the ground! You can tell there's a lot of base jealously from me about the fact he gets to wear the cape! But we found it really easy to get on. It's really nice to have a repartee when you're trying to do complicated things in rough conditions. It's also a good thing being able to simply finish a day's work and being able to have a regular conversation with a bloke over a beer without it being some big to do and breaking some sort of contemporary taboo like: 'We don't do that in Los Angeles.'"

Christian also revealed that people thought he was mad to work with Crowe, who once had a reputation as a hard-drinking troublemaker. In 1999, Crowe was involved in a scuffle at the Plantation Hotel in Coffs Harbour, Australia, that was caught on security camera. Two men were later acquitted of using the video in an attempt to blackmail him.

In 2002 Crowe got into an argument with TV producer Malcolm Gerrie when part of his appearance at the BAFTA (British Academy of Film and Television Arts) awards was cut to fit the BBC's tape-delayed broadcast. The Aussie actor let rip with a barrage of four-letter words. Though he later apologized, saying: "What I said to him may have been a little more passionate, now in the cold light of day, than I would have liked it to have been."

And in June 2005, Crowe was arrested and charged with second degree assault by New York City Police after he threw a telephone at the Mercer Hotel employee who refused to help him place a phone call when the system did not work from his room. After being charged with fourth degree criminal possession of a weapon, the telephone, Crowe was sentenced to conditional release and later paid $100,000 to settle a civil lawsuit out of court with the employee, who received treatment for facial lacerations. Crowe later said: "This was possibly the most shameful incident that I've gotten myself in and I've done some pretty dumb things in my life."

So it was easy to see why those around Christian were concerned that he was going to be working with Crowe.

Christian told a reporter: "We had never met before. Whenever people asked me what I was doing next and I said that I was going to be working with Russell, they would kind of look at me and go: 'Oh right, you're going to be in for a tough ride with him.' You find an awful lot and I don't mean to talk out of school but a lot of actors sort of complain and wince and do everything to avoid actually getting on with the work, so it's nice when you're working with someone like Russell when you can just get to the point and you can have blunt conversations about the scenes and it just makes it easy. Obviously he doesn't have to be told what to do because he's a bloody good actor and it's a pleasure to work with someone as good as that."

Crowe has cleaned up his act and stayed out of trouble since the phone-throwing incident, but soon Hollywood—and the rest of the world—would be looking on stunned as his costar Christian would be the one hitting the headlines for all the wrong reasons.

14

The Curse of Batman—
It's No Joker

"You can't help but find that violence is endlessly fascinating—
and I mean true violence, not action-movie violence, just because it is used as the answer to so many problems. We're all
taught as kids not to be violent but you can't help but also see
that violence is what works very often. Bullies thrive."
—**Christian Bale, *New York Magazine* 2006**

"The Dark Knight Is Cursed!"

That was the headline that screamed out around the world
after a series of mishaps, threats, and deaths struck the cast and
crew of the new *Batman* movie. Christian had once again got
his physique into shape and eagerly hit the set along with Heath
Ledger, Gary Oldman, Michael Caine, Morgan Freeman, Maggie
Gyllenhaal, and Aaron Eckhart.

Filming had begun on the highly anticipated *The Dark Knight*
in April 2007, but almost immediately things began to go wrong.
A series of catastrophes would hit the $185 million film. Before
the movie was even released, two people would be dead and

Christian would be arrested for attacking his own mother and sister in a hotel room, while just a month after *The Dark Knight* hit movie screens another actor would be involved in a near fatal car crash.

The first unfortunate accident happened in September 2007 when a special effects technician was killed while filming a stunt. Conway Wickliffe was operating a camera from the backseat of a Nissan 4x4 when the vehicle failed to negotiate a turn while driving alongside a stunt car at 20 mph.

The crew was setting up a test run for a scene where the Batmobile is blown up, and an old American police car, similar in size and weight, was being used as the unmanned "rocket car," which was being fired off a ramp by a black powder cannon while pyrotechnic explosions inside the car were set off. Wickliffe was in the backseat leaning out of the window and facing backwards to capture the shot when the accident happened. The Nissan struck a tree and Wickliffe suffered severe injuries and was pronounced dead at the scene at the site at Longcross, near Chertsey in Surrey, U.K., where the stunt filming was taking place.

The cast and crew were devastated by the accident and the film's closing credits carried a dedication to the cameraman. But that wasn't the only shocking death to hit the movie.

Actor Heath Ledger was found dead of a drug overdose in his New York apartment on January 22, 2008—just two months after filming ended.

The hugely talented Ledger played The Joker in *The Dark Knight*—a role originally brought to life with full comic force by the legendary Jack Nicholson in Tim Burton's 1989 *Batman*. When Ledger was first cast in the role, Hollywood was happily buzzing with the news that the critically acclaimed actor, who had earned great reviews and an Oscar nomination for his role as a gay cowboy in *Brokeback Mountain*, would face off against Christian.

Warner Bros. President of Production proclaimed: "We can't wait to see two such formidable actors as Christian and Heath face off with each other as Batman and The Joker."

And as filming got under way, there were whispers on the set of exactly how formidable Ledger was. Unlike Nicholson's previous outing, Heath made The Joker a darker and more clearly disturbed character. Before the movie had even finished, people were talking Oscar nomination for Ledger and in one interview Christian told a reporter that his costar had done "one hell of a job," as The Joker.

So it was a huge surprise, after production had wrapped, when the news broke that Ledger, just 28, had been found lying dead next to his bed surrounded by bottles of pills. He reportedly had six types of drugs prescribed in his name at his home—mainly generic versions of anti-anxiety medications. Two types of sleeping aids were also found next to his body.

He was found facedown at the foot of his bed by his masseuse, Diane Lee Wolozin, who tried to wake him for an appointment. As she failed to get a response she used Ledger's phone to call Mary Kate Olsen, telling the actress: "Heath's unconscious, I don't know what to do," before screaming: "I think he's dead!" Both Olsen and Wolozin called 911 and Wolozin tried to resuscitate Ledger until paramedics arrived at 3:33 pm. However, nothing could be done and the actor was pronounced dead in his apartment at 3:36 pm.

The world mourned the loss of a great movie star as news of his untimely passing hit every newspaper, blog, radio, and TV show around the world. Yet his *Dark Knight* costar Christian refused to watch any coverage of Ledger's death.

Christian explained: "I paid no attention to it. I knew him, I knew the family and why the hell would I sit there listening to idiots who don't know anything at all? I literally didn't read or watch anything after he died. If I happened to be watching anything that came on, I switched over straight away. It's incredible the way the voyeuristic outlook is accepted as news."

But Christian and the rest of the cast and crew of *The Dark Knight* were in shock. No one had expected anything like that to happen to Ledger, who had seemed happy and stable and enjoying life as a dad to Matilda Rose, his daughter with ex-fiancée and former *Brokeback Mountain* costar Michelle Williams.

And when the coroner released his final report, proving Ledger died of an accidental overdose of prescription drugs, his family and friends were still struggling to cope with their loss. Ledger's father, Kim, said: "It's a pretty sad time, we're finding it difficult to cope." While Michelle Williams released a statement that simply said: "My heart is broken."

Just a few months later, Ledger became the second actor in history to win an Academy Award posthumously. Ledger's Best Supporting Actor Oscar was also a rare exception to the rule that Academy voters overlook action-hero movies.

But Ledger's compelling performance, together with worldwide interest in one of his final films, helped power *The Dark Knight* to a global box office gross of more than $1 billion, which made Academy members sit up and take notice. Eyebrows were raised at Warner Bros.' poster campaign, which featured a deranged Ledger as The Joker, looking corpselike in whiteface and smeared makeup, with the tagline "Why so serious?"

Accepting the Oscar on behalf of his son, Kim said: "This award tonight validated Heath's quiet determination to be truly accepted by you all here, his peers, in an industry that he so loved."

While all of Ledger's family flew in from Sydney for the Oscars, one person noticeably absent was Christian, who also did not attend Ledger's funeral.

He did not attend the ceremony although he told a reporter: "Heath winning Best Supporting Actor was fantastic. He was a fantastic guy and we had a lot of fun on set. Heath was infectious;

his death makes me angry because I know our friendship would have blossomed had he not died."

He went on to tell *Details* magazine, "He was incredibly intense in his performance but incredibly mellow and laid back. Certainly there was this great anarchistic streak to it, just getting dirtier than anybody's envisioned The Joker before. The film was something I wanted to share with him and expected to do so. And I can't do anything else now but hope that it will be an absolutely appropriate celebration of his work."

But while Christian was praising his *Dark Knight* costar, a pal was telling other reporters that Christian was himself feeling especially cursed. According to the Famous Scandal blog, a pal claimed: "Christian's been more than gallant in praising Heath while promoting the film but privately he's telling close friends that the film had turned into more of a wake for Ledger than a career building blockbuster for him. Christian believes he gave the best performance of his life in Dark Knight—but no one's going to notice!"

That sentiment appeared to be true as Christian received no nominations at all for playing Bruce Wayne and his alter ego, while Ledger scooped up a number of trophies during the awards season. In addition to the Oscar he also won a Golden Globe, BAFTA, Screens Actors Guild, and a slew of American and Australian critics' awards. And movie actors, directors, and producers all greeted each win with standing ovations.

While praise for Ledger's portrayal of The Joker was unanimous and global, Christian's performance as Batman was being debated by the Bat-fans. *Screenrant* wrote, "A civil war has brewed amongst fans on whether Bale's husky voice work is good or bad since he first appeared as the Caped Crusader in *Batman Begins*."

A YouTube spoof of the Batman/Joker interrogation scene has attracted over 12.4 million views, and helped to popularize that

Christian sounded as if he had "throat cancer." Christian's voice for Batman was, some fans complained, incomprehensible.

Voice actor Kevin Conroy has portrayed the Dark Knight longer than anyone else; be it animated series, film, or video games. He is considered by many fans to be the true voice of Batman.

Conroy commented on Christian's gravelly 'throat cancer' Batman voice at the 2010 C2E2 convention in Chicago. "He just got steered wrong. Obviously, someone should have stopped him and said, 'You sound ridiculous!'"

The fans erupted in cheers.

"I thought Christian was excellent as Bruce Wayne, but I didn't understand his choices (with his portrayal of Batman). I thought it was over the top and distracted from his scenes as Batman."

Before Ryan Reynolds landed the lead as *Green Lantern*, Bradley Cooper had been up for the role but confessed that he blew his audition by imitating Christian's growl. Said Cooper, "The trouble was that when I auditioned, it being a superhero movie, I couldn't help but do my Christian Bale Batman voice. I don't know why. Needless to say I didn't get the job."

With all the accolades being heaped on Ledger, it is perhaps easy to see why Christian would not be in the best of moods as the movie readied to debut. The movie was released on July 14, 2008, in the U.S., while the London premiere was scheduled to follow a week later.

Christian prepared to return to his native England a conquering hero—the young boy who had once been bullied at school for being in a Steven Spielberg movie was now back in the U.K. as one of the biggest A-list stars on the planet. The now-confident star had his face splashed all over the front of Britain's biggest tabloid newspapers the day after the London premiere, but it wasn't to promote the movie.

Instead the headlines blared:

BATMAN ON BAIL:
SUPERHERO STAR ARRESTED!

KAPOW COPS NAB BATMAN

BATMAN STAR BALE QUESTIONED BY POLICE
OVER ASSAULT CLAIM

Christian had been arrested for allegedly attacking his own mum and sister. He spent four hours being grilled by police over the family bust-up at the five-star Dorchester Hotel in central London. He had his fingerprints, mugshot, and DNA taken before being released on bail without charge although he had to return to the police station in September to find out his fate.

Police ended up allowing Christian to attend the glittering London premiere for *The Dark Knight* though, just hours after mum Jenny and sister Sharon accused him of assault. Jenny, sixty-three, claimed she was pushed during the row in the actor's suite at the hotel. Jenny and Sharon reported the alleged assault the morning after it happened, which left police with the dilemma of whether or not to arrest Bale before the premiere that night.

He was eventually allowed to walk the red carpet with wife Sibi as adoring fans screamed his name—unaware what had happened just hours earlier. But the next morning Bale voluntarily went to a police station in the posh Belgravia district of London to be questioned.

Different reports claimed different reasons for the row with everything from Christian being depressed over Ledger's death, to his marriage to Sibi being on the rocks, to his sister Sharon begging him for money.

The evening was supposed to be a happy night out before Christian's premiere. Jenny, Sharon, and Christian's three young nieces made the four-hour journey from Bournemouth to see Christian and Sibi in London. His nieces, all under twelve, had been looking forward to the premiere for months and had saved up their own money to buy dresses for the premiere. In particular, Christian's eldest niece, Ruby, eleven, worshipped her uncle as a hero. Ruby had dreams of being an actress as well and was hoping to visit Christian on the set of *Terminator Salvation*.

The Sun newspaper claimed that Christian had flipped out after Sharon, forty-three, asked him for £100,000 to help bring up her own three children. But when he refused, a row broke out in the hotel suite and Christian was alleged to then have pushed mum Jenny, who, sources claimed, inflamed the situation by hurling insults about his wife, Sibi.

Sharon tried to set the record straight in early 2010 when she was forced to file for bankruptcy. She refused to reveal how much debt she was in but gave an interview along with Jenny to the *Daily Mail* newspaper in which they revealed, they decided to report Christian to police because they were "so terrified" of his temper—especially in front of his nieces.

Jenny said in the same interview: "He just exploded with anger like I have never seen. He never gave us a chance to find out what it was all about before he frogmarched us out of his suite. We hadn't all been together for about a year. I was dying to see him and his family, especially his little girl. He'd e-mailed a few times. In the last one he signed off saying: 'See you at the Dorchester for the premiere, perhaps we'll have dinner.' So that's what we were expecting.

"I know getting arrested annoyed him and I know that being all over the papers annoyed him too, but I don't think that's why he's not talking to us. He was furious with us before we'd even opened our mouths. Probably before we walked into the suite. We just don't know why.

"He's not talking to us now. It's not the other way round. He has changed his phone numbers and he ignores letters, e-mails, and birthday cards I send. As awful as that night was and although I rack my brain every day about what could have made him behave like that, I'd happily forget it happened if we could go back to being a family. That's the most important thing. We miss Christian terribly. But it's been more than 18 months now and it's hard to see how this will ever end."

Sharon added: "We walked into his suite and he didn't say much. It was clear that he was angry for some reason. He left the room to take a phone call, so we sat down as I took out some muffins that I'd made. Then he walked in and immediately started shouting at us. He was saying how angry he was that we had left arrangements to the last minute—which made no sense as we'd been planning it for weeks with all the people around him. Perhaps the messages weren't getting through, we just don't know.

"He was screaming at mum: 'It's not on! It's not on!' He kept saying it was rude. We weren't being respectful. Despite what the papers said afterwards, this was not a two sided argument. We have no idea what set him off. He was filming *Terminator Salvation* at the time, so he was huge and muscular, the girls were terrified. They were screaming and crying.

"He had his face to mine and was bellowing and swearing about how I never called or e-mailed. His wife, who I have met a few times and always got on with, was standing across the room. I kept asking her: 'Why is he doing this?' but she just shrugged. I was shaking. It was so frightening. I said: 'But Christian, we call you all the time.' It didn't make any sense. It probably went on for about ten minutes before he physically marched us out of the room and into the lift.

"Living on opposite sides of the world makes things especially difficult. Over the years, he has become harder and harder to contact. We would leave messages and never be sure they were getting through. We wanted him to have more to do with the family but accepted that he was very busy and very involved in his work. The more work he did the more strained our relationship became. It's not true, I've never asked Christian for a penny. We have never spoken about money—his or mine. It was completely untrue.

"I was incredibly angry but I can see now that I was naïve too. I expected to get a phone call the next day saying he'd calmed down, explaining what went wrong, but we waited and there was nothing. It was clear we were expected to leave.

"I went to the police hoping that some big policeman would go round there and have a quiet word with him. I just wanted someone bigger than him to tell him that what he'd done was wrong. A slapped wrist. It was clear his wife wasn't going to do that. But there were two things I hadn't realized. First, that the police would arrest first and talk later. Second, that it would be such a big deal. I hadn't taken into account the fact he is such a big star now and the news got out fast."

While Sharon and Jenny professed to the *Daily Mail* that they had no idea what caused Christian to fly into such a rage that day, they had privately told friends a different story.

Just days after Christian was arrested, Sharon confided in a family friend that they believed the reason for Christian's terrifying outburst was over his wife, Sibi. She revealed that both she and Jenny had withdrawn their statements just two days after the incident because of the ongoing publicity their actions had caused.

She also said that while she had never "begged" her brother for money she did once ask him to invest £100,000 in a property business venture but that he never agreed and believes that the e-mail she sent him asking about the investment opportunity was leaked to the press.

Sharon told the friend: "The police have confirmed that the Crown Prosecution Service has agreed with us on dropping any further proceedings. Mum and I actually both withdrew our statements two days after the event as we realised that family members, friends and neighbours were suffering as a result.

"Money was not even mentioned by Mum or myself and we were not arguing about money and had no intentions of doing do. We went there to see family and go to the cinema.

"Mum put the phone down on Sibi about four months ago because Sibi was being confrontational. Sibi then phoned and apologized. On the night we met, Christian began an argument with Mum over never putting the phone down on his wife again. We have all been getting on fine, there was no need for an argument at all. We were really looking forward to an evening together after so long.

"I went to the police and asked them to talk to Christian before he left as we felt his verbal and physical actions and no show of remorse afterwards, especially in front of three children under the age of 12 years, needed to be pointed out to him as wrong. Normally the police would do this but the media intercepted the police files and were already making their own assumptions of what took place even before Christian spoke to the police.

"The next day—as this all happened at 11pm at night—we took the kids shopping to try to alleviate the sorrow they were feeling after this trauma, I then drove them home, a four hour journey and then went out on my own to the police station.

"We are all very sad about the press accusations of us wanting money off him. We have never asked for money ever. The 100K must have come from an e-mail I sent Christian asking if he wanted to invest in a property investment via a property broker/ investor and the solicitors dealing with the investments. I gave him an example figure of what the returns were if he were to invest 100K. How he ever thought I was asking him to lend me money for myself is beyond me, I would however have gained commission from his investment just like I do other investors I introduce to this organization. I even sent him an e-mail a few month ago asking if he wanted me to assist him financially with the £450 he pays monthly for the house he owns that Mum lives in, that Sibi seemed to be upset about but I never heard back from him."

"We do not know why Christian got so angry over nothing that night, it has had a lot of knock on effects with the children as well which is upsetting us all greatly."

The reaction in the media to Christian's alleged assault ranged from confirming his rumored temper to attacks on estranged relatives hitting him up for money. In particular, Christian's hardcore fans naturally assumed Christian could do no wrong. And the damage his late father, David, had done to his ex-wife, Jenny, was coming back to haunt her. Cruel jokes about Jenny being a circus clown (a job she held for just one summer) were on the Internet. And even when it was revealed that Christian had exploded in front of his three young nieces, nasty commentators snickered that Sharon was a welfare mom who should not have had children she could not afford.

Christian was due back at the police station in September 2008, but before he could even think about the charges he might be facing, the curse of Batman struck again, taking the heat away from him.

This time on August 4, 2008, Morgan Freeman, who played Wayne Enterprises' CEO Lucius Fox in both *Batman* films, was involved in a horrific car accident and had to be cut from the wreckage.

The then seventy-one-year-old actor was listed as critically ill after he was airlifted to the hospital after the late-night crash on a road in rural Mississippi. His car became airborne in the smash and flipped over several times before landing in a ditch.

The Hollywood legend's injuries were listed as several broken ribs along with arm, leg, and shoulder wounds while a female passenger in the car with him suffered "bumps and bruises."

The female passenger in the car later sued Freeman for negligence. She claimed he had been drinking the night of the accident and that he was driving her car when it veered out of control. She claimed the accident ruined her life because following the crash, various reports claimed she was Freeman's mistress.

The crash and Freeman's recovery were still dominating headlines when just ten days later the Crown Prosecution Service (CPS) quietly announced it would not be filing charges against Christian.

A CPS statement read: "We can confirm that we have advised the Metropolitan Police Service that the actor Christian Bale should not face any charges following an incident which occurred in relation to his mother and sister at the Dorchester Hotel on July 21 this year.

"Whilst the CPS treats all incidents which take place in a domestic context seriously, it is important that the views of the complainants are also taken into account when making decisions in such cases.

"Taking all the factors into consideration, the decision had been taken that there is insufficient evidence to afford a realistic prospect of conviction and accordingly the police have been advised that no further action should be taken against Mr Bale."

So thanks to Jenny and Sharon who had already withdrawn their statements, the CPS did not have enough evidence to charge him. This time the matter quietly disappeared with just a few paragraphs in a few papers reporting Christian would not face any charges.

But it wouldn't be long before Christian's temper once again reared its ugly head. Only this time it was caught on audio tape for everyone to hear.

[15]

The Fighter

"Listen, I know I have a potty mouth. Everyone knows this now. I was out of order beyond belief. I was way out of order, I acted like a punk."
    —Christian Bale

By the time Christian had apologized for his "punk"-like behavior and expletive-laden rant on the set of *Terminator Salvation*, practically everyone around the world had heard him let rip. Shocked fans busily remixed the rant into a number of hit club songs, scoring millions of hits and views on YouTube. Video mashups featured Christian yelling at babies and a remixed *Newsies* trailer had become a viral hit. During the blowup on the set, Christian dropped an astonishing thirty-six F-bombs in just four minutes.

Christian became enraged on the set of *Terminator Salvation* in the summer of 2008, when the Director of Photography, Shane

Hurlbut, entered the actor's sight line, removing some lighting equipment while the cameras were still rolling. The star exploded with curses and even threatened to walk off the set if the error was repeated.

As he let rip, the sound crew let the tape keep rolling and caught the entire rant on audio. Existence of the tape was covered by TMZ on July 22, 2008, but the actual audio of the tape was leaked several months later on Friday, January 30, 2009 (Christian's birthday), and made headlines around the world.

Bale can be heard screaming: "I will kick your ass. I want you off the f****** set. No, don't just be sorry. Think for one f****** second. What the f*** are you doing? Am I going to walk around and rip your f****** lights down in the middle of the scene? So why the f*** are you walking right through? You do that one more f****** time and I'm not walking on this set if you're hired."

By the following Monday, the *Today Show* hosts Matt Lauer and Meredith Viera asked their crew on the air: "What would happen to any of us if we were to say to you, or treat you in the way that Christian Bale treated a member of his movie crew?" The crew collectively shook their heads.

The BBC, the largest broadcasting network in the world, then accidentally broadcast Christian's rant uncensored and without any bleeps on *BBC Breakfast News*. They quickly had to apologize to the astonished public.

The rant left both fans and industry insiders stunned. Even though it is usually acknowledged that movie sets can be tense places to work with many actors deeply immersed in their characters, long hours, and sometimes dangerous stunts, no one had ever heard of an actor behaving so irrationally before. Actors blow takes all the time, so why was Christian so angry?

Even Christian's fellow British actor Gerard Butler acknowledged he had stepped out of line in an interview in March 2010 while promoting his movie *The Bounty Hunter*. Butler revealed to the BBC: "I'm pretty good on set and I think I have a reputation for that. But I do play pretty heavy roles sometimes. It's not that I go as far as the Christian Bale outburst but I can get a bit into it sometimes. It doesn't make me the nicest person but I always try to be."

It was a sad vindication for Christian's mother, Jenny, and sister Sharon. After the Dorchester Hotel incident, cynical press and fans called them gold diggers. But now the world could finally hear what Christian's temper sounded like.

In a *Daily Mail* interview, Sharon said: "What most people don't know is he has a brilliant sense of humour. He's funny and used to laugh a lot. You never see that now. All you see is this po-faced guy in a cap and sunglasses, pushing the paparazzi away."

Added Jenny: "I watch him giving interviews on the TV and I think: 'Come on Christian, give us a smile.'"

For many of Christian's fans, it seemed like the actor had finally gone too far. First he had allegedly attacked his own mother and sister in a hotel room and now this.

It didn't help that it took Christian four days to publicly apologize for the rant, and even then he didn't issue an apology directly to Shane Hurlbut but instead went on a local Los Angeles radio show to talk about the incident.

He started off by telling the show's hosts, Kevin Ryder and Gene "Bean" Baxter: "It's been a miserable week for *me*." He continued: "The thing that I really want to stress is I have no confusion whatsoever. I was out of order beyond belief. I was way out of order. I acted like a punk. I regret that. There is nobody that had heard that tape that is hit harder by it than me. I make no excuse for it. It is inexcusable. I hope that is absolutely clear. I'm embarrassed by it. I ask everybody to sit down and ask themselves, have they ever had a bad day and have they ever lost their temper and really regretted it immensely?"

Despite Christian's apparent contrition for his outburst, the damage was already done. The movie performed disappointingly at the box office. While the production cost of *Terminator Salvation* was estimated at $200 million, it grossed only $125 million domestically. Adding insult to injury, the much anticipated reboot of the *Terminator* franchise failed to open at the top of the box office on its opening weekend—instead, beaten by *Night at the Museum: Battle of the Smithsonian*. In just a couple weeks, *Terminator Salvation* would drop off the Top Ten movies, beaten soundly by the similarly budgeted *Transformers: Revenge of the Fallen*. A survey taken by respected trade publication *Ad Age* went as far to suggest that Christian's drawing power at the box office may have taken a hit because of the incident.

He even acknowledged himself that he was worried his behavior would overshadow the movie. Christian revealed just before the film opened in summer 2009: "I was worried that it could completely overwhelm the movie itself. There's so much hard work that's gone into this. We had 77 days of smooth running and four minutes of me just going too far—and that shouldn't characterize the making of the movie. My concern was that people would unfairly judge the movie based on my bad behavior."

It was also a film that Christian had initially had his own concerns about and had even been warned against taking. Christian revealed he was sent the script while he was still working on *The Dark Knight* in London, and he immediately vowed it would be a movie he would never make.

The movie franchise was being resurrected by director McG— not a huge name in Hollywood with just a couple credits to his name—the TV show *The OC* and two *Charlie's Angels* movies with Drew Barrymore, Cameron Diaz, and Lucy Liu.

The game company Halycon had purchased the *Terminator* franchise in 2007 from producers, Mario Kassar and Andrew Vajna, for a reported $25 million. The franchise had been very good to its original star, Arnold Schwarzenegger, and director, James Cameron. And Schwarzenegger's star power could still propel his third *Terminator* movie (without Cameron at the helm) to outgross Christian's *Terminator Salvation*.

Christian revealed: "I went: 'No, I don't even have to read this.' I just thought, the mythology was dead. I mean, I did flick through it because you can always be surprised. But I wasn't surprised by what I read in that one. I had people telling me: 'Don't do it Christian, don't go with that guy.'"

Christian initially turned down the role, wanting instead to concentrate on the *Batman* franchise. But when director McG, who is afraid of flying, got on a plane to London to beg Christian to be his John Connor, the star finally changed his mind. McG believed that Christian was the only actor who had both the "intensity and the integrity" to re-kickstart the sci-fi franchise.

Christian eventually agreed to star in the film, but with two conditions: He got to pick his costar and the script had to be rewritten. He immediately handed over the script to Jonathan Nolan, the screenwriting brother of *Dark Knight* director Christopher Nolan. Nolan went to work on the script, overhauling the story line, fleshing it out, and beefing up Christian's role as Connor. After Nolan worked his magic on the screenplay, it was then handed over to additional writers, including Oscar winner Paul Haggis, who has written such award-winning movies as *Crash* and *Million Dollar Baby* as well as the scripts for *Casino Royale* and *Quantum of Solace* for the newly revamped Bond franchise.

So, by the time the movie opened on May 14, 2009, there were high expectations. Yet *Terminator Salvation*, which cost over $200 million to make, took in just $125 million in the U.S. The movie eventually grossed $372 million worldwide, but with the budget and the millions of dollars spent on marketing it only just turned a profit.

And to top it off, the star getting all the attention from the press this time was newcomer Sam Worthington to whom, ironically, Christian had given his seal of approval for the role. Worthington then went on to star in another James Cameron blockbuster, *Avatar*, the 3-D spectacular that became the world's biggest grossing movie ever. Then he starred in the hit 2010 remake of *Clash of the Titans*, yet another box office smash. In *Terminator*, the hunky younger star wasn't even top billing. Christian was the lead as savior John Connor. Yet it was the unknown Australian actor in his first big American blockbuster who blew the critics away.

> Hollywood *Variety* wrote: "Heath Ledger stole *The Dark Knight* away from Bale and Sam Worthington heists *Terminator Salvation* from Bale for the most ironical of reasons: In a movie that poses man against machine, Worthington's Cyborg is the far more human character."

> In the *San Francisco Chronicle* review, Mick LaSalle noted: "When Christian Bale allowed himself to play Bruce Wayne in *Batman Begins*, he was slumming—and to good effect. But with *Terminator Salvation*, this ostensibly serious actor takes up residence in the action ghetto and it's not a good fit."

> And respected movie reviewer Roger Ebert said: "Edward Furlong was infinitely more human as John Connor than Christian Bale in this film."

It was as if bad karma haunted the role of John Connor. Edward Furlong, the original John Connor in *Terminator 2: Rise of the Machines*, was replaced by Nick Stahl for the sequel. Another former child actor, Furlong's post-*Terminator* career was ailing after a couple of arrests and incidents. The TV series *The Sarah Connor Chronicles* was canceled just months before the opening of *Terminator Salvation*. Thomas Dekker, who portrayed a teen John Connor in the series, was charged a few months later for felony DUI. And perhaps creepiest of all, in February 2010, news broke that the New Mexico house where Christian was staying during the shoot of *Terminator Salvation* had a dead body buried in the yard—a murder victim who had disappeared eight years prior.

Christian definitely breathed more life into his next role as FBI Special Agent Melvin Purvis in *Public Enemies*. Starring alongside one of this generation's greatest actors, Johnny Depp, and playing bank robber and Depression-era folk hero John Dillinger would have been nerve-racking for any actor. But Christian stood his own, garnering great reviews for his portrayal of Purvis, who made it his mission to track down and arrest Dillinger in the 1930s.

But it seems as though his *Terminator Salvation* rant may have cost him an Oscar nomination for *Public Enemies*. On the show *Inside Edition*, *Los Angeles Times* columnist Tom O'Neill said this about Christian: "How a star acts off camera is as important as how they act onscreen."

The movie fared modestly at the box office when it opened to strong reviews in June 2009. *Public Enemies*, directed by Michael Mann, cost an estimated $100 million to make and took in $214.8 million worldwide. But Christian admitted that working on *Batman*, *Terminator Salvation*, and *Public Enemies* back to back left him burnt out.

He vowed to take a break from filming after revealing in early 2009: "*Terminator's* coming out, then *Public Enemies* is coming out after that, and then I'll just wait and see for the first time ever. I kind of felt burnt out and just knowing that if I took on any movie right now, I wouldn't be able to commit myself properly. But variety is essential for me. I love watching a Michael Mann movie. I love watching a Christopher Nolan movie. Just to talk about my stuff, I enjoy a *Machinist* kind of movie, a *Rescue Dawn*, a *3:10 to Yuma*, an *American Psycho*, whatever. But I also love watching *Terminator* movies, I love watching Batman movies . . . For me it's less important that following the *Termi-nator* that I quickly get *Public Enemies* out there. I'm just not as strategic as that but for my own personal satisfaction I need to vary it up. I couldn't for instance follow up *Terminator* by doing another *Terminator* straight away."

Yet despite his proclamation that he was "burnt out" and wanted to spend time away from movies, Christian jumped straight into his next project. After spending just a month hanging out with Sibi and their then three-year-old daughter, Emmaline, in Los Angeles after the premiere of *Public Enemies*, Christian was back on a movie set. (As another example of Christian's uneasy relation with fame and publicity, even his daughter's birthdate and birthplace were not immediately revealed. Emmaline is a public name while Christian has compartmentalized facts among his inner circle. To some members of his family, his daughter is known as Luka Isabella.)

This time he was starring alongside Mark Wahlberg in *The Fighter*. And once again Christian did what he does best—he completely transformed himself for the role. Just like he did for *The Machinist*, the star began losing weight for his role as Dicky Eklund, the famous boxer turned crack addict.

The Fighter opened in limited release in the U.S. on December 10, 2010, just making it eligible for the Academy Award nominations. The movie made just $300,000 in its opening weekend, but it was a huge critical success.

Movie reviewers began falling over themselves to praise the film, in particular Christian and his costar Melissa Leo who played Alice Ward, the mother of Dicky and Micky Ward, played by Mark Wahlberg.

Roger Ebert of the *Chicago Sun-Times* wrote: "The weakness of the film is the weakness of the leading role. That's not a criticism of Mark Wahlberg who has quite a capable range but of how he and Russell see the character. That's not the case with

Dicky, Alice and Charlene and those characters are where the life is. Christian Bale, who has played Batman and John Connor in the *Terminator* and for Werner Herzog played a man who survived the jungles of Laos, so successfully transforms himself that you see a career as a cutup in the Jackass movies."

Peter Travers of *Rolling Stone* wrote: "After Matt Damon and Brad Pitt turned down the role of crackhead Dickie, Wahlberg lucked out big time with Christian Bale. I have one word for Bale: phenomenal. He dropped 30 pounds to play the skinny, loose-limbed, demon-driven Dickie. But his hilarious and heart-breaking performance cuts deep under the surface. Bale's eyes reflect the man Mickey grew up hero-worshipping and the 'pride of Lowell' who might find that pride again as Micky's trainer."

Claudia Puig of *USA Today* raved: "Bale is astounding as a strangely charismatic weasel, giving probably the best performance of his career. Suave Bruce Wayne of 2005's Batman is long gone, Bale's handsome face is almost unrecognisably gaunt. Bale's knockout performance should not be missed. Dicky steals the show, much like he does his family's attention."

And Anne Hornaday from the *Washington Post* added: "The title character of the *Fighter* might be Micky—played here in a straight-up, stalwart, hugely sympathetic performance by Mark Wahlberg. But it could just as easily pertain to the hardscrabble Dicky, especially as he's channelled by Christian Bale. Down 30 pounds, Bale is nothing less than revelatory as the skinny, skeeved-out crackhead, who, against all odds, commands the audience's attention and, improbably, a few laughs."

The buzz around the little boxing movie began to grow and before the end of 2010, Christian was being mentioned as the front-runner of the awards season. The movie went on to make $93.5 million at the U.S. box office alone—not bad for a film with an estimated budget of just $25 million.

The rave reviews for *The Fighter* were perfect for the all-important Christmas moviegoers, generating buzz ahead of the award nominations season that would culminate with the Oscars. Christian reluctantly did his publicity duties to promote the film. It was the first time he was in front of the press since his *Terminator Salvation* rant had gone viral. To head off any potentially embarrassing or provocative interrogation, Christian's ground rules about the format of the interview were clear: Q&A format only. No personal questions. Christian's cover interview with *Esquire* would bring his bad boy image back to the forefront with what *Esquire* described as a "testy encounter." *Esquire* writer John H. Richardson scolded Christian, "There's nothing that's more of a dick movie-star move than to say, 'It has to be printed as a Q&A.' That's movie star. You and Tom Cruise back in the day are the only people who do that shit."

> "I want to be able to just act and never do any interview, but I don't have the balls to stand up to the studio and say, 'I'm never doing another interview in my life!' So I tip my hat and go, 'Okay mister! All right mister! I'll go do the salesman job!'"
> —Christian Bale, *Esquire*, December 2010

Ironically, after Christian had lost more than 60 lbs. for his role in *The Machinist*, he received mixed reviews and precious few award nominations. For *The Fighter*, Christian was careful not to bandy about the exact weight loss figure; instead he just stated that he had to look like a welterweight (140–147 lbs.). Of course, *The Machinist* came out before Christian was the star of *Batman* and was widely considered difficult to watch. *The Fighter* would have that Rocky crowd-pleasing vibe, and Christian's fans would see the hunky man who had been Bruce Wayne transformed into a sweet crackhead.

January 2011 would be an exciting month for Christian as he began to rack up acting award nominations and wins for his performance in *The Fighter*. Up against the hugely popular *The Kings Speech* and its Best Supporting Actor front-runner, Geoffrey Rush, Christian scored nominations from BAFTA and the National Society of Film Critics to name a couple. However, Vegas odds-makers were taking notice when Christian won Best Supporting Actor awards from the Screen Actors Guild, the National Board of Review, and most importantly, a Golden Globe Award.

For his Golden Globe acceptance speech, Christian astonished viewers with a frank admission about the Hollywood Foreign Press Association—the people who had voted for him to win the Golden Globe. He said: "Thanks to the HFPA. I never really knew who those guys were. I'd always leave the press junkets going who were those oddball characters in that room?"

The Golden Globe Award win tilted Hollywood pundits to favor Christian for an Oscar nomination. And on February 27, 2011, Christian would see his hard work for *The Fighter* honored with a gold statuette. Christian beat out front-runner Geoffrey Rush (*The King's Speech*), John Hawkes (*Winter's Bone*), Jeremy Renner (*The Town*), and Mark Ruffalo (*The Kids Are All Right*).

When Christian walked up to the podium to accept his award, he took a self-humored jab at his potty mouth reputation, saying, "I'm not going to drop the f-bomb like *she* did, I've done that plenty before." He was referring to his *Fighter* costar Melissa Leo, who had earlier taken home the Best Support Actress Oscar and said "fuck" on live TV. Thanking the cast and crew of *The Fighter*, Christian astonished the audience by seemingly forgetting his wife's name. With hesitation and fumbling, obviously charged with emotion, he concluded: "And of course [pause] mostly, my wonderful wife, [pause] I didn't think I was like this. My wonderful wife who's my mast through the storms of life, I hope I'm likewise to you darling and our little girl who's taught me so much more than I'll ever be able to teach her. Thank you, thank you so much."

Five thousand miles away, Jenny Bale proudly sent her son an e-mail of congratulations. No response. She had not heard from her son in the three years since the incident at The Dorchester Hotel.

Award Season

"The way Christian Bale's arm is around his wife reads like she probably can't take a shit w/out his okay."
    —Sarah Silverman, via Twitter

"Christian Bale looks ready to slay Grendel."
    —Seth McFarlane, via Twitter

Christian stunned everyone during the 2011 awards season by looking like a scruffy, homeless person. He joked about his bushy beard, laughing it off as being "too lazy" between movies.

When actors are in between projects during their "downtime," you'll see their candid shots in entertainment magazines—unshaven and unkempt on the beach or at the supermarket. But rarely do you see actors looking disheveled during a publicity tour. They're selling a movie and, of course, they're selling themselves. In 2010, Joaquin Phoenix declared that he had quit acting and showed up notoriously on David Letterman with a shaggy beard, looking like, in Letterman's words, the Unabomber. Though

Christian was doing publicity duties to promote *The Fighter*, it seemed that his Joaquin Phoenix–like appearance during the press junket and especially during award shows was his way of telling the press that no matter how many big movies he starred in, he was never going to be a typical movie star.

After the end of his publicity tour, he did manage to get cleaned up and to head off to China to start his next film. On paper, *The Flowers of War* looked like a master stroke for Christian's career. With more and more movies relying on foreign markets for profits, a film by China's best known filmmaker, Yimou Zang, seemed like a smart move for Christian to build his Chinese box office presence outside of Batman. And making a Chinese movie also got Christian around China's foreign film quota.

Christian was never a great scholar of history, but he was always curious—he loved to ask why things were a certain way, just like a kid. When the U.K. had to return Hong Kong to China in 1997, he asked me to explain why. I told him about the infamous ninety-nine-year lease and what I knew of the Opium Wars, but Christian was thinking about England's 1982 victory over Argentina contesting the Falkland Islands and wondering aloud why the British Navy couldn't simply win a war with China to secure Hong Kong permanently.

"A war with China," I told him with just a touch of ethnic pride, "wouldn't be the same as the Falkland War." Christian smiled back at me, equally confident of the Royal Navy's abilities.

While Christian was researching for his role in *American Psycho*, he was eager to read about atrocities to understand more about the human capacity for cruelty. I presented him Iris Chang's landmark book *The Rape of Nanking: The Forgotten Holocaust of World War II*, the first English-language account of the Nanjing Massacre when hundreds of thousands of Chinese civilians and unarmed soldiers were murdered and tens of thousands of Chinese women were raped by Japanese soldiers after the city was captured on December 13, 1937. He and I sat up late one evening poring over the horrific photos in the book of the dead and mutilated. It was important for me to have my friend learn a little history.

The Flowers of War was based on Geling Yan's novel, *The 13 Flowers of Nanjing*, which is set during the Nanking Massacre. The novel is the story of thirteen prostitutes taking refuge in a church who offer to trade places with thirteen school girls to save them from being raped by Japanese soldiers. Yan is a very successful Chinese-American writer who may be the only person to be a member of both the Writers Guild of America and the Writers' Association of China. A number of her works have been adapted into movies in China.

On the Chinese side, moviegoers were impressed that a major Hollywood star like Christian Bale would be in a Chinese film—his first major shoot in China since *Empire of the Sun*. But outside of China, Yimou Zang's reputation had been tarnished in recent years. Zang's career began as one of China's most daring new directors, known for powerful dramas and stunning primary-color palettes. Films like *Red Sorghum* (1987), *Ju Dou* (1990), and *Raise the Red Lantern* (1991) earned Zang an international reputation as one of China's best directors and launched the career of actress Gong Li.

But his 1994 film *To Live*, which depicted life and hardship during China's Cultural Revolution, not only earned him the Grand Jury Prize at the Cannes Film Festival but also a *two-year ban* from filmmaking by Communist China. Its star, Gong Li, also suffered a two-year ban because, it was said, the Chinese government felt that the film took a negative stance toward certain aspects of Chinese history.

The ban seemed to have affected Zang's career as he shifted gears from dramas to big historic epics like *Hero* with none-too-subtle messages that some critics complained toed the

Communist Party line. By 2008, Zang impressed China and the world with the spectacularly elaborate opening ceremony for the Beijing Olympics, but as the *New York Times'* Edward Wong noted, it looked as if Zang had become "China's Leni Reifenstahl."

The Flowers of War, a big wartime drama about the Rape of Nanking Massacre during World War II, earned both Christian and Zang negative reviews. On one hand, it was the most expensive Chinese movie ever made, with a reported budget of US$100 million. The shoot took over six months, with a part of Beijing used to look like wartime Nanjing. Christian enjoyed the shoot, telling the *Los Angeles Times* that "one of the things he liked about shooting so far away is the relative anonymity, not to mention the remove from Hollywood." It was also one of the top grossing films in China, earning $83 million in its first 17 days of release.

On the other hand, *The Flowers of War* earned a Golden Broom nomination for Worst Picture. The Golden Broom is China's equivalent of the Razzie Award. Some movie critics decided that Christian was miscast and that Zang had made a big-screen spectacle out of a war tragedy. The reviews were not kind.

> "Zhang Yimou, one of China's best-known filmmakers, deserves a great big lump of coal in his holiday stocking thanks to his ludicrous soap opera *The Flowers of War*."
>
> —*New York Post*

> "If Warner Bros. had made a film with this plot back in 1942, it would have made effective anti-Japanese propaganda and probably absorbing drama in the bargain. Today it just plays like hokum."   —*The Hollywood Reporter*

> "With *The Flowers of War*, Zhang mostly just proves that there's

no tragedy too terrible that it can't be turned into an operatic pageant—human suffering reduced to visual showmanship."

—*Village Voice*

The Flowers of War was China's biggest film production, ready to open on 8,000 screens on December 13, 2011—the anniversary of the Nanjing Massacre—and backed by a nationwide promotion campaign. Its script had to be approved by government censors. It was China's submission for an Academy Award nomination, with the hopes to win China's very first Oscar. On Sunday, December 11, the film premiered in Beijing in a government building called The People's Political Consultative Conference. Little wonder that at the Beijing premiere, Christian seemed annoyed when asked whether he had made a propaganda movie for the Chinese government. "I think that would be a bit of a knee-jerk reaction," he said. "I don't think they're looking closely enough at the movie."

A few days after the Beijing premiere, Christian and a CNN news crew drove out to meet with Chinese dissident Chen Guangchen, but were stopped and shoved back by security guards blocking the road to his village. Chen is a blind lawyer who has become a cause célèbre as he's taken up the cases of women in China who have been victims of its aggressive one-child policy that includes mandatory sterilizations and abortions. As Christian and the CNN crew drove back, he said, "I'm not being brave doing this. The local people who are standing up to the authorities and insisting on going to visit Chen and his family and getting beaten up for it and my understanding is getting detained for it, I want to support what they're doing."

CNN declared, "Actor Christian Bale, CNN crew roughed up trying to visit Chinese activist" and featured the video of the incident on the front of its Web site as well as on the CNN network. However, some were amused at what cynically looked like a publicity stunt—whether by Christian to distance himself from *The Flowers of War*—or by CNN to use a celebrity to run a blockade. After all, Christian is not known for any Angelina Jolie-style political activism.

Adam Minter, of *Bloomberg* in Shanghai, tweeted, "News orgs that want to maintain their credibility in China don't set up confrontations between cops and celebrities, at celebrity request." Shaun Rein, of *Forbes*, wrote, "Shame on CNN for its Christian Bale stunt. CNN's China team, in a complete failure of journalistic integrity, decided last week to become the news rather than just report it."

In China, the incident was partially censored from the Internet—CNN's video of the incident was blocked—but as an Internet meme, it was portrayed on China's social networks as PandaMan versus Batman. "Batman couldn't do it alone," tweeted a Chinese commentator on Sina Weibo, a Chinese social network. "But if he takes Spiderman, Superman, the Hulk, Wolverine, Captain America, and Harry Potter, they can get it done, right?"

The Chinese government criticized Christian for the incident. Foreign Ministry spokesman Liu Weimin said that Christian "was not invited to create a story or shoot film in a certain village." Liu continued, "I think if you want to make up news in China, you will not be welcome here."

However, Hollywood insiders considered the incident a major public relations nightmare for China and its very expensive bid for an Oscar, for its hopes for a big box office hit in the U.S., as well as for Christian's prospects of ever shooting in the Middle Kingdom ever again.

Additionally, whether it was because of the film's subject matter, Christian's CNN incident, or poor reviews, *The Flowers of War* bombed in the U.S. market, earning just $1,619 per location in limited release in December. *The Wrap* declared, "Christian Bale couldn't entice U.S. moviegoers to go see *Flowers of War*, the most expensive movie in Chinese history. Nor could director Zhang Yimou of *Hero* fame."

(On January 24, 2012, the Oscar nominations were announced. *The Flowers of War* was China's official submission for a 2012 Best Foreign Language Film Oscar, but it failed to earn an Oscar nomination.)

But before all of that happened, back when Christian had just started filming *Flowers of War*, he was already thinking ahead. He was transforming his body, knowing that he'd have to bulk up again for his role in the third Batman movie, *The Dark Knight Rises*.

Christian initially signed up for three *Batman* movies before he'd even made *Batman Begins* as Warner Bros. was banking on the movies being a smash success. Jonathan Nolan revealed in March 2010: "Will we do a third movie? It's got to be the right story. You can't make something like *The Dark Knight* and then come out with something disappointing. The fact is I have to! I've signed up! Chris doesn't. So I'm in a bit of a fix if he says he doesn't want to!"

As he spoke those words, Jonathan Nolan was already working furiously on a script with Christopher who hates giving away any spoilers, simply revealing: "My brother is writing a script for me and we'll wait to see how it turns. He's struggling to put it together into the epic story that you want it to be! Without getting into specifics, the key thing that makes the third film a great possibility for us is that we want to finish the story. And in viewing it as the finishing of a story rather than an infinitely blowing up the balloon and expanding the story. We have a great ensemble, that's one of the attractions of doing another film, since we've been having a great time for years."

The challenge for Nolan then would be to find a villain, or villains, who not only matches up to Christian's Batman portrayal, but matches up to that of The Joker by the incomparable Heath

Ledger. Fans had been hitting the Internet for months, ever since it was confirmed there would be a third film and had been pushing their own favorite villians to take on the Caped Crusader. Many fans wanted Johnny Depp as The Riddler or Angelina Jolie as Catwoman or even Phillip Seymour Hoffman as The Penguin. But Nolan had dozens of villains to choose from and remained tight-lipped on which one, and even which A-list star, he wanted in *The Dark Knight Rises*. All he said as casting began, with a wry smile, was: "It won't be Mr. Freeze."

By April 2011 the cast was confirmed. Anne Hathaway would play Catwoman and British actor Tom Hardy would be Bane, considered one of Batman's most deadly and powerful foes. Bane's strength is matched only by his superior IQ and in the graphic novels, he is one of the few villains who was able to deduce Batman's identity within a year.

And Hardy's *Inception* costar Joseph Gordon-Levitt was cast as Alberto Falcone, the son of mob boss and major *Batman Begins* villain Carmine Falcone, who was played by Tom Wilkinson. Oscar winner Marion Cotillard (*Inception, La Vie en Rose*) was cast as Miranda Tate, a Wayne Enterprises board member eager to help a still-grieving Bruce Wayne resume his father's philanthropic endeavours for Gotham.

Fans of Batman were also delighted with the news that David S. Goyer was involved with the script. Goyer has a huge comic book, graphic novel, and superhero background and has been involved in both previous Batman movies, providing the story for both and cowriting the screenplay for *Batman Begins*. He also wrote and directed the hugely popular *Blade* vampire movies starring Wesley Snipes as well as *Crow: City of Angels* and produced *Ghost Rider* with Nicolas Cage. Goyer is also screenwriting *Ghost Rider 2* and *X Men Origins: Magneto* and collaborated with Nolan on a new *Superman* franchise with the first movie, *Superman: Man of Steel*, slated for release in summer 2013.

Ironically Christian almost ended up as Superman instead of Batman after auditioning for the role back in 2003 before *Batman Begins* and Bryan Singer's *Superman* hit screens. Director Wolfgang Petersen was all set to direct *Batman vs. Superman*, a big budget outing to set two of DC Comics biggest superheroes against each other.

And Christian was one of two actors shortlisted for the part of Krypton's favorite son, the other one being *Black Hawk Down* star Josh Hartnett. The movie almost happened but then Warner Bros got a single script for a Superman film from JJ Abrams while Nolan began working on Batman, so the studio decided to go with two separate movies. Abrams ended up making *Superman* with Brandon Routh as the Man of Steel while Nolan pushed ahead with Batman and Petersen went off to film *Troy* with Brad Pitt.

Petersen revealed: "It was pretty close. And then the studio got a single Superman script I think from JJ Abrams at that time and Warner Bros chief Alan Horn was so torn because it was such a fascinating concept to do a Batman versus Superman film. And I think it still would be fun to do that. But the studio decided to try separate versions of Superman and Batman and then maybe think about down the road if they want to bring them together in one film."

However, Nolan seems adamant that he won't be putting Superman and Batman into a film together anytime soon. He revealed: "A lot of people have approached Superman in a lot of different ways. I only know that the way that has worked for us, that's what I know how to do. Batman exists in a world where he is the only superhero and a similar approach to the Man of Steel would assure the integrity needed for the film. Each serves the internal logic of the story. They have nothing to do with each other."

It appeared that Christian would be free to concentrate on *Terminator 5* after finishing with *The Dark Knight Rises*. *Terminator*

Salvation director McG had already begun working on a script as early as March 2010, and he revealed that John Connor is a big part of the movie and would possibly show up in *Terminator 6*, too.

McG revealed: "We're very far down the line with the story for that—for the next picture and even the picture after that. We can't wait to get back at it and show the world what becomes of that war and how we master time travel because we stayed away from time travel in *Salvation* and I missed it. John Connor is going to travel back in time and he's going to have to galvanize the militaries of the world for an impending Skynet invasion. They've figured out time travel to the degree where they can send more than one naked entity. So you're going to have hunter killers and transports and harvesters and everything arriving in our time and John Connor fighting back with conventional military warfare, which I think is going to be awesome. It will be more of a chase movie with a new Terminator on your ass! I also think he's going to meet a scientist that's going to look a lot like present-day Robert Patrick, talking about stem cell research and how we can live as idealised younger versions of ourselves. I think the next film is going to be very pleasing and very surprising to the fans. That's the goal."

However, by March 2011, McG was out and other directors' names were being thrown into the mix. While Universal Studios was in the process of enticing a director to jump on board after Ridley Scott, Steven Spielberg, and James Cameron all reportedly turned down the offer to helm *Terminator 5*, and the next Terminator movie had been dropped from Christian's IMDb page.

But there is hope the fifth movie in the franchise will make it to the big screen as Justin Lin, director of *The Fast and the Furious: Tokyo Drift* and *Fast Five*, revealed he had been in talks with original *Terminator* star Arnold Schwarzenegger after the former governor of California told his reps to start looking for movie offers once he stepped down from political office.

Lin said: "*Terminator* was one of my favorite films growing up. And I feel I have a take that I would love to see and I've talked with Arnold and we've talked and we'll see. Again, I would love to do it but it has to be the right circumstances. It has to be with the right people. And there're other projects too. But I'm in a position now that I can choose more than I could a year ago, two years ago. So that's something that is potentially in my future."

As for Christian, it remains to be seen if he's asked to return to the role of John Connor but he spent most of 2011 filming *The Dark Knight Rises* for a July 2012 release. After that his schedule was pretty open, with just two future movie projects listed.

One is *The Last Photograph*, in which he will play one of two men who are inspired to travel to war-torn Afghanistan by a photograph they see. The other is *Concrete Island*, in which he will star as an architect who finds himself stranded on a man-made island between two highways with only the contents of his car in his possession. Both movies are scheduled for release in 2013.

As Christian's career progresses, he has been trying to steer clear of the Hollywood machine that happily eats up and spits out its stars. He's forged a career on his own terms. You won't see Christian at parties or red carpet premieres for movies other than his own. He continues to be notoriously private, yet at the same time, he acknowledges that his fans have sustained him through a career that has had its share of ups and downs.

Throughout Christian's twenty-five years of making movies, he has always done things his way. He's refused to play the Hollywood game and, indeed, has managed to do an end run around Tinseltown's establishment, bypassing traditional publicity for Internet marketing, defiantly bearded and unshaven on a publicity tour.

The Q Scores are the industry standard for measuring familiarity and appeal. Stars like Tom Hanks, Clint Eastwood, and Will Smith are routinely ranked at the top for both familiarity and their Q Score. Henry Schaefer, Executive Vice President of Marketing Evaluations, The Q Scores Company, said this about Christian: "His awareness is at 55 percent familiarity among the total population but because he won the Oscar in 2011, his Q Score actually went up to 16 percent.

"Christian Bale's family disputes, which were publicized shortly after the release of the movie, and the overwhelming coverage of the Heath Ledger death most likely suppressed a lot of the positive acclaim he could have potentially achieved as a result of the success of *The Dark Knight*. While Christian Bale benefited greatly with respect to his awareness, it did not translate into a significant gain in his appeal overall.

"However in the past couple of years, the demographic that follows Christian has changed slightly. He is now more popular with men in the 18 to 35 age group, but he appeals more to women 35 and over. But he is still below the average Q Score for male stars, who generally are in the 20 percent range."

It is perhaps a perfect description of Christian's image. He remains an enigmatic contradiction—famous but not popular. To some of his critics, Christian's approach to acting is all dazzling technique—with the weight losses and the accents, but he hasn't made a deeper emotional connection with the audience. Said John Farr, *Huffington Post*, "His acting chops are prodigious, but he seems to me to be all technique and no heart; we get buckets of perfectly formed ice, but very little fire. I see nothing behind his eyes."

In the spring of 2010, when news outlets reported that Christian was about to apply for U.S. citizenship, the British media tried to gauge reaction. A number of U.K. celebrities living in America change their citizenship, and the reaction can be quite negative. Pierce Brosnan became a U.S. citizen in 2004 but assured his native Ireland, "I found a whole new life and identity in America but my heart and soul will be forever Irish." Welsh-born

Anthony Hopkins angered his hometown of Port Talbot when he became a U.S. citizen in 2000; however, he declared, "America has been very generous to me, magnanimous really. I thought it would be good to give something back." Hopkins added, "I love Wales where I was born."

But when James Campbell, the mayor of Haverfordwest, Wales, Christian's birthplace, was asked if people would be angry if Christian became a U.S. citizen, he replied, "It's not as if we're losing a national treasure."

True Baleheads understand and appreciate this star who does not seek fame. Christian summed it up when he said: "At first I was somewhat hesitant to do the role of Batman. I mean, after all, Batman is an icon. But I remember, clear as a day, being at the grocery store the day the movie opened and this little boy saw me. He couldn't have been more than five years old. He just walked right up to me and hugged me and hugged me. He hugged me and I was so moved by it that I hugged him back. Then he looked up at me and said: 'You're my hero.' And in that moment, I knew that not only as an actor that I had done my job but that I had made the right decision to play Batman."

And while he's never looked back, Christian has also pushed the way forward not only for himself but for others, opening up the gates to make it acceptable for young British actors to play American superheroes. There would be an outcry if an American was chosen for a role as quintessentially British as Bond. Producers tried once to use an actor that wasn't British, the Australian George Lazenby, and it was a total disaster. Lazenby was hired in 1968 more for his fighting skills than his acting prowess for *On Her Majesty's Secret Service*, and he quit as Bond before the movie had even premiered. Sean Connery was soon brought back out of Bond retirement for *Diamonds Are Forever* in 1971 before Roger Moore took over the role. Even before Daniel Craig was hired as the latest incarnation of Bond, the actors being bandied around for the much-sought-after role were all British—Colin Farrell, Clive Owen, Ioan Gruffudd, and Christian's old pal Ewan McGregor.

For years it worked the same across the Atlantic in the U.S., with movie producers hiring Americans for their superhero roles, not for a second believing a stiff-upper lipped Brit could take on the role or physicality of their dynamic superheroes—until Christian turned that idea on its head and proved that super-heroes didn't have to be American.

Following the success of *The Dark Knight*, Andrew Garfield (who calls himself British after moving to the U.K. with his parents when he was just four) landed the lead in *The Amazing Spiderman*. Fellow Brit Aaron Johnson played the lead in the superb 2010 antisuperhero movie *Kick Ass*. And Henry Cavill, best known for his hit Showtime costume drama *The Tudors*, is none other than Superman, doing his bit for truth, justice, and the American way. Batman, Superman, *and* Spiderman? That's the Holy Trinity of American superhero movie franchises.

Now we're not talking advances in civil rights, but Christian's success with Batman demonstrated a change in the Hollywood mind-set. It was considered very risky for a studio to hire a relatively unknown British actor to play an American lead in a franchise movie. If *Batman Begins* had bombed at the box office, Christian would have been promptly replaced. Money talks! (*Hulk*, anyone?) Before Christian's successful run with the Dark Knight, British actors had been typically relegated to the roles of Nazis, Romans, or wise wizards. But these all-important franchise movies—"tent pole" blockbusters to carry a studio's summer season—depend on worldwide appeal. Christian's worldwide fan base on the World Wide Web demonstrated that a British actor could carry the world on his shoulders—and take home an Oscar, too.

As his mum e-mailed on Oscar night, February 27, 2011, "Well done, son! Well done!"

Appendix A

BALE: Kick your fucking ass!

HURLBUT: Christian, Christian . . .

BALE: I want you off the fucking set you prick!

HURLBUT: Christian, I'm sorry.

BALE: No, don't just be sorry, think for one fucking second. What the fuck are you doing? Are you professional or not?

HURLBUT: Yes I am.

BALE: Do I fucking walk around and . . .

BRUCE FRANKLIN: Christian, Christian . . .

BALE: No, shut the fuck up Bruce! Don't shut me up!

FRANKLIN: I'm not shutting you up.

BALE: Am I going to walk around and rip your fucking lights down, in the middle of a scene? Then why the fuck are you walking right through like this in the background. What the fuck is it with you? What don't you fucking understand? You got any fucking idea about, hey, it's fucking distracting having somebody walking up behind Bryce in the middle of the fucking scene? Give me a fucking answer! What don't you get about it?

HURLBUT: I was looking at the light.

BALE: Oh, good for you, and how was it? I hope it was fucking good, because it's useless now, isn't it? Fuck-sake man, you're amateur.

BALE: McG, you got fucking something to say to this prick?

MCG: I didn't see it happen.

BALE: Well, somebody should be fucking watching and keeping an eye on him.

MCG: Fair enough.

BALE: It's the second time that he doesn't give a fuck about what is going on in front of the camera. I'm trying to fucking do a scene here, and I am going "Why the fuck is Shane walking in there? What is he doing there?" Do you understand my mind is not in the scene if you're doing that?

HURLBUT: I absolutely apologize. I'm sorry, I did not mean anything by it.

BALE: Stay off the fucking set man. For fuck-sake. Alright, let's go again.

MCG: Let's just take a minute.

BALE: Let's not take a fucking minute, let's go again. You're unbelievable, you're un-fucking-believable. Number of times you're strolling and fucking around in the background. I've never had a DP behave like this. You don't fucking understand what it's like working with actors, that's what that is. That's what that is man, I'm telling you. I'm not asking, I'm telling you. You wouldn't have done that otherwise.

HURLBUT: No, what it is, is looking at the light and making sure, that you are . . .

BALE: I'm going to fucking kick your fucking ass if you don't shut for a second! Alright?

BALE: You do it one more fucking time and I ain't walking on this set if you're still hired. I'm fucking serious. You're a nice guy. You're a nice guy, but that don't fucking cut it when you're bullshitting and fucking around like this on set. I ain't the one walking. Let's get Tom and put this back on and let's go again. Seriously man, you and me, we're fucking done professionally. Fucking ass.

Appendix B

Bill for David Bale to get a green card

106th CONGRESS
2d Session
S. 2945
For the relief of David Bale.
IN THE SENATE OF THE UNITED STATES
July 27, 2000

Mrs. FEINSTEIN introduced the following bill; which was read twice and referred to the Committee on the Judiciary

A BILL
For the relief of David Bale.
Be it enacted by the Senate and House of Representatives of the United States of America in Congress assembled,

SECTION 1.
PERMANENT RESIDENT STATUS FOR DAVID BALE.

(a) IN GENERAL—Notwithstanding subsections (a) and (b) of section 201 of the Immigration and Nationality Act, David

Bale shall be eligible for issuance of an immigrant visa or for adjustment of status to that of an alien lawfully admitted for permanent residence upon filing an application for issuance of an immigrant visa under section 204 of such Act or for adjustment of status to lawful permanent resident.

(b) ADJUSTMENT OF STATUS—If David Bale entered the United States before the filing deadline specified in subsection (c), he shall be considered to have entered and remained lawfully and shall, if otherwise eligible, be eligible for adjustment of status under section 245 of the Immigration and Nationality Act as of the date of the enactment of this Act.

(c) DEADLINE FOR APPLICATION AND PAYMENT OF FEES—Subsections (a) and (b) shall apply only if the application for issuance of an immigrant visa or the application for adjustment of status are filed with appropriate fees within 2 years after the date of the enactment of this Act.

(d) REDUCTION OF IMMIGRANT VISA NUMBER— Upon the granting of an immigrant visa or permanent residence to David Bale, the Secretary of State shall instruct the proper officer to reduce by one, during the current or next following fiscal year, the total number of immigrant visas that are made available to natives of the country of the alien's birth under section 203(a) of the Immigration and Nationality Act or, if applicable, the total number of immigrant visas that are made available to natives of the country of the alien's birth under section 202(e) of such Act.

Acknowledgments

Harrison would like to thank:

Harry, Lillian, Leslie, and Laurie Cheung—my family, for their unwavering love and support, even after I ran away from home.

Nicola "Nickels" Pittam—my co-author and dear friend. You are the only true superhero in Los Angeles. Thank you so much for sticking with me on a project that was literally years in the making!

Jennifer De Chiara—my agent, for your persistence and belief in my writing all these years.

Linda Gamst—for years of preparation and fortification, without which, this book might not have happened.

Jean McKay—for your guidance and support since day one—with love and affection.

Jennifer Lac Kamp—je suis mon coeur aussi.

Laurie Reid—the very first Balehead—and John McFetridge. You know, Bea, we could have saved Rupert Graves instead!

Dodger and Odessa—the home guard! Greenies all around!

Harrison and Nicola would like to thank:

Glenn Yeffeth, Jennifer Canzoneri, Erin Kelley, Lindsay Marshall, and the great team at BenBella Books.

Angelica Jopson—we were so lucky to have you on our team. Thank you for your drive, initiative, and perseverance.

Henrick Vartanian—thank you so much for literally going the extra thousand miles for marketing support.

Ryan Doherty—the Big R for Big Web help!

Zac Witte—for marketing support and brainstorming

Dan Hogan, Bournemouth University

Michael Stead, Bournemouth Library

Scott Harrison, Bournemouth Daily Echo—thanks for letting us harass you.

Mark Passera, Edinburgh Napier University—for rolling the ball.

Jay Leno—a true gentleman; we hope this explains all!

Patrick Antosh—the cock-sock inventor!

More acknowledgments:*

African National Congress	*Bournemouth County Court*
Alamo Drafthouse Cinema	*Bournemouth Daily Echo*
Austin School of Film	*Bournemouth School for Boys*
Avonbourne Girls School	*Bournemouth Public Library*

* Production budgets and box office figures are estimates sourced from IMDb.com and Boxofficemojo.com.

Bournemouth University

BraveNewHollywood.com

Brian Boeckman

British Midland

British Airways

British National Archives

City of Los Angeles

Hallmark Publicity

Haverfordwest, Wales

I.B.M.

London Metropolitan Archives

Mark Lynch

Middlesex Crown Court, U.K.

NBC Publicity

N.F. Mendoza

Palm Springs Film Festival

Paramount Pictures Publicity

Peter Jeffrey

PR by the Book

Q Scores Company

Screen Actors Guild

State of California

Sundance Film Festival

Ted Fay

Toronto International Film Festival

United Kingdom Civil Aviation Authority

U.S. Bureau of Citizenship and Immigration Services

Westlaw